THE DIGITAL CROWN

This book is courtesy
of our sponsor

www.tealeaveshealth.com

THE DIGITAL CROWN

WINNING AT CONTENT
ON THE WEB

Ahava Leibtag

AMSTERDAM • BOSTON • HEIDELBERG • LONDON
NEW YORK • OXFORD • PARIS • SAN DIEGO
SAN FRANCISCO • SINGAPORE • SYDNEY • TOKYO

Morgan Kaufmann is an imprint of Elsevier

Acquiring Editor: *Meg Dunkerley*
Development Editor: *Heather Scherer*
Project Manager: *Malathi Samayan*
Designer: *Matthew Limbert*
Photo Credit: *FeeBee Photography*

Morgan Kaufmann is an imprint of Elsevier
225 Wyman Street, Waltham, MA 02451, USA

Library of Congress Cataloging-in-Publication Data

Leibtag, Ahava.
  The digital crown : winning at content on the web / Ahava Leibtag.
    pages cm
  Includes bibliographical references and index.
  ISBN 978-0-12-407674-7 (pbk.)
1. Internet marketing. 2. Branding (Marketing) I. Title.
  HF5415.1265.L447 2013
  658.8'72–dc23
                                                    2013022878

British Library Cataloguing-in-Publication Data

A catalogue record for this book is available from the British Library

ISBN: 978-0-12-407674-7

Printed and bound in China
14 15 16 17   13 12 11 10 9 8 7 6 5 4 3 2 1

For information on all MK publications visit our website at www.mkp.com

CONTENTS

PART I CONTENT IS A CONVERSATION

1 Understanding Branding, Content Strategy, and Content Marketing **3**

The Problem Grows 3

The Challenge of the Web 4

    Crowdsourcing: Information from Trusted Sources 5

    Should Businesses Really Care? 6

Understanding Content 6

The Art of Conversation 8

Branding: A Brand Is a Promise 8

    What Is a Brand? 9

    Defining Brands 10

    Who Defines a Brand? 10

    Managing the Brand 11

    Brand Definition 12

    Employee Training About the Brand 12

    Brand Consistency 13

Build a Process: Content Strategy and Content

Marketing Reinforce Branding 14

    What Is Content Strategy? 14

    Systems Create Freedom 14

    What Is Content Marketing? 18

    That Better Way Is Content Marketing 18

Moving Forward with New Understanding 19

    The Five Basic Questions Answered 19

Summary 20

Rule #1 Start with Your Audience **23**

2 Making the Case for Content **33**

Understanding Business Objectives 34

Defining Business Objectives 36

    Meeting the Achievement Threshold 36

    Understanding Your Sales and Business Cycles 37

    Different Types of Media 39

Analyzing the Current State of Affairs 40
Approaching the C-Suite 41
Understanding the C-Suite 42
What the C-Suite Cares About 43
How to Explain Content to the C-Suite 43
How to Convince Each Member of the C-Suite
About Content 45
How to Explain Content Strategy and Customer
Engagement (for B2B and B2C) 46
Content Cheat Sheet to Convince the C-Suite 47
Overriding the Objections 47
Summary 48

Rule #2 Involve Stakeholders Early and Often 49

Case Study: XONEX 61

PART II   CONTENT FLOATS

3 **Constructing the Conversation** 69
The Internet Is the Room of Requirement 69
Magic Content: Making Diamonds Out of Coal 70
Understanding Substance and Structure 70
Creating a Content Framework 71
The Content Framework 71
Content Is Where Information Lives and Thrives 71
The Three Parts of Content 72
Content Formats That Flex 72
Content: Formats, Platforms, and Channels 73
Supporting the Sales and Buying Process Cycle 74
Understanding the Buying Process 76
The Law of Trust 78
Business Is about Relationships 79
Controlling the Content Experience 79
Understanding and Creating a Content Mix 80
Types of Content 84
Summary 85

Rule #3 Keep It Iterative 87

4 **Publishing Content for Everywhere** 101
Unlearn What You Have Learned 101
Content as a Concept 102
Attracting Surfers 102

Intersection of People, Process, and Technology 102
What Is Multichannel Publishing? 103
    Making Your Content Accessible on Any Device 104
    They Say How **and** When 104
    Changing Patterns of Content Consumption 105
    Pages Are Dead 105
    Strip Content from Display 106
    So If It's Not About Pages, Then What? 107
    Where We Fix Your Problem 107
    Defining Some Terms 108
    Why Design Isn't Always the Answer 109
    Adaptive Content to the Rescue 110
    How to Structure Your Content 112
    Welcome to the World of Hip Hop 113
    Content Modeling 115
    Content Management Systems (CMS) 116
    It Comes Down to People, Yet Again 116
A New Type of Content Consumption 119
Are You Planning for Content Properly? 120
Summary 120

5 Engagement Strategies 123
The Medium (Channel) Is the Message 123
    Deciding on the Right Channels to Distribute Content 124
Defining Channels 125
The Rise of Social Media, Digital Channels, and the
Multi-Screen World 126
Think Engagement—Think Community 128
Identifying the Community and Its Channels 129
    Find Your Audience on the Right Channels 130
Engaging the Community 131
    Entertain and Be Relevant! 132
    Keep the Conversation Going 132
    Invite Them to Engage Further 134
What to Do If the Community Doesn't Commune? 135
How and When to Build a Community 135
    It Isn't Social Media—It's Audience Engagement 136
    The Mind-Shift to a Culture of Community 136
    Figuring Out What to Measure 138
    Showing the C-Suite that Content Is Worth It 138
    Just to Reiterate … 139
Summary 140

Rule #4 Create Multidisciplinary Content Teams   **141**

Case Study: REI   **151**

PART III   EFFECTIVE CONTENT STRATEGY: PEOPLE, PROCESS, AND TECHNOLOGY

6   Understand Your Customers   **157**

About Personas   157

The Answers You Need   158

What Is a Persona?   159

    Personas Represent Your People   159

    Why Use Personas?   160

How to Create Personas   161

    Personas Workshop   161

    Backing Personas Up with Data   163

Three Categories of Journey Maps   168

    Seeker Maps   169

    Decision Journey Maps   169

    Interactive Scenarios   172

The Challenges of Using Personas in Large Organizations   175

Align Content Development with the Largest Persona Group   175

Summary   176

7   Frame Your Content   **179**

Why Frame?   179

What Is "Framing Your Content"?   180

Identity Pillars   180

    Brand Attributes   180

    How Do We Define Our Brand?   181

    Brand Attributes Versus Identity Pillars   181

    Creating Identity Pillars   182

    Example #1: Hospital Cure   182

    Example #2: American Faucet Maker   183

Messaging Architecture   184

    Creating a Messaging Architecture   184

    Establishing Pillar Priority   185

Voice and Tone   188

    Defining Your Voice   188

    Defining Your Tone   189

    Gogo—Getting Voice and Tone Right   190

The Payoff of Framing   191

    How Do We Express These Guidelines?   191

Summary   192

8   The Content Strategists' Toolkit   **195**

Thinking Like a Publisher   195

Ready to Execute   196

Focus on the Tools in the Box   197

Framework: People, Process, Technology   198

Content Strategy: Tools You Can Use   199

Plan   199

    Content Audits   200

    Centralized Style Guide   205

    Content Testing   205

Competitive Analysis   207

Create   208

    Goal Matrix   208

    Editorial Guidelines and Style Guide   209

Publish   209

    Editorial Calendars   209

    Workflows or Publishing Guidelines   210

    CMS Documentation   211

    Archiving Guidelines   211

Distribute   212

    Channel Mapping   212

    Policies and Guidelines for Distribution

    (Social Media)   212

Analyze   212

    Analytics Data   213

    Engagement Metrics   214

    Site Search Analytics   214

Govern   214

Summary   215

Rule #5 Make Governance Central   **217**

Case Study: HipHopDX   **231**

PART IV   CREATING CONTENT: TALKING AND LISTENING

9   Content Marketing Sustains the Conversation   **239**

    Promoting a Business in Today's Marketplace   239

What Is Content Marketing?   241

    Content Marketing Goals   241

    Content Marketing Tools   242

Content Marketing Solves Certain Problems   243

    Ads Don't Have the Same Power   243

Reduced Attention 243

Lack of Brand Loyalty 243

Social Sharing 244

Content Marketing to the Rescue 244

How Content Marketing Captures Today's Consumer 245

Get Buy-In for Content Marketing in Your Organization 247

Establish a Content Marketing Program 248

The 1-7-30-4-2-1 Approach 249

Match Your Content Marketing Efforts to Your Identity

Pillars and Messaging Architecture 250

Measure and Publicize Your Results 251

Summary 253

10 The Dream Digital Team **255**

You Need Great Talent 255

The Digital Strategy Talent You Need 255

Finding the Money (Spending Like a Publisher?) 257

Making Output Matter 257

Having a Back End and a Front End 257

Multidisciplinary Digital Strategy Teams Are Best 260

Kissing Disciplines 260

Pick the Right Talent 260

Captain Web 261

User Experience Professionals 262

Publication and Distribution Advocates 266

Business Advocates 268

Summary 270

Rule #6 Workflow That Works **273**

11 Talking About Design **289**

It's What's Inside the Box 289

However, Let's Get Real 289

The Relationship of Content to Design 290

Marry Content and Design 290

Design Before Content Reason #1: People React Visually 290

Design Before Content Reason #2: Bringing in Content Too Late 291

Design Before Content Reason #3: *Lorem Ipsum* 292

The Design Process 293

Site Maps 293

Flowcharts 295

Wireframes 295

Visual Designs 296

Content Tools to the Rescue 297

Page Specs 298

Content Testing 299

Usability Testing 300

Microcopy Testing 300

Summary 300

Rule #7 Invest in Professionals and Trust Them **303**

Case Study: Stefanie Diamond Photography **311**

Conclusion **315**

Acknowledgments **319**

Author Bio **321**

Index **323**

DEDICATION

For my greatest teachers, my children:

Tzophia, Amaya, and Navon

You are my glorious crowns.

To actually improve user experience in a sustainable way—that is, while achieving business goals—we need to help organizations deal with the revolutionary changes that the web has created in their business models, operational structures, and customer relationships. Denial isn't a strategy.

—Jonathan Kahn

FOREWORD

"A few strong instincts and a few plain rules suffice us." – Ralph Waldo Edison

As toddlers, they keep us safe: don't touch the stove. Look both ways before you cross the street. Dessert comes after broccoli.

In school, they keep us orderly: Raise your hand. Get to class on time. No running in the hallways.

And the older we get, the more we have to remember: Pay your bills on time. Use your turn signal. Don't wear white before Memorial Day. Call your mother.

To be honest, I don't spend a whole lot of time thinking about rules, at least not when it comes to my work. As Thomas Edison once said, "Hell, there are no rules here—we're trying to accomplish something!"

And yet, when it comes to content, I think the main problem we face is that we don't have *enough* rules. Or, in many cases, any at all.

Why? Is it that, like me, we often find them unnecessarily restrictive—as in, "These shouldn't apply to me, because I am a unique snowflake?" Is it just too hard to fight the battle, so we stay with the status quo? Or is it simply that we don't know where to start?

Over the past ten years, I've worked with clients of all shapes and sizes, from small startups to Fortune 100 enterprises. But no matter where I go or who I talk to, time and time again, I hear the same woeful complaints:

- "We have too much content."
- "We don't have enough content."
- "Our content is off-brand/inconsistent/out-of-date/inaccurate."
- "We don't know where all our content is or where it's coming from."
- "Content is being produced in silos."
- "No one is in charge of the content."
- "The technology we use/don't use to manage our content doesn't work the way we want it to."
- "We can't keep up with the [fill in a scary number] digital properties we've launched over the past [fill in a scary number] of years.

This, my friend, is what we call chaos.

I'll tell you what, though. The one that always breaks my heart is when people say:

- "This is all so very embarrassing."

There is no need to feel embarrassed, dear reader. Visit any website and do a little digging, and you quickly realize that you are not the only one whose content could use some help. And although you may be in caught in a quagmire of content ickiness, it's important to understand that most likely, you, personally, haven't done anything wrong. You are a simply working for a company that lacks the infrastructure that supports the ongoing creation, delivery, and governance of content people actually care about.

But, really. Why would we expect your company—any company—to have that in place? That's what a *publisher* does. You are not a publisher. You are a service or product provider. That's where your core competencies lie.

Except, of course, the minute you launched a website … the minute you put up a Facebook page, or started a video channel, or signed up for Twitter … you assumed the mantle of publisher. You're creating content. You're curating it. You've started a conversation people expect you to continue for as long as that digital property lives on.

Welcome to your new reality.

Here's something to consider. The more work I do with organizations, the more convinced I become that there is, in fact, a finite set of content problems to be solved. This implies that, perhaps, there are some common solutions that might be shared among anyone who deals with content. We've been sold on a variety of silver bullets—buy this expensive CMS! Let your users create all the content!—but, frankly, nothing has really, truly addressed one of the core problems that exists within organizations: when it comes to content, people often either don't get it or don't care.

The Digital Crown will go a long way in changing that. By offering seven hard-and-fast rules for delivering valuable content to your core audiences, Ahava has provided you with an extraordinarily valuable framework to build sustainable, *profitable* content marketing campaigns. Her seven unbreakable rules are real-world solutions that will help you get on track for both today's complex content environments and tomorrow's unpredictable challenges.

Finally, here is something that every marketer needs to understand: when it comes to winning at digital strategy, *you are not an exception to the rules.* For too long, companies simply have refused to step up and acknowledge that content—far from being a simple byproduct of necessary business activities—is in fact a valuable business asset that deserves our strategic consideration.

In order to fully realize its value, it's critical that we invest our thought, time, and resources to get it right … not just the first time, but every time.

The Digital Crown changes the content game. Follow the seven rules, and you'll win. Beat that!

Kristina Halvorson
CEO, Brain Traffic
Author, *Content Strategy for the Web*

INTRODUCTION: WHY CONTENT MATTERS

Information in This Chapter

- Solving the Content Problem
- Managing Content with a System
- Knowing Your Audience
- Using the Right Talent

Whether you are a marketing executive, a small business owner, a content professional, or the chief technology officer of a Fortune 1000 company, chances are you're freaked out by the demand for online content. Bill Gates famously said in 1996, "Content is King." Everyone keeps repeating that quote, but some people have no idea what it really means—how to achieve content excellence, ascend the throne, and wear the crown.

If you need to understand the how, why, when, and who of creating great content for your audience to consume, then this book is for you. You may feel unequipped to create and deliver fabulous content experiences for a variety of reasons: not enough money in the budget, not the right staff, not enough content, too much content. If you've noticed that focusing on video, or blogging, or search engine optimization (SEO), or social media, or the next hot digital thing isn't getting you where you really want to go, then you're in the right place. Together, learning the theory of content, as well as tactics and tools for content success, we will build a roadmap toward digital strategy victory.

SOLVING YOUR CONTENT PROBLEM

Chances are you picked up this book for one, two, or maybe all three of these reasons:

1. Your business isn't performing the way you want it to and you're suspicious that after two expensive redesigns the problem may not lie with design.
2. You've been on too many website and digital strategy projects that have failed and you're looking for a new way to think about digital strategy.
3. You buy any book with the word *content* in the title.

The reason that websites and other digital strategy projects fail is because the people managing them don't focus on what really matters. They begin changing things for the sake of change, to "update," without first asking themselves why. They usually also forget to ask what the update will accomplish. This creates a focus on the wrong priorities.

In the case of any strategy for a business, not-for-profit organization, government agency, or other organization, the first question we must ask is: Why are we doing this? This question is otherwise known as the business case.

A business case demonstrates the reason we do something that costs resources such as money or someone's time. If you want your digital projects to be successful, you need to move your focus away from doing what everyone else is doing to "keep up." Instead, start focusing on your audience—what they want to say as well as what they want to hear. Start with a conversation. In the digital world, content makes conversations happen.

In the digital world, content makes conversations happen.

Your design can look good, it can even win design awards, but without the content to attract the audience, keep them there, and get them to buy something or use your service, your pretty website or social media page does not meet the needs of your business. *Meeting the needs of your business is what content is about*: content supports the sales process.

THE INHERENT TENSION IN CONTENT

Our challenges with content lie with two different but interrelated challenges:

- How do we capture the information we need from our internal sources?
- How do we create a publishing system to release that content into the world?

The information you need from inside your organization is the content your audience needs and wants. *Content consists of all of the information assets of your company that you share with the world*.

And, it's not just text. Mind-shift time: We need to stop thinking about content as articles, blogs, and catalogs. *Content is the information, resources, and materials that you want to communicate to your audience.* This includes, but is certainly not limited to, written text, photographs, graphics, infographics, PDFs, documents in other formats, reviews, video, audio, and so on.

Getting all those information assets out to the public in a systematic, sensible process feels overwhelming. Publishing has become so instantaneous that it's (almost) impossible to keep up with your audiences' demands—four years ago it was Facebook. Eighteen months ago, Google+. Now, if you don't have an infographic, you're not relevant (that's Pinterest). Vine exploded just a few months back. Apparently, even MySpace is back. How can any organization, especially smaller ones with very limited budgets, keep up?

If you are responsible for the content on a website or for a brand, then it's not just the written word you need to think about, but also any type of content that communicates about your brand. In fact, user-generated content (UGC) is also your responsibility. How do you publish, regulate, and manage all of that content? (Without the use of illegal or prescription drugs?)

CONTENT IS MESSY. IT'S COMPLICATED. IT'S TIME-CONSUMING

People typically go wrong with content because they want to finalize it. Finish with it. Forget that, too. Things change too quickly in today's marketplace for us to get to "perfect" and feel that a project is finished. It's not like writing a book or a brochure that is printed (and even books have second and third editions). Content is something that keeps changing, so by definition it does not really end.

When content teams seek perfection, they freeze in this fast-paced world and don't create or publish *anything*. Some organizations don't act because they lack a clear strategy for what they can accomplish with their content. Instead, they throw things on the wall and see what sticks. (I call this a spaghetti content strategy.) Sometimes, because of this immense pressure, they put the wrong types of information out there, or even worse, incomplete information, further stymying that great conversation they intended to have.

While the CFO would never allow that strategy in the finance department (can you imagine how the books might look?), many marketing departments behave in precisely that manner because they don't have a systematic content process. Then, when content doesn't perform the way they expect, they give up. Or, *they redesign*.

The Mess That Can Be Managed

Feeling frustrated? I hear you. You probably feel like my ten year old who, while doing her math homework, will throw her pencil across the room and exclaim, "I'm bad at math!"

If you feel that you are not good at this content thing, or you are so overwhelmed with your to-do list that you are frozen, like peas, you've made the first right step: You've picked up this book.

WHY FOLLOWING A SYSTEM IS KEY

If you want to manage anything, you must follow a system. Content is no different. Systems, by their design, create freedom. Rules are there to help people. Take driving, for example: If one driver decides to ignore a stop sign, others get hurt.

The goal of content strategy is to create a framework around the execution of content so that creativity can flourish.

Systems help us modify our behaviors which is vital for organizations that want to create great content. This is why in this book I introduce and evangelize the adoption of seven rules to keep your content processes healthy and adaptive. These rules will give you a system for creating engaging, robust, reusable content. Once you and/or your digital team master these seven rules, you will have a map, a road to follow—in other words, freedom from chaos and panic. In essence, a company has to experience a cultural shift in order to create outstanding, winning content. Shifts only happen with guiding principles and support. These rules provide that structure.

Together, we're going to explore content—first, how to think about it. Then, we will learn how to create a content publishing strategy that works for your organization, builds your business, and makes you and your team content rock stars.

PART 1: CONTENT AS CONVERSATIONS

In Part 1, we'll explore the idea of content as a conversation. For a great exchange we need give and take. To do that, we need to know whom we are, which is why we need to understand our organization's branding.

We also need to know how we're going to have those conversations, which is why we'll explore the concepts of content strategy and content marketing. We'll learn why it's so important to know who it is that we're talking to, which is why the first rule is ….

RULE #1: START WITH YOUR AUDIENCE

Content is the fuel that drives your organization's sales engine. Your audience will buy something, use your service, or donate money because of your content. Therefore, you need to know the following about these people (because *they are people*):

- Who are they?
- Why are you creating content for them?
- What types of content do they truly want to consume?
- How do they want to find and/or receive that content?

In Chapter 2, we will tackle how to build a business case for content and position that business case for your senior and executive leadership (you may even be that leadership).

Making a business case for content can be challenging. However, your executives—or you—need to understand how important content is to an organization's sales process, or achievement threshold. Identifying some of those executives and senior leadership as stakeholders will bring us to the next step on our journey …

RULE #2: INVOLVE STAKEHOLDERS EARLY AND OFTEN

We all know the expression, "Let's get the right people in the room."

I cannot tell you how many times I have seen content projects and entire web projects derailed because nobody consulted the senior stakeholders about content early in the process. What is scarier is how many times I've seen projects derailed because *junior* stakeholders were not brought into the process early enough.

It's important to understand who makes decisions *and* who has important knowledge that affects content. Get to know the lay of the land so that you invite the right people into the right discussions, which will ultimately affect the production and management of content.

PART 2: CONTENT FLOATS

You goal is to have a great conversation with your audience in order to build a relationship. How do you know what to say? How do you get your content packaged so that it meets your audience when they are in a mood to listen? What tools do you use to listen to the audience? How do you make sure you are saying the right things?

We will learn how to create content based on our business objectives as well as use content to support the decision-making process our customers make. We'll also learn that we must follow …

RULE #3: KEEP IT ITERATIVE

Iterative describes a process in which you continually re-think and refine, making changes and remaining flexible and sensitive to the flow of ideas and input, until you achieve the final product. We all agree that in the constantly changing digital world there is no such thing as a final product.

Online we can change so much so quickly, which means we can always iterate. Plus, technology is always changing, so serving great digital content means we have to learn to adapt to change.

We'll talk about how to approach projects from an iterative point of view, always looking to improve but not being stymied by paralysis through analysis.

In Chapters 4 and 5 we'll learn how to structure your content so that it's future-ready. We'll also learn that your content is not your website, or your blog, or your YouTube channel. Content is the information you have displayed on your website, blog or YouTube channel. Those channels are just delivery methods—ways to get your content to the people that want it.

Which brings us to …

RULE #4: CREATE MULTIDISCIPLINARY CONTENT TEAMS

I spent seven years writing healthcare digital content and the major buzzword during that time (and still) in the healthcare industry was "multidisciplinary." Medical professionals use that word to describe different specialists who work together to plan and coordinate treatment for complex diseases.

In our digital strategy world the same approach applies. Only multidisciplinary digital teams can produce *and* deliver great content. Having designers who understand how people read on a mobile device or a developer who picks the right platform for content delivery will make or break your digital strategy. You also need people throughout the organization who understand all the different types of conversations you need to have with your audience. That's where finding the right people to drive certain content projects transforms into the art of skillful management and breaking down organizational siloes.

PART 3: CONTENT STRATEGY: PEOPLE AND PROCESS

In Part 3, we'll learn how to set up an effective content strategy—an online publishing system—and all about the tools you will need to do so. The management of content requires a firm understanding of people, process, and technology. In Chapters 6, 7, and 8, we'll talk about understanding your customer, how to map out what you want to say, different phases of a content strategy, and how to align your content teams so that they are running efficiently.

Which brings us to …

RULE #5: MAKE GOVERNANCE CENTRAL

Governance describes the process of keeping content consistent, fresh, and organized. You must maintain governance if you want people to connect to your brand. Did you ever have that friend who was hot and cold? On Monday you were best friends and on Wednesday she gave you the cold shoulder? No one likes those types of people because you cannot trust them. You certainly do not want your customers to perceive your brand as inconsistent and unreliable. Consistency is powerful and the only true path to change. This brings us to content marketing, which is a vital approach to maintaining a consistent relationship with your target audiences.

PART 4: SUSTAINING THE CONVERSATION

Content marketing is using content to build an audience that trusts you, shares your content, and recommends you to friends. After we describe how to create effective content marketing programs, we're going to learn about our final two rules …

RULE #6: POSITION THE RIGHT TALENT IN THE RIGHT ROLES

Too often, when I consult with companies I learn quickly that the wrong talent is in the wrong roles. Creatives are trying desperately to be project managers, personnel responsible for creativity don't have the proper training, or people with great execution skills are responsible for theory and strategy. For obvious reasons this creates friction, inefficiencies, and workflow challenges—not to mention nausea and exhaustion. We will talk about the importance of workflow and change management and how they lead to creating and managing winning content.

Then, in Chapter 11, we'll touch upon design because just like a beautiful diamond shouldn't be set in a less than spectacular setting, so too, your content should be displayed in a supportive design. Which will bring us to our final rule:

RULE #7: INVEST IN PROFESSIONALS AND TRUST THEM

You need to know when you don't have the internal resources you need to do the job. That might mean a SEO expert, or a digital writer, or a mobile developer.

If you don't have the financial resources to outsource, you might be able to find an enterprising person on your team who is willing to try to wear that hat. Ultimately, however, you will find you have wasted valuable time and money in potential revenue if you don't bite the bullet and find a way for an expert to look at your problem.

Hire the right professional who can help you look at your challenge and find the solution that's right for your budget and your team. Then trust that person. It's his or her *job* to solve the problem—not yours.

Along the way, we're going to meet businesses of all sizes that faced content problems and mastered them. By peering inside their world, you will get a glimpse of the tools and tactics others have used to succeed at content.

YOU ARE GOING TO BE GREAT AT THIS

The goal of *The Digital Crown* is to arm you with the steps you need to create winning online content. If you follow the seven rules in this book, you will feel primed to take control of content production within your company, or for your clients, and move it forward toward success.

No one has the Holy Grail on how to be successful on the web. You need a strategy in place—one that is elastic enough to keep up with the speed of innovation but structured enough so you feel confident of your overall direction. You need a Lycra® blend content solution, which is why the seven rules are so important: They provide a structured system to aid in winning the digital content game.

More than ever people need information and they want to have a conversation. It's your job to give both to them. Along the way, you can entertain, delight, enchant, and persuade. Because content is king, it needs to be your starting and ending point. It lives in a cycle of conversations with your audience and it's out there waiting to be mastered.

Shall we begin?

CONTENT IS A CONVERSATION

The Net is a real place where people can go to learn, to talk to each other, and to do business together. It is a bazaar where customers look for wares, vendors spread goods for display, and people gather around topics that interest them. It is a conversation.

(Levine, 2009)

CHANGING PATTERNS OF CONTENT CONSUMPTION

We live in a world of networked markets. To build great relationships with our customers, we must focus on content as conversations.

The marketplace shifts rapidly. People research everything they buy online; they can even talk to other people *around the globe* before they buy.

Our audiences typically have more than one device to access content. They surf multiple channels at once, having conversations on multiple devices and different sized screens, moving seamlessly from one conversation to the next. They interact and share daily with friends, colleagues, and peers within huge social networks previously impossible to imagine.

If you are the person responsible for managing content creation and execution, you may not be sure where to start. When you don't know who someone is and you want to learn more about and share with them, where do you begin?

You begin with a conversation. A conversation is a dialogue, the exchange of information between two parties. Sometimes we listen, and sometimes we talk.

UNDERSTANDING THE POWER OF DIGITAL CONTENT

The axiom goes, "If you want to be treated differently, act differently." In the case of content, we need to think about it differently so we can treat it differently. In Part 1, we're going to learn how to think about content differently so that we can build long-lasting, true relationships with our audiences. By learning to think about content in a different way, we will break down some of the organizational barriers and silos that occur when we try to create and publish content.

So, we are going to learn how to have a conversation with our customers. To do that, we must understand:

- *Our brand*: Who we are
- *Digital content*: The most effective way to converse with our audiences
- *Content drives sales*: Content is a critical asset within the business

In Part 1, we're going to cover all of the above. Together, we will also learn the first of the seven rules for creating winning content for your brand:

- Rule #1: *Start with Your Audience*
- Rule #2: *Involve Stakeholders Early and Often*

Let's begin by learning about the interplay of branding, content strategy and content marketing.

REFERENCE

Levine, R. (2009). *The Cluetrain Manifesto*. New York: Basic Books, p. 81.

UNDERSTANDING BRANDING, CONTENT STRATEGY, AND CONTENT MARKETING

Are you a person who is frustrated by the content process within your organization? You may be the vice president of marketing, the owner of a small business, the director of web strategy, or a content communications professional.

For a moment, I want you to imagine that instead of being responsible for your organization's content or website, you are actually responsible for a retail store—an actual storefront with a physical address and an entrance. It's a beautiful store, with fabulous merchandise arranged in pleasing detail to entice your customers.

However, when your customers enter there is no one to greet them. Not one person in the store picks up his head to say, "Hello, can I help you?" In some cases, the salespeople in the store don't speak the same language as your browsing customers. When your potential buyer asks about products in the store, those salespeople are missing critical information.

Does the content on your digital properties (websites, social media channels, blogs) function like this? Does the content support the user experience? Can people find the information they need? Is the product information complete? Are there enticing stories that compel visitors to dive in deeper? Do they sign up for continued communications with your organization or do they bounce like rubber balls right off of the page?

THE PROBLEM GROWS

How many times does someone call you on the phone and ask why your company is not showing up on Google as the first result of a search for a certain term? How many requests pass across your desk to change something on the website? Do your superiors tell you that this is not your problem, only to have various people in the organization then point their fingers at you when something goes wrong on the website or on social media? Are you the person consistently reporting to the CEO, or other members of the C-suite (senior executive management, so named because many of their titles begin with C, for Chief), and falling short every time? Worse, are you not able to articulate the full mess you are managing every day?

Around the globe, organizations of all sizes are struggling to communicate online—to make sales, encourage brand ambassadorship, communicate information, and persuade public opinion. The word *web* suggests interdependence, something large multinational organizations understand. Yet, these very same organizations do not know how to align their web operations so they are consistent, efficient and have reporting mechanisms that speak directly to the bottom line.

Before you decide where you want to go, you need vision. You must begin with the end in mind. To get there, you need a roadmap. Together, we are going to learn to create a digital strategy roadmap for your organization. We will learn about the unique interplay between people, processes, and technology that are vital for effective and successful web content.

THE CHALLENGE OF THE WEB

> The web gives us the power of information through exchanges and conversations.

In many ways, the virtual world of the Internet is better and worse than the actual physical world. In the real world, you can smell a Cinnabon. Stroke a mohair jacket. Taste a salted caramel latte. Not true online. You can't touch products, try them on, taste them, or really discern if that shirt is teal, turquoise, or cerulean.

In the actual physical world you can't read what others think about the shirt, if they found the fit true to size, and what color they thought it looked like when they pulled it out of the box. The web gives us the power of information through exchanges and conversations.

Marketplaces rely on conversations: the web is a modern marketplace. Conversations between people matter in ways they have not mattered before, as communication technologies facilitate wider and deeper exchanges of information than ever in the history of humankind.

Starting the Conversation: The Beginning of the Internet

There is some controversy as to whether or not the military started the Internet as a way of maintaining communication in time of war. Some say this is an urban myth. As Gordon Crovitz writes, "For many technologists, the idea of the Internet traces to Vannevar Bush, the presidential science adviser during World War II who oversaw the development of radar and the Manhattan Project. … Bush defined an ambitious peacetime goal for technologists: Build what he called a 'memex' through which "wholly new forms of encyclopedias will appear, ready made with a mesh of associative trails running through them, ready to be dropped into the memex and there amplified" (Crovitz, 2012). Yet another theory is that a famous computer scientist named Bob Taylor invented the Internet so that universities could share resources.

Let's not worry about the who, but rather, let's appreciate what the creation of the Internet has meant for all of us— the start of our ability to engage in incredibly wide reaching and meaningful conversations. And, for many of us, it's created careers we never could have dreamt about in high school physics classes.

The Internet was built for creating conversations through the input of real people (called crowdsourcing), which is why content has become so important in modern marketing. We are in a world of constant conversations and exchanges of information. People want to know what they want to know—and they want to know instantaneously.

CROWDSOURCING: INFORMATION FROM TRUSTED SOURCES

In the real, actual world, you share doctor referrals, recommendations for dance classes for your kids, and golf tips, across the proverbial white picket fence. Now, you jump on Facebook and ask your social network for their recommendations. Or, get on YouTube and watch videos about golf. Use Google or Bing to research dance classes. You are seeking information from trusted sources—and the web supplies that demand. It is the technology platform that facilitates global interactions.

It should come as a comfort that human behavior remains the same; we still seek recommendations from others. New communications technologies facilitate those normal interactions—but wider and deeper than ever before. And, more public, as we are allowing others to "eavesdrop" on those conversations.

You have always chatted with your friends about your favorite supermarket; now you can post a statement on Facebook about the store. Before you know it, everyone is shopping there—something that would not, and could not, have happened before our new communication technologies. The reverse is also true—one convincing negative review and a person may choose not to buy a product or service.

While you can find thousands of articles on how texting, the web, and current mobile technologies are changing human interaction, I would say that we are actually just facilitating MORE of the interactions we've always had. More than anything, the instantaneous and awesome power of the Internet is that it has flattened our white picket fence.

TripAdvisor: Powerful Exchanges Between Strangers

According to Google, we spend an average of about 2.5 hours on research before making a travel decision. It is very likely that a lot of that time is spent on TripAdvisor (Morison, 2012). What's unique about this site is that people from all over the world post their personal experiences with specific locations, hotels, restaurants, and travel destinations. The rankings on the site are created according to audience input, not some vague industry standard. And today, hotels are fighting to be in TripAdvisor's list of the top five hotels for a particular city. If you see a review critiquing the cleanliness of a hotel room, or the surliness of its staff, you will more than likely choose another hotel with better reviews, and the travel industry knows this.

Behold the power of the conversation—TripAdvisor reported in 2011 that page views of its content had some influence on roughly $2.6 billion worth of business.

SHOULD BUSINESSES REALLY CARE?

Yes. The reach people now have is almost immeasurable. People make assumptions about your brand based on their encounters with it in the actual physical world and online. Then they will talk about it—with their spouses, peers, colleagues, and strangers—when they post an online review. As a business, you need to control that conversation. This book shows you how.

UNDERSTANDING CONTENT

If you want to control the conversation people have about your brand, you need to understand what content is, how it performs, and how people choose to share and consume it. Content is information that is organized and arranged in a format. Embedded in that format is information—the solution to someone's problem or question.

For example, if a company issues a press release, they know that journalists will see it and think, "That piece of content is for me." When you see an ad in a newspaper, you recognize it as an ad—embedded within it is a piece of information about a brand, store, or sale. When someone hands you a form to fill out, you know what you need to do.

These content formats are recognizable to you because you've seen them so many times. Someone designed them to provide you with the information you seek, or to capture information that someone else needs.

Once you make that transformation of information into content, you choose which channels (print, broadcast, web) you wish to use to distribute the content (Figure 1.1).

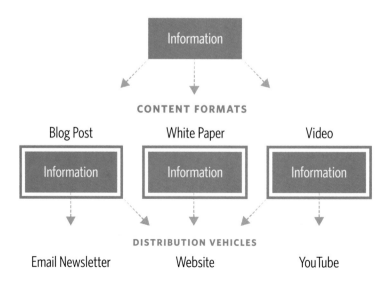

Figure 1.1 Content: From Information to Distribution. Ahava Leibtag. All Rights Reserved.

In other words, we take information we want to share with our audience and turn it into a content format they will quickly recognize. Then we choose the channels where we think they spend their time and make sure our content is there for them to find.

Media planners spend thousands of hours each year choosing TV shows that promise to attract the audience they believe will buy their products. If you are a media buyer for a denture cleaner company, chances are you're not going to spend your precious advertising dollars on a network like MTV,

When information takes the form of something we recognize, that is content.

Choosing the Right Ads—Or Not

The ad world is full of horror stories about bad ad placement. For example, Aflac, the insurance company, posted an ad featuring their duck mascot on the same page as an article about anatidaephobia—the fear that you are being watched by a duck (Figure 1.2).

In real estate, they say location is everything. This is true in ad placement as well.

Figure 1.2 An article about fear of being watched by a duck is mistakenly placed alongside information from an insurance company whose mascot is … a duck.

a channel that shows music videos and reality TV shows geared toward teenagers and young adults. People who use denture cleaners probably aren't watching MTV.

Digital marketing strategy has many similarities to traditional marketing. The focus is still about offering your information in a format that will attract your audience. Yet to do this right, and get the results you want, you need to think strategically about how people communicate online.

If you want to be in control of the conversation people have about your brand, you must understand the unique interplay between:

- Branding
- Content Strategy
- Content Marketing

Developing and managing successful content is dependent on understanding all three, which in turn will help you have great conversations with your audiences.

> Strategy is about having a plan that gets you where you want to go. Tactics are methods you use to get to that place.

THE ART OF CONVERSATION

Branding, content strategy, and content marketing are harmonious when it comes to creating great conversations around your brand. To understand this concept, let's talk about what a great conversation looks like.

Great conversationalists know six rules about leaving a lasting effect:

1. Know who you are
2. Know who you are talking to
3. Listen
4. Ask good questions
5. Have thoughtful answers
6. Understand there are different types of conversations

Branding, content strategy, and content marketing are all designed to help you build great relationships with your target audiences, make the sale, persuade the donor, inform the prospect, and so on. Let's understand how they help you build your digital and content team's understanding of artful conversations.

BRANDING: A BRAND IS A PROMISE

Tiffany & Co., the famous jeweler with the unmistakable robin's egg blue packaging, ran a print ad many years ago. In the black and white photograph, a man holds a ring box in his hand behind his back. Looking at the ad, you felt the immediate suspense of an imminent marriage proposal.

The tagline on the ad captured the moment perfectly. It said, "It's a promise."

The copywriter and photographer conveyed two simpatico ideas using a very simple black and white image and tagline:

1. This man was about to give his bride-to-be a classic, quality engagement ring from one of the finest jewelers in the world, demonstrating his promise of eternal love. "I will take care of you forever," he is saying.

2. The ring, a product of this world-famous jeweler, is, in itself, a promise. The diamond set in that ring, with a perfect platinum band stamped with Tiffany's brand, is a lifelong promise about the ring and its classic, eternal value.

I use this example to demonstrate what a brand really is—a brand is a promise. For some, the promise is a good one. For others, who have had negative encounters with a particular brand, the promise is one of poor customer service or products being too expensive or too cheap. It depends on the encounter, or series of encounters, the person experiences with that brand over time.

WHAT IS A BRAND?

A brand is the amalgamation of all the different experiences and encounters a consumer has had with products, salespeople, marketing, advertising, and retail experiences (if there are retail stores). That's why a brand is a promise; people have an expectation of how their encounter with a brand will go based on

---

Short History of Brands

Historians and archaeologists believe that brands may have begun as far back as the Middle Ages. The word "brand" is derived from the Old Norse *brandr* meaning "to burn." It refers to the practice of producers burning their mark (or brand) onto their products (Ritson, 2006). The Italians were among the first to use brands, in the form of watermarks on paper in the 1200s (Colapinto, 2011).

Centuries later, industrialization moved the production of many household items, such as soap, from local communities to centralized factories. When shipping their items, the factories would literally brand their logo or insignia on the barrels used, extending the meaning of "brand" to that of trademark. In the 1700s and 1800s, American cowboys would brand their cattle with a specific logo that identified the cow as a member of a particular herd.

previous encounters, what they have heard in the media, what their friends have told them, how the salesperson greets them when they walk into the store, and so on.

Brands are NOT logos, or typefaces, or colors, or spokespeople, in the same way that a person is not their name, weight, age, or profession. Rather, those are brand attributes.

Just like people, brands have different facets and aspects—like different people you know have different personalities. One way to think of a brand is how most people might express the brand in three words. (How would people describe *you* in three words?).

DEFINING BRANDS

How do we define brands? Here is a quick exercise:

What do you think of when you consider the following world famous brands?

- McDonald's
- Coca-Cola
- Apple
- Nike

Fill in the following table:

	Logo	Tagline	Represents	Makes You Feel (Brand Promise)
McDonald's				
Coca-Cola				
Apple				
Nike				

The items you filled in above are *brand attributes*, in the same way that a person's demographics and identifying features are characteristics. They do not define the brand, just as the color of your hair does not define you.

Before we get into deeper thinking about brand definition, let's discuss who should define a brand.

WHO DEFINES A BRAND?

In a perfect situation, a company defines its brand. That's why the above four brands are internationally known, well respected, and unique within their competitive marketplace. The branding teams behind those companies spend countless hours and dollars to develop what billions of people around the world think and feel about those brands.

A brand community is a community formed because of attachment to a product or service. In a less than perfect situation, the leadership in a company has allowed the *brand community* to define the brand. They have allowed the brand audience to take control of the conversation in a negative manner.

The famous homemade video "United Breaks Guitars" is an example of a brand audience taking control of a conversation. United Airlines' baggage handlers damaged a musician's guitar in the course of loading it and unloading it on the plane. After getting no response from the company after repeated attempts to resolve his claim, the musician made a video, posted it on YouTube and got more than 12 million views. This was publicity and a conversation that United didn't need. The good news is that they eventually apologized, reimbursed him for his guitar, and use his video in their customer service training (Kelleher, 2013).

The United story had somewhat of a happy ending but it did damage. Instead of an active, determined, strategically planned brand, those outside of the organization defined United as the airline that damages luggage. Branding damage happens because there is no executive control over the brand and no plans in place to deal with emergencies. There is no control over the conversation.

People create brand communities by the way they interact with a brand, including:

- Products
- Salespeople
- Marketing
- Advertising
- News media
- Retail experiences

The brand's image will suffer if the media reports that the brand's latest product has bugs. If you have a negative encounter with a brand, you might post about it on your social networks. Depending on how many people see it, the brand might suffer. Good brand management happens when the company handles both negative and positive interactions well.

Let's talk about good brand management.

MANAGING THE BRAND

Customers develop their own ideas about brands based on hundreds of virtual interactions and perhaps very few *real-life*, or physical interactions. This creates conflict for you if you're responsible on any level for the brand. Why? Because you have no real control over how, when, and why consumers will interact with your brand. If you sell a variety of products under your umbrella brand, like the four brands we listed above, consumers may have a perception of one product that they tie to your overall umbrella brand. For example, Apple sells the iMac and the iPhone. Consumers may confuse these two products under the major brand umbrella. If they have a bad experience with one product, it confuses their image of the brand.

So, the big question is: How do you create a powerful brand that consumers will associate with your products and services and that will truly differentiate them from everything else out there?

You need three things:

1. Brand definition
2. Employee training about the brand
3. Brand consistency on all your communication channels

BRAND DEFINITION

Defining the brand is something that should be decided by the senior-most executive leadership. However, brands evolve and change over time. In fact, companies sometimes hire new executive leadership to change brand perception.

If you need to know more about your brand, ask around. Talk to people within the organization. If you have the budget, time, and emotional reserve, consider hiring a branding firm to help you. Most of the time, people within the organization know the brand. What they are afraid of is how to articulate what they think.

Too often companies are afraid to tell the truth about their brand. But that's silly. Not everyone is going to shop at a high-end department store. Some people will want to shop at a more affordable department store. The affordable department store should make it clear to their target audiences that they deliver fashionable clothing at reasonable prices.

EMPLOYEE TRAINING ABOUT THE BRAND

Employees fail to deliver on their brand promise because brand alignment is lacking throughout the organization. Most organizations have difficulty maintaining the brand promise throughout all levels of service. Test this by asking employees to describe the company brand in three words. See if there's a gap between what your marketing department says and what your employees say.

Apple is a phenomenal example of branding alignment across employees and staff. When you walk into an Apple store, it's usually busy. When you approach the Apple salespeople, they are friendly, helpful, and knowledgeable about any product in the store. This is probably because Apple recruits enthusiastic job seekers and trains them to channel that enthusiasm into their work.

Apple educates employees about the brand promise on their first day of work. On their first day, new Apple employees start their training by entering a room filled with current employees; they then receive a standing ovation. While the clapping and whistling may be a bit overwhelming, it also inspires the newbies.

During their training, a huge amount of time is devoted to role-playing, emphasizing etiquette, empathy, and honesty. For example, before touching a customer's product, an employee is trained to ask permission to do so. Trainees hear repeatedly that their job is to "enrich people's lives," which instills in them the sense that they are doing much more than fixing or selling products (Segal, 2012).

Specifically, Apple employees are trained in what is called the Apple Five Steps of Service (Gallo, 2012):

- **A**pproach customers with a personalized, warm welcome
- **P**robe politely to understand all the customer's needs
- **P**resent a solution for the customer to take home today
- **L**isten for and resolve any issues or concerns
- **E**nd with a fond farewell and an invitation to return

BRAND CONSISTENCY

Everyone in the company has to be in alignment with the brand so that you communicate effectively with your consumers. If you run a Fortune 1000 company, you probably have an entire branding staff to help you on this complex journey. If you're a part of a small company, then you probably don't. Don't despair: sometimes in small companies branding is easier because you can align a smaller group of people on the brand promise.

Brand consistency is an art you must practice. There are many tools we will learn about to help you develop and maintain brand consistency across your content in Rule #5.

Consistency Across Channels

Now think about your encounter with a brand online. It's different in some ways from in-store experiences but the basic challenge remains the same. Well-known and trusted brands do this so well—they maintain the brand as a promise.

Part of the reason that I have focused on retail consumer brands is to highlight a perceived difference between digital marketing and real-world marketing. The toughest challenges in digital marketing are that many marketers perceive the web to be a completely different place than the real world. Is this true?

Well, as we said at the beginning of this chapter, in some ways the web is a different marketplace because the technology facilitates fast and wide interactions—and in many cases with no consequences. So while you might be willing to rank a book anonymously on Amazon.com, you may feel more inhibited doing so in front of the author.

The web is a marketplace like any other, which means that people want consistency. If they encounter your brand one way in real life they want it to be that way on the web. That is why brand definition and management is the starting point for any online content and marketing strategy.

Once you define that promise, the next step is to decide how to communicate that promise.

BUILD A PROCESS: CONTENT STRATEGY AND CONTENT MARKETING REINFORCE BRANDING

If the key to any great conversation is knowing who you are—and you discover that through branding—then how do you begin to communicate with your audience in a strategic way? That's where content strategy and content marketing provide systems and structures for your digital strategy efforts.

WHAT IS CONTENT STRATEGY?

Content strategy describes the production cycle for your digital strategy. (Remember: don't confuse content strategy with messaging strategy. As we explained earlier, messaging is one way brands encapsulate their goals and offerings for customers.) For now, when we say content strategy we mean a production cycle for creating and managing digital content.

SYSTEMS CREATE FREEDOM

Content strategy is a system that an organization uses to plan, create, publish, analyze, and govern content. Systems create freedom; they make it much easier to make decisions and implement them. Many people feel hindered by the rules. But rules keep everyone in check, as we talked about in the introduction.

Kristina Halvorson, who wrote the defining book on content strategy, *Content Strategy for the Web*, explains, "Content strategy plans for the creation, delivery, and governance of useful, usable content" (Halvorson, 2010). Richard Sheffield, who wrote *The Web Content Strategist's Bible*, says [Content strategy is a] "repeatable system that defines the entire editorial content development process for a website development project" (Sheffield, 2009).

Both of these definitions are helpful because they give us two focus areas:

- Useful, usable content
- Repeatable system

What Is Useful, Usable Content?

Halvorson explains that content strategy has two purposes:

1. It aligns your content with your business objectives
2. It helps your users accomplish their goals

Halvorson uses the example of putting the little weather widget on the home page of a website. While having this widget on your site is certainly fun, if you are a bank, the weather probably doesn't really matter to users when they are interacting with your site. They want to find out how much money they have, how to set up a savings account, or how to apply for a loan. In other words: Don't give them a totally different conversation than the one they came to you to have—that defeats the purpose of content supporting the sales process.

If the "information" you want to put on your website does not align with your business objectives *or* help your users accomplish their tasks, then forget about developing it into content. It won't help you make more money (or reach your achievement threshold—your organization's measurement of success). It won't help your customers and therefore it's a waste of time.

What Is a Repeatable Lifecycle?

Those are some scary words, right? But, a repeatable lifecycle is something we are all familiar with—it is like a recipe. Think of the barista at your favorite corner coffee store. (Have a particular logo in mind right now? See, the power of branding at work!)

When you walk in and order a decaf skinny vanilla latte with extra foam, do you think the barista goes to find the recipe and refers to it while he is making the drink? Unless he just started working at this coffee shop, I'd vote no. He has made that drink so many times that the bottle of sugar-free vanilla syrup is replaced at least once a day. He certainly does not need to refer to the recipe; he just does it the same way each time.

In the same way, the repeatable lifecycle Sheffield mentions refers to the idea that each of the types of content you create in your organization gets created the same way each time. That means a defined workflow is in place for your team and they know exactly who will:

- Plan
- Create
- Publish
- Distribute
- Analyze
- Govern

In this way, an effective content strategy removes all the guesswork out of execution. Just think—if your creative team didn't have to think about all the steps needed to create and publish a piece of content, they would be free to think creatively about content.

There are many different versions of the following figure that illustrate the different phases of a content strategy. However, this is the one I feel most comfortable with; as I think governance should be the center of all activities on the web (We will learn more about that in Rule #5) (Figure 1.3).

You can see many other versions of the repeatable content strategy lifecycle by doing a Google Image search on content strategy lifecycle. We will return to this graphic as we discuss content strategy in depth in Chapter 8.

Figure 1.3 Governance as the Center to Content Strategy. Ahava Leibtag. All Rights Reserved.

Talk About What the Consumer Wants to Hear

The other critical piece that makes implementing a content strategy so successful is that it puts the focus back on your audience. In many organizations, marketing professionals will say they are creating content they think people will like. In reality, they are just creating content for themselves or their bosses. This is why so much content on the web is a waste of everyone's time.

By aligning your content with your business objectives *and* your users' tasks, (helping them do what they need to do), you are directing a spotlight onto your audience and customers. If you want to help your users accomplish their tasks, then you need to inquire who they are and what they need. You will learn more about this in Rule # 1 and Chapter 6.

Focus on the Customer

There's a great story Sandler Selling System® trainers tell about this type of thinking:

One day, a young man named Brian starts working at a big box store. The philosophy at this store is that you put salespeople on the floor and train them by the sink-or-swim method—either they get it or they don't. The general manager of that particular location is rather busy, so he shows Brian to the few aisles he will be in charge of that day—the small appliances section. Brian looks around the aisles for a few minutes, trying to familiarize himself with the products.

After about half an hour, an older woman comes into Brian's section. He approaches her eagerly, and she tells him she wants to buy a space heater. Brian remembers where the space heaters are and he leads her down to that aisle. He then begins an instructive dialogue with her:

Brian: "Ma'am, what kind of space heater are you interested in buying?"

Woman: "I don't know much about space heaters. Can you tell me about them?"

Brian: "Well (and he remembers what he saw on the boxes before she came in) there are two types of heaters: gas or kerosene."

Woman: "I don't want a gas heater. I've heard those can catch fire."

Brian: "Well, we have two types of kerosene heaters. The difference between them is the heating element. One is made of ceramic and the other tungsten. How big is the room you want to heat?"

They proceed to look through the different types of space heaters and the woman leaves the store with her purchase. Along comes another prospect, and Brian helps that person. Before you know it, by the end of the week, Brian has made enough sales to put him on the list of top salespeople *in the entire store.*

The general manager of the store is so excited about Brian's potential that he sends Brian for product training. At this training, different manufacturers present their products and features and explain their products' competitive advantages. After training, Brian returns to the big box store and the general manager puts him in charge of personal electronics.

What do you think happens? Do you think Brian continued to be one of the best salespeople in the store?

Of course not. Brian didn't make a sale that entire week following training. Why? Because Brian stopped focusing on the customers' needs. He stopped asking them questions that would help narrow their choices so they could make an educated purchase. Instead, Brian wanted to talk about everything he knew and had just learned about the products.

Content Strategy Will Save You from Being a Brian

Don't worry—eventually Brian learns to combine both sales techniques and becomes the best salesperson at the store. The point of the story is that we don't ever want to lose our focus on the people who consume our content because they ultimately lead us to reaching our achievement threshold (profits, donations, patients, enrollees, and so on).

We can learn from Brian's experience—we must always think about the kind of information our audience needs to accomplish their tasks. Otherwise we run the risk of delivering the wrong type of information and losing their attention.

We now understand that content is information you place in a format that is easily recognizable to potential customers. Content strategy is a system that gives you a step-by-step process, with analysis built-in, to publish your content successfully. So, what role does content marketing play in our process of creating a system around our digital content?

WHAT IS CONTENT MARKETING?

Joe Pulizzi, one of the first advocates of content marketing, poses the following problem: "Consumers have simply shut off the traditional world of marketing. They own a DVR to skip television advertising, often ignore magazine advertising, and now have become so adept at online 'surfing' that they can take in online information without a care for banners or buttons (making them irrelevant). Smart marketers understand that traditional marketing is becoming less and less effective by the minute, and that there has to be a better way" (Pulizzi, 2012).

THAT BETTER WAY IS CONTENT MARKETING

Content marketing brings content and marketing together—creating and distributing online content so that users develop an awareness of your brand.

Once that seed of awareness takes root, customers are more likely to return to you when they are ready to engage. Think of it as conversational bait—if we get to talking and exchanging information long enough—you will become the service or product they choose to buy. Great content marketers understand how to have artful, thoughtful conversations.

Once the consumer is aware of your brand and trusts your content, you have achieved two vital things:

1. You've become a trusted resource

2. People will buy from you (or donate money or rave to their friends about you)

Consumers will seek your content for information they trust and their social interactions online will work to create a coveted brand audience. This audience in turn becomes a community so that when asked for a recommendation—online or in person, they will always recommend your product or service.

Conversations Facilitate the Sale

Brian Clark, the founder of copyblogger, a popular online blog, asks, "How do people decide to buy? … The evidence is unmistakable—the Internet has completely upended the lead generation and sales process. Prospects are not waiting to be sold to—they're proactively gathering information, soliciting peer recommendations, and making decisions about you and your competitors … before you realize anything is happening" (Clark, 2012).

In other words, content marketing is an incredibly powerful strategy:

- You publish your content and make it freely accessible in many different places.

- When a consumer is in a buying frame of mind, he or she will "stumble" upon your content—or come to you because you are a known, respected, and trusted entity—and understand that your product or service is probably the best one.

MOVING FORWARD WITH NEW UNDERSTANDING

With a solid understanding of your brand's identity, you can now set up an effective digital content program. We can think of it like this:

- Branding→Foundational

- Content Strategy→Execution

- Content Marketing→Tactical

THE FIVE BASIC QUESTIONS ANSWERED

Remember as a fourth grader your teacher taught you how to write a story? Didn't s/he say, "You must answer the following five questions: Who, What,

Figure 1.4 Branding Supports Content Strategy and Content Marketing. Ahava Leibtag. All Rights Reserved.

Where, When, and How?" Well, you've made it way past fourth grade but you're still asking the same basic questions. The beauty of thinking about branding as foundational to content strategy and content marketing is that you answer these questions automatically (Figure 1.4).

If you want content marketing to provide results for you, you must define your brand. Then you need to develop and distribute content using content strategy. Content marketing happens when you have an execution strategy.

So where do we begin? Well the right place to begin is with Rule #1. To understand what types of content to create and what will resonate with our audience, we must understand:

- Who they are
- How they think
- Where they spend their time
- How they consume information

SUMMARY

Content begins as information, is set into a recognizable format for your audiences, and is distributed through different channels—both traditional and online. Brands are promises that define who you are as an organization and what you can deliver to your audiences.

Branding is foundational to creating content online because if you don't understand who you are (encapsulated by your brand), you can't properly communicate to your users. Content strategy is an online publishing strategy that accounts for the planning, creation, publishing and delivery, analysis, and governance of content.

Content marketing is about creating content that educates your consumers and befriends them. Then, when they need your services, they engage with you by buying from you, sharing with their friends, and recommending to others.

Ready to talk about starting with your customers? Let's go.

REFERENCES

Clark, B. (2012). *The business case for agile content marketing*. http://www.scribecontent.com.

Colapinto, J. (2011). Famous names: Does it matter what a product is called? *The New Yorker*. http://www.newyorker.com/reporting/2011/10/03/111003fa_fact_colapinto. Accessed 03.10.11.

Crovitz, G. (2102). *Who really invented the internet?* http://online.wsj.com/article/SB10000872396390444464304577539063008406518.html.

Gallo, C. (2012). Apple store's secret sauce: 5 steps of service [video]. *Forbes Magazine*. http://www.forbes.com/sites/carminegallo/2012/05/16/apple-stores-secret-sauce-5-teps-of-service-video/. Accessed 16.05.12.

Halvorson, K. (2010). Content strategy for the Web. Berkeley, CA: New Riders.

Kelleher, B. (2013). *The good, bad and ugly. Social media's impact on your brand. RIS Media*. http://rismedia.com/2013-03-07/the-good-bad-and-ugly-social-medias-impact-on-your-brand/.

Morison, A. (2012). *People power: TripAdvisor and customer hotel reviews*. http://www.babusinesslife.com/Stuff/Travel/People-power-TripAdvisor-and-customer-hotel-reviews.html.

Pulizzi, J. (2012). *What is content marketing?* http://contentmarketinginstitute.com/what-is-content-marketing.

Ritson, M. (2006). *Mark Ritson on branding: Norse fire smokes out bland brands*. http://www.marketingmagazine.co.uk/news/534969/Mark-Ritson-branding-Norse-fire-smokes-bland-brands/?DCMP=ILC-SEARCH.

Segal, D. (2012). Apple's retail army, long on loyalty but short on pay. *The New York Times*. http://www.nytimes.com/2012/06/24/business/apple-store-workers-loyal-but-short-on-pay.html. Accessed 23.06.12.

Sheffield, R. (2009). The web content strategist's bible: The complete guide to a new and lucrative career path for writers of all kinds. Atlanta: ClueFox Pub.

RULE 1

START WITH YOUR AUDIENCE

First, a note on the seven rules. Putting a digital strategy roadmap together is fun and exciting, but you need a system in place. I designed the seven rules to give you a clear path and framework so you can easily map where you are, envision where you want to be, and create a plan for what you need to do to get there.

WHO IS ON THE OTHER END OF THE LINE?

When we begin creating a digital strategy roadmap, we always start with "Who are we talking to?"

As a digital strategist and web writer, I have sat in countless planning meetings for web projects. Called, with ever so much optimism, "kick-off" projects, they usually consist of some of the stakeholders, a marketing manager, some of the digital team, and me.

The conversation often goes something like this:

- "Ahava, we need you to write about X because our users really care about that."

- "Sounds good. How do you know your customers care about that?"

- "What do you mean?" Blank stares all around. "We just know."

The above interchange is ubiquitous. Too often, companies, with the best of intentions, but in error, assume they know what *types* of content their customers want and, more to the point, which *information* about their product or service those customers want. Why does most digital content feel empty and disappointing? Because someone in the organization decided *this* is what customers wanted to know about without doing any research to determine if that was true.

WHO *ARE* THESE PEOPLE?

Your content audiences are real people. They are your customers or potential customers. They might also be patients, gardeners, astrology buffs, shoppers, obsessive celebrity addicts, moms, professional athletes, writers, researchers, economists, lawyers, doctors, children, adolescents, and senior citizens.

First of All, Stop Calling Them Users!

Nomenclature matters. If you ask yourself why we ignore our customers, the answer might be that we don't see them as people like us; instead we refer to them as "users." Gerry McGovern highlights the problems inherent in the term *user* in his article, "We Have Customers, Not Users." He begins with a quote from Jack Dorsey, the creator of Twitter:

> " 'It's time for our industry and discipline to reconsider the word user,' Jack Dorsey, creator of Twitter and founder and CEO of Square recently wrote. 'We speak about user-centric design, user benefit, user experience, active users, and even usernames. While the intent is to consider people first, the result is a massive abstraction away from real problems people feel on a daily basis.' I couldn't agree more. The single biggest challenge I have faced since I started consulting on web issues in 1994 is getting my clients (and me) to truly understand that real, human, flesh and bone people come to their websites."
>
> (McGovern, 2012)

So, the first rule is: these are real people, customers, not "users" and we will call them customers for the rest of *The Digital Crown*.

Depending on your organization's product or service, they can span many ages, interests, and educational levels.

The first rule in marketing is "Know Your Audience." Often you read content on a company's website and find their focus is completely on themselves: what they can do, how great they are at everything, how amazingly their products will change your world forever. Don't they know the only person the reader cares about is the reader?

Readers think about what they need. What they don't want is to hear a company toot its horn; it's a massive turn-off. They want the company to demonstrate the value of the product or service they are seeking.

WHAT DO OUR CUSTOMERS WANT?

We know our customers are looking for information. We also need to know the state-of-mind they might be in while they are searching: What's most important to them at this moment?

Let's think of it like this: If I asked you to build me a house, would you just start building? Or would you find out what type of house you should build? You'd probably ask me the following before you started (Leibtag, 2010):

- How many people will live in your house?
- What is your budget?
- What size is the plot of land?

- How many bathrooms do you want?
- How many kitchens do you want?

If I asked you to buy me a car, you'd probably ask:

- How big a car do you want?
- How many people will you be transporting on a regular basis?
- What is your budget?
- Is the cost of gas important to you?
- Do you prefer leather or fabric seats?
- Do you like the feel of a racecar underneath your fingertips?

It's no different with content: We can't possibly create content unless we know what will make sense for our customers. We are having a conversation with them; it's our job to make them feel the conversation was *worth their time*.

Creating content is like creating any other product. And, as with a car or house, you can't possibly give the customer what he wants if you don't know him. So let's get to know him.

GETTING TO KNOW YOUR CUSTOMERS—THE TOOLS

Never make assumptions about your customers. Instead, spend time getting to know who they are. Once you make the commitment to get to know your audience *instead of assuming you already know them*, you need to have a framework for this discovery. Luckily, there are tools and criteria that provide you with a full, rich characterization of your intended audience.

These tools and criteria for defining your audience should include:

1. Customer Personas (also called user personas, but we're trying to banish that word from our vocabularies)
2. Audience Research
3. Understanding Content Access

#1: CUSTOMER PERSONAS

A customer persona is a full-blown description of your customer. To fully understand someone, you need to know as much as you can about him or her. An excellent metaphor for this type of research is falling in love. That type of obsessive curiosity is necessary so you can truly get to know your target audiences.

Do you remember the first time you fell in love? Or, maybe *every* time you did? There is something so delicious about that all-consuming feeling of wanting to know everything about the other person: What kind of childhood did he have?

Is she thinking about me as much as I'm thinking about her? What's his mother like? What does she like to do on the weekend?

You spend those thrilling first months exploring that other person so you know everything. That insatiable curiosity is critical to the survival of our species. If we didn't fall in love, we wouldn't consider the possibility of a future with that person. We ask all of those questions to know if that person is right for us for the long-term.

THAT is how you should approach your audience—with passion and deep curiosity. Just like lovebirds, marketers need to know everything about the audience whose attention they crave, so they can communicate with them effectively.

You have to become your customer to understand your customer. And yet, so many of the executives I meet and work with have very little or no exposure to their audiences (Leibtag, 2012).

You can become your customer by developing one or more of these "customer personas." In marketing, we refer to it as audience—or customer—segmentation. Think of "customer personas" as real people—the actual individuals that you are trying to reach—Mary, Kate, Joe, and Mike. Your team should create several of them and breathe life into them, making them real.

In Chapter 6, we will discuss persona development in greater detail. We will also talk about a tool called interactive scenarios, which will help you understand

Knowing Your Customer—Avoid the Dreaded "Marketing-Up" Syndrome

If you are a marketing executive, chances are you have a degree, went to university or college, and have advanced professional qualifications. This means your life may look different from your target audience. So, as fascinating as you are, you don't look like your audience, sound like your audience, or act like your audience. In short, you're suffering from "marketing-up syndrome." This means that you are marketing to an audience like yourself, but not to the audience you're really trying to reach.

I have written a tremendous amount of content for healthcare organizations: Plain language and concepts are critical for customers. If a hospital's website reads like a Ph.D. thesis, patients may be concerned that the doctors will talk to them using words they have to look up in a dictionary. I spend time educating medical professionals that we must use simple vocabulary if we want patients to feel a sense of comfort and security while reading their content.

People don't want to have to sit with a dictionary and decipher content. They prefer plain language, conversational tones, and engaging content. Plain language is not dumbing down your content. It's about picking words customers understand.

So how do you cure marketing-up syndrome? Go spend time where your audience spends time. If you're marketing for hospitals, spend time with patients. If you're selling cars, hang out at car dealerships. If you're marketing higher education, spend time with seniors in high school who are choosing colleges or adults who are considering going back to school.

how and when your audience accesses your content. By sketching these various use case scenarios, you will be able to make better decisions about where, when, and in what formats you publish your content.

#2: AUDIENCE RESEARCH

Your goal is to create a picture of each of the members of your audience. You want to find out why they would want to buy your product or donate to your cause. To do this, you must have data. This means research.

Strong research gives you a wide platform on which to base your decisions, and concrete data with which to make good decisions now and later. Popular online marketing blogger Delray Phoenix says it well, "Market research cost and effectiveness, if done right, will become invaluable to a company that is starting a campaign … and getting their products evaluated. Without researching the target audience, their wants and needs, and effective cost control measures, companies would be taking big shots in the dark with their products and services, potentially losing tons of money in the process" (Delray, 2011).

Try to triangulate your data to ensure you are coming to the right conclusions. With three different research approaches, you will see where the data converges and your customer personas will bubble to the top. The three approaches for audience research are:

- Customer Research
- Interactive Data
- Ethnographic Studies

Customer Research

Customer research involves a scientific approach to gathering data about your audience. Don't call it market research—like the term "users," the term "market research" de-personalizes what you are doing. Your company will probably need to outsource this research. While the mere thought of spending that money may scare the C-suite, this may be the best money your company ever spends.

The Three Questions You Need to Answer

There are three critical questions you need to answer to know your customers:

1. Who are our customers?
2. What do they care about?
3. Where do they spend their time so we can engage with them?

You can use the following types of research to learn about your customers:

- *Focus groups*: Facilitators ask a group of people their opinions about a product or service in an interactive setting where they are free to speak with other group members.

- *Surveys/Polling*: Individuals fill out questionnaires or respond to in-person interviews as a way of gathering data. Ad tracking research, also known as post-testing or ad effectiveness tracking, is research that monitors a brand's performance, including brand and advertising awareness, product trial and usage, and attitudes about the brand versus their competition.

- *Consumer trends by geographical markets*: Use this to analyze consumer behavior by geographic location.

Interactive Data

Let's consider a customer: Sarah is buying a couch and needs to do price research on different styles. Customer Sarah comes to your furniture store website every other day. She looks at the home page, uses the interactive comparison to check on the prices of a few products, and then she exits your site. Sometimes she goes ahead and puts the product in the shopping cart, but she never buys. Why does Sarah leave your site without paying for the items in her cart?

To really know that answer, you'd have to ask Sarah. She may not have enough money. She may want to think about it for a while. Sarah may not be able to decide between bisque and mushroom color paint, so she doesn't want to commit to a couch until she makes that decision. By examining the following metrics, you can understand key behaviors:

- Search data

- Analytics data (we discuss this further in this Rule)

- Click-through rates from your digital ads

- Facebook likes

- Engagement on social media

Patterns often emerge from your data; you can draw conclusions about why potential consumers behave the way they do. By better understanding customer behavior, you can discover what you'd like to change. Then, you can experiment using different types of content and layouts to see if those changes affect customer behavior patterns. When you compare two different designs and/or content to each other, it's called A/B testing. "A" stands for the first, and "B" for the second. Depending on which one "wins" the testing, you can move ahead with that format.

Ethnographic Studies

Ethnography is the practice of observing a group of people in order to determine how they live, interact, and work. Ethnographic studies in marketing include:

- *Mystery shopping*: A mystery shopper performs specific tasks such as purchasing a product, asking questions, registering complaints, and then provides detailed reports or feedback about his experiences.

- *Observational studies*: Researchers watch customer behavior in a real setting—sometimes covertly.

- *User experience assessments*: Consumers interact with a product and comment on their experience.

Ethnography is helpful because you can learn about how people interact in a real-world environment.

#3: ACCESS TO YOUR CONTENT

You need to know how and when your audience accesses content. What devices (smartphones, tablets, laptops, and so on) do they use? When are they most likely to read your content? What is their preferred method of accessing your content? The answers to these questions will give you powerful knowledge about when and how to publish your content.

You can learn the answers to these questions with an analytics program. An analytics program gives you important information about how many people visit your site, how long they stay, which pages they use to enter and exit, as well as where your visitors come from. Analytics programs run in the code behind your site and tally these vital statistics.

Google Analytics is a popular, free option, but there are many analytics packages available. By analyzing this data, you can know when and with which devices your audience accesses your content.

NOW YOU HAVE TOOLS

After you collect and collate the data, you should have a good picture of what your customers look and act like. Assembling all this data will result in strong personas you can use to create content moving forward. As I mentioned above, we will discuss how to create and use customer personas in Chapter 6.

Once you know who they are and how they behave, it's much easier to describe their motivation for engaging with your brand or product. And once you do that, you're in much better shape to target them.

CASE IN POINT—NIKE

In a CNNMoney article, Scott Cendrowski explains how Nike completely changed its marketing between 2010 and 2011. In a reassessment of its marketing strategy, Nike came to an interesting conclusion—its "… core customer [is] a 17-year-old who spends 20 percent more on shoes than his adult counterparts, [and] has given up television to skip across myriad online communities." (Cendrowski, 2012).

Not only does Nike think it can do without the mega-TV campaigns of old, the company makes the bold assertion that the digital world allows the brand to interact even more closely with its consumers—maybe as closely as it did in its early days, when founder Phil Knight sold track shoes out of his car in the 1960s. That's a major change in marketing direction for a global company. As Nike CEO Mark Parker explained in the article, "Connecting used to be, Here's some product, and here's some advertising. We hope you like it [but] connecting today is a dialogue." In other words, brand connection comes through conversations.

In addition, there was a realization that today's consumers are not as into hero worship as the world once was. Instead, today's consumer depends more on his or her peers for their opinions. In making this change, Nike didn't abandon the ad agency it's been using for decades, but instead, broadened its advertising interests among other companies, some of whom are experts at social and digital media.

Lesson learned? Customer research pays. Even the largest, most successful companies don't stop assessing and re-assessing who their customers are and what they want. In fact, the most successful companies are constantly defining and understanding their customers: That's why they're successful. You can't take your eye off the ball for a second, and the ball is your customers.

SUMMARY

In order to create a robust and successful digital strategy, you must do research on your customers: who they are, what they read, how they read it, what types of content they consume, what they care about, what resonates with them, etc.

Understanding your different audiences is complex in an environment in which you may have dozens of persona types. But it's important to know who you are talking to before you start thinking about content, delivery, and design. Once you understand your audience, it's much easier to put the building blocks in place for elegant and robust content. In order to understand your customers, you must:

- Do market research on who they are
- Look at your analytics data for insight into your customers' behaviors online

- Spend time with them to see what they care about
- Create personas for them (see Chapter 6)
- Know how they consume media and which devices they use to do so

Now that we've discussed Rule #1, about putting your audience first and keeping them there always, we're going to talk about how to make the business case for content with your senior executive management. Understanding how content fuels the sales process will prove invaluable as you ask for broader organizational support for content.

REFERENCES

Cendrowski, S. (2012, February 13). *Nike's new marketing mojo*. Retrieved from http://management.fortune.cnn.com/2012/02/13/nike-digital-marketing/.

Delray, P. (2011, November 15). *Market research cost and effectiveness*. Retrieved from http://market-research.ezinemark.com/market-research-cost-and-effectiveness-31abce6a943.html.

Leibtag, A. (2010, September 21). *What a content strategist needs a web designer to know* [Blog post adaptation]. Retrieved from http://onlineitallmatters.blogspot.com/2010/09/what-content-strategist-wants-web.html.

Leibtag, A. (2012, June 26). *Stop marketing up* (Adapted). Retrieved from http://www.econtentmag.com/Articles/Column/Content-Ahas!/Stop-Marketing-Up-83389.htm.

McGovern, G. (2012, October 21). *We have customers, not users* [Blog]. Retrieved from http://www.gerrymcgovern.com/new-thinking/we-have-customers-not-users.

MAKING THE CASE FOR CONTENT

Content drives the sales process. Even if your job title doesn't include the word *sales*, you are still trying to achieve something. Content is responsible for getting you there. Think of it as the fuel in an engine. Now, consider what we've done in our society to ensure we have enough fuel to power our cars and homes. *That's how important content is to your business.*

Not everyone understands this in your organization. But you do. That's the first step. Now you have to convince the right people that to move the business in the right direction, they need to invest in content: Content production, distribution, and management. How do you do that?

We know information is the critical building block of any type of content. Using the right kind of content helps us to get our information into the right hands—our target audiences. If we want to do this well, we need to have budget dollars for content. Budget approval for content means appealing to the C-suite and convincing them to invest in this all-important fuel. In this chapter, we learn how to make the case for content within your organization and to your C-suite.

First, a story about why content is so important.

Who Is in the C-Suite?

The term *C-suite* refers to the top executives within your company:

- Chief Executive Officer (CEO)
- Chief Operating Officer (COO)
- Chief Technology Officer (CTO)
- Chief Financial Officer (CFO)
- Chief Marketing Officer (CMO)
- Chief Information Officer (CIO)

Figure 2.1 Misleading hotel web page.

When people research vacations, they often look at different hotel websites to learn more about their amenities, rooms, and services. Last year, while planning a vacation, I went to a hotel's website and made sure that the suite had a small kitchenette, because sometimes I like to make my own food instead of dining out for every meal. There were six types of rooms available and each one had its own web page. On each of the six pages, a shaded box (see Figure 2.1) appeared on the page. The name of the room changed depending on which type of room it was: a one-bedroom suite, a two-bedroom suite, and so on.

After seeing the box on every single page, I assumed that every type of room had a fully equipped kitchen. But, when I arrived at the hotel, guess what? No kitchen. The Village Guestroom, I learned, was not one of the types of hotel rooms that had a kitchen. Those were only available in the top four tiers of rooms. I shared this misleading/incorrect information with both the hotel and the travel credit card company who had booked my stay. The travel credit card company agreed with me and *asked* the hotel to upgrade my room. *Free.*

Because someone in charge of the website did not understand the importance of content, my stay cost the resort about $400 in revenue. The descriptions about what amenities to expect in every room are confusing. If you multiply that amount across the resort, that one mistake in their content could be costing them thousands of dollars every year. Why? Because there is a lack of understanding about how important content is to the bottom line.

UNDERSTANDING BUSINESS OBJECTIVES

In Chapter 1, we talked about understanding business objectives and thinking like an executive. To sell the importance of content to the C-suite, you must understand how the C-suite thinks and what is important to them as leaders of the company. As a content professional, you must understand the business from the ground up and recognize the need to increase profit, be cost-efficient, and out-do the competition. You need to identify and share stories like the one above to demonstrate how important content is to the business.

In the workshops about content strategy that I teach, I often show the audience a picture of Jack Welch, who was the CEO of General Electric (GE) for more than 20 years. I talk about GE's management strategy, which is world famous. At GE, they review every employee's performance annually. If you perform in the bottom 10%, you are most likely let go. If you perform in the top 20% of the workforce, the executives at GE recognize you as a potential GE rock star (Knudson, 2012).

At that point, the management team tells the employee she has what it takes to rise to the ranks of management at GE. They make her an offer: "We will move you around the world, every two years, into many different positions. If you want to learn about refrigerator cooling, we'll send you to China to learn about refrigerators. If you want to learn about accounting, we'll send you to accounting. If you want to learn about digital strategy, we'll move you to digital strategy." The goal is to teach these potential future executives at GE *the* paramount lesson: How the company makes money.

Learning about how a company makes money is not just the job of the executives-in-training or the executives already sitting in the C-suite. It must also be the primary goal of a content professional. A content professional is responsible for two things:

1. Marry content development to the business and communication goals of the organization

2. Support the customers in accomplishing their tasks

Growing Leaders at GE

General Electric is world renowned as a company that knows how to grow leaders. Its focus on future leaders absorbing everything they can about the company is hailed as a brilliant strategy. The process starts with the traits they insist all leaders have:

- Imagination

- Clear Thinking

- Inclusiveness

- External Focus

- Expertise

Harry Elsinga, Manager of Executive Development at GE, explains the importance of "external focus." Elsinga says, "The external focus trait is simply: do you understand your markets, are you known in the industry and do you know your industry?" Elsinga is reinforcing the importance of Rule #1. Design for them, build for them, and sell to them.

As a content professional, you need to understand the organization's business and communications objectives. (In some cases, those goals are murky. We will talk about that later.) Until you master those objectives, you cannot create great content.

DEFINING BUSINESS OBJECTIVES

Your business objectives are what your company plans to do to grow. Most businesses plan for growth. To grow, executives may consider introducing different products or services, adding to the sales team, enlarging the marketing department, and looking to move into new industries or verticals.

If you are a content professional, your job is to comb through the business plan and identify precise goals for growth. Then you need to marry your content plan to those business objectives.

MEETING THE ACHIEVEMENT THRESHOLD

Everyone has an achievement threshold. Even if you work for a not-for-profit organization, and don't necessarily have a profit-driven growth strategy, you still have plans and goals. Your job is to work toward expected achievements. This is the achievement threshold; to meet that threshold, your company must have a business strategy.

For example, you may work at a government agency collecting and analyzing data about the use of Social Security benefits such as food stamps in the United States. Lawmakers will use this data to analyze the value of these benefits. (Food stamps are stipends given to low-income households to buy food staples.) Your achievement threshold is providing lawmakers with up-to-date and current data. If your business strategy doesn't help you meet that threshold—say your department's data gathering programs are not up to par—the analyses will be poor and you will be reporting incorrect information on a very important program affecting millions of people.

To review:

- *Business objectives*: The goals your organization has to grow or succeed in.

- *Achievement threshold*: How you measure whether you have reached your business objectives. (In many industries, the achievement threshold is profit, but in other industries, it may be something else.)

Find out your organization's business objectives, as well as the achievement threshold. Armed with these facts, you can create content that makes a difference.

Achievement Threshold=Profit Motivation

From now on, when we talk about your profit motivation, we'll be talking about your achievement threshold. So if you do work for a government, association, NGO, or not-for-profit organization, know that I'm still thinking about you.

UNDERSTANDING YOUR SALES AND BUSINESS CYCLES

Sales people like to talk about sales cycles. A sales cycle is the length of time it takes to close a sale. For some businesses, this is 30 days. For others it can be 3–5 years. You must know how long it takes to close a sale when thinking about marrying your content objectives to your business goals.

If you're not familiar with the sales process, it is important that we review it here. For those of you who have this down cold, take a minute and read it again, so that we're all on the same page. I'm including a sales cycle description so that we all understand how a sales cycle works. Then your content can be developed to accomplish the business objectives efficiently.

Sales and marketing professionals talk about a sales funnel (Figure 2.2). As Michael Hogenmiller, a media professional I work with has pointed out; the sales funnel should really be a sales loop, which we will refer to as a customer loop (Figure 2.3) (Leibtag, 2013). We always want to have contact with our customers so we can continue our relationships with them. Instead of talking about a sales funnel, we are going to talk about a customer loop.

Let's define some terms that sales and marketing professionals use when they talk about creating, nurturing, and generating leads:

- *Leads*: Leads are prospects that you potentially have the opportunity to do business with, or get donor dollars from, etc.

- *Lead generation*: When we talk about generating leads, we're talking about how we typically acquire prospective customers. Many websites use Request for Information, or RFI forms, to generate leads. They offer a piece of content in the hope a prospect will supply an email address to download the content he wants.

- *Lead nurturing*: Once you have a lead's contact information, you nurture that relationship. Think about the last time you bought a pair of shoes online. The company starts sending you emails, reminding you to shop on its site, and sending you coupon codes. They're courting you, nurturing the relationship, hoping you'll bite. In Business to Business, or B2B marketing, lead nurturing typically happens in the form of email newsletters, direct mail, and phone calls.

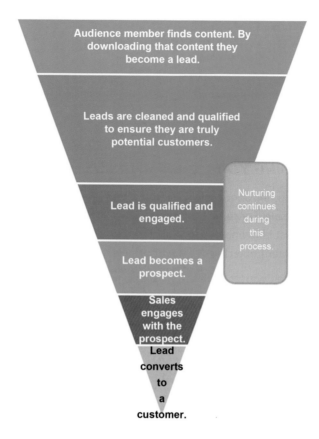

Figure 2.2 The classic sales funnel.

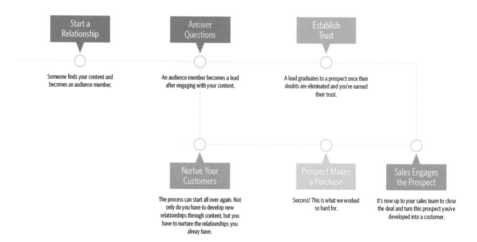

Figure 2.3 The customer loop.

- *Buying stage*: This is where you try to determine the stage at which your lead is in the buying process. For example, is he ready to buy? Just looking around? Not sure if he even wants to buy? When I did a project for a higher education institution, we developed two downloadable pieces of content: *12 Reasons to go back to school in 2012* and *Are you ready to go back to school?* Depending on which piece of content the lead chose to download, we learned something about where he was in the decision process. Knowing the buying stage helps with the next item— lead scoring.

- *Lead scoring*: Sophisticated organizations use lead scoring to decide which leads to pursue and which leads will probably end with no business. By scoring leads via a series of metrics, you can determine which leads are qualified. Qualified leads have the budget and interest to do business with your organization.

- *Lead conversion*: Conversion happens when the lead becomes a customer, meaning they buy! Then they might reenter the customer loop and become a new lead all over again, as they decide on their next purchase. However, their score may be higher now because they became "converted" to a paying customer. If, however, they don't return for a long time to buy from you again, depending on your sales cycle, that lead's score may fall.

The more you read about marketing, the more familiar you will become with the types of marketing funnels and loops that filter and qualify leads. Some are quite sophisticated, depending on the type of organization and its business objectives.

One of the goals of content is to continue this customer engagement cycle via the customer loop. By continuing to engage with customers on a regular basis through content, you can keep the conversation going. Let's talk about the different types of media you can use to spark those conversations and interact with your target audiences.

DIFFERENT TYPES OF MEDIA

With the incredible deluge of data and information that businesses have now, we all have to keep up with the different forms of media, and how quickly things change and mutate. Let's define the different types of media an organization can take advantage of to achieve its business objectives:

- *Paid media* includes search engine marketing, advertising, and paid search (pay-per-click campaigns) that you can purchase from third-party organizations.

- *Owned media* is all the media *you* develop and use for your organization, including the digital content that lives on your website and other digital properties, like social media channels.

- *Earned media* is media generated by someone other than your own company: Journalists, media outlets, bloggers, and public relations vendors working to create buzz about your products or services.

When you're making the case for content, understanding the value of different forms of media will help you make better decisions about the types of conversations you want to have with your target audiences. There are also certain things you can do to control the conversation. Understanding the different forms of media will help you to do this. Let's see why.

Paid media is a way to pay for attracting traffic and attention to your digital properties, so you can start new conversations with new prospects, and continue to nurture existing prospects. You are controlling the conversation when you use paid media by corralling your audiences toward your content.

Owned media is critical to establishing yourself as an important voice within your space. Creating your own content and engaging with your customers means you now have a direct line to them. You have a better chance of controlling the conversation if you use owned media because you are producing content that speaks in your brand's personality.

Creating your own content, in most cases, is cheaper than trying to earn media. Most companies engage public relations firms to capture the attention of major media outlets. With the rise of social media and changing patterns of content consumption (people don't necessarily watch the nightly news anymore), earned media may not be the best way for your organization to attract your target audiences.

Earned media can gain you lots of credibility—if the vibe is good and positive. However, as we all know, there are also the negative reviews, comments, and blogs that frighten the C-suite back into the decade of broadcast advertising and direct mail. It's true that earned media can be extremely powerful. However, you must have plans in place for what to do in case it goes awry.

ANALYZING THE CURRENT STATE OF AFFAIRS

Now that we are all on the same page about business objectives, as well as how sales teams think, it's important you analyze in great detail the current state of your content before you waltz into the C-suite to make your case for why content is the fuel that drives your organization's growth.

These are some of the questions you should have the answers to *before* you talk to your decision makers:

1. How much content do you currently have?

2. Where is it?

    a. Does it live on your website or inside your social media channels?

    b. Does it live elsewhere on the web?

    c. Do you have user-generated content (content that your customers create, like comments)?

3. How does the current content perform? Does it attract leads?

4. Do you have to use paid media to attract leads to your digital properties?

5. Do earned media help you drive leads toward your digital properties? (Think of a review in a popular magazine about your product. Did that spike an increase in traffic to your website?)

6. Do you have analytics in place to measure your content's performance?

7. What's working? What's not?

Gather as much information as you can about the overall state of your content. You may also want to pick one or two specific examples to back up your points.

APPROACHING THE C-SUITE

We have talked about knowing your audiences in terms of creating content. At the start of your content process, you will need to convince your most difficult audience—the C-suite—that content is vital to the success of the company. You need to be well prepared to present an honest story to them. Remember, as with any audience, you need to understand where they are coming from before you walk in the door.

Executives and leaders make decisions based on certain criteria: data, business objectives, workforce issues, and what will generate decisive results. Investing company dollars in content is not necessarily one of those things that is an easy or clear sell. One of the approaches I advocate is to propose a pilot project. This way, your executive leadership feels they are making a small investment to see if you are right about the power of content. Once that pilot project is complete, you should have the data you need to convince them to invest in content full-force.

The following story illustrates how a pilot content project helped one of my clients to begin investing in content to fuel their sales cycle. The sales force had a challenge—they felt they were in the midst of what they considered a long sales cycle—six months. They wanted to find a way to shorten it. *That* was their business objective: Shorten the sales cycle.

When I asked them what they did to nurture leads, they looked at me with blank faces. "We call them every month to check in?" responded one of the sales people.

Content Works

Business objective: Shorten the sales cycle

Solution: Create a lead nurturing program with available resources (a list of 800 previous and potential customers)

Outcomes: Converted a prior customer to a customer for another product within three months

Conscientious about entering leads into their sales database, this company had accumulated more than 800 email addresses to nurture leads. I helped them design an email newsletter that went out twice a month to those leads, based on the company's messaging architecture. (We'll talk about messaging architecture in Chapter 7.) The company offered a suite of four products, so every two weeks we rotated through those four. This meant that each lead received four newsletters in two months that covered all of the organization's products and services.

The strategy paid off. Instead of waiting passively for customers to contact them, the company had aggressively promoted products in a systematic way, gaining interest from at least some of the 800 leads they had gathered. After receiving the email newsletter, a previous customer that used this organization for one product called to ask about a different product. The customer didn't know this company sold the other product—and ultimately the company made the sale.

In this case, the sales cycle for a completely different product was created and completed in one shot. It was a surprise, and a happy one. Hopefully, the "new" customer will go on to recommend the product to others.

If your job is to sell content within your organization, find a story like the one above to sell your case. Or, present the problem and describe how you think better content will help solve the challenge, like the wrong hotel room description at the beginning of this chapter. Explain that using content as an outreach channel builds relationships that lead to smoother deals *and* supports the communication and business goals of the organization. Start with something small so that no one feels that the risks are outlandish.

UNDERSTANDING THE C-SUITE

The members of the C-suite are the first stakeholders in your development of content. They are also your most important and challenging audience. Knowing what motivates them, and what they care about, will help you present the best possible case for why they should invest in content. In the same way you carefully prepare your customer personas, work with your team to prepare the personas of your C-suite. Ask around your organization about different executives and the data that matter to them. Use that knowledge to drive the examples you choose to present.

Executives are goal oriented; they are interested in growing the business, making a profit, and cutting expenses. Illustrate to them how the content is critical to the revenue generation process. Convince them of its value. They each have their own goals to meet as part of the business's overall strategic plan, so you need to show how you can support them with content. Explain that content is a conversation always taking place between the organization and its customers. If that conversation is poorly mapped, or doesn't even exist, how can the company expect to do business?

WHAT THE C-SUITE CARES ABOUT

The C-suite cares about:

- Increasing profit
- Increasing productivity
- Reducing communication, travel, and other costs
- Improving employee job satisfaction (Gogo, 2012)
- Outdoing the competition (Harris, 2012)

Most important to the C-suite is making a profit. They are judged every year on how much money the company makes. So don't forget about how much they focus on the bottom line. When you can demonstrate—as in the example of the lost revenue from the wrong description of the hotel room—how you can trace a direct line from revenue to content, you will probably see them show a lot of interest.

HOW TO EXPLAIN CONTENT TO THE C-SUITE

When you need your C-suite to green light a budget to create a content project, make sure you first explain the relevancy of content in general. Below are some tips on explaining content marketing to the C-suite:

1. *Priorities, priorities*: The first thing you need to think about is how to tie the impact of content marketing to business priorities. The C-suite doesn't care about clicks and opens; they care about increasing revenue and decreasing costs. Build a business case for content within your organization, even if you have to tell a bad story.

2. *Customer personas*: Why not create content that is persona-driven to convince your executive team? Find out specifically what they care about that content can address, and create a series of emails to convince them how you would reach one particular type of customer.

3. *Return on investment*: See the sidebar "What ROI Is All About" on the next page.

4. *The competition*: It won't hurt to include examples of your competitor's content to make your case. Has a competitor launched a new eBook? Ask your C-suite, "What if all the engagement from a new eBook could

be ours?" If you can prove that your company has performed poorly against the competition in online content, you are making a very strong case.

5. *Sales impact*: Get the VP of Sales on your side and have him/her go to bat for you. Work together to forecast what the revenue impact could be if salespeople were able to increase their close rate due to having more highly qualified leads (Harris, 2012).

6. *What do they do?* Ask them to think about how THEY access content: According to a recent survey from SiriusDecisions, targeted digital content is the ideal entry point into the lives of busy executives. It stands to reason that if your C-suite depends on you selling prospects, they will give you the budget dollars you need to do that (Pisello, 2011).

7. *Talk the talk*: Talk in their language (not "engaging" customers, but in terms of $$). Sixty percent of online marketers intend to increase

What ROI Is All About

When you're talking to the C-suite, you must measure Return on Investment (ROI) in a way that makes sense to them. ROI is a finance metric, so you need to be able to track actual dollars coming in or dollars saved. If you cannot show actual money changing hands, then you are not measuring ROI.

However, you can demonstrate that proper content management improves the productivity and creativity of your staff. There's return on time and there's also return on investment. Both count to the C-suite (Pisello, 2011).

Return on Time Examples

*   *Improved efficiency*: Publishing content becomes easier and smoother with the introduction of a content strategy, which is a production cycle for your digital content. Systems create freedom, which means your team spends more time being productive.

*   *Fewer mistakes*: With good governance standards, it is less likely your team will have to "fix mistakes on the website," leading to better productivity.

*   *Sales tracking*: The sales force is better able to engage leads that are primed to buy because they consistently engage with the content (open emails, comment on blogs, and so on).

Return on Investment Examples

*   *Content drives sales*: You can actually track the relationship between certain blog posts or eBooks and customers who entered your customer loop and converted.

*   *Fewer missed sales*: With better content, you miss fewer sales (think of the site that doesn't tell you how high the coffee table is, or that doesn't tell you how long it takes to ship).

*   *Do more with less*: With an effective content publishing system, you can accomplish more projects with the same employees (Smith & Leibtag, 2012).

their content marketing budgets. Therefore, if a company doesn't aggressively enter this space, they risk falling behind competitors. While businesses that offer professional services top the content marketing adoption scale at 94%, even blue-collar industries such as manufacturing and processing (83% adoption) intend to get more involved. In other words, no company can afford to ignore content. The most effective content professionals spend more of their company's advertising budget (up to 31%) on content marketing and have fewer objections from the C-suite. They also use a more diversified approach, using a bigger mix of articles, social media, YouTube, blogs, and other outlets (Pisello, 2011).

8. *Customers!* Show them where the customers are. This is an excellent opportunity to share your research on personas. Convince them to spend time with their target audience. It will open their eyes to the meteor-like impact the right content can have on the sales cycles.

HOW TO CONVINCE EACH MEMBER OF THE C-SUITE ABOUT CONTENT

Here are some tips for selling content to the C-level executives (Dale, 2012):

- *Chief Executive Officer.* CEOs want buyers to choose their product or service over the competition, while simultaneously keeping budgets in line. You need to make the case to the CEO that customers learn about what your company offers by engaging with your content. If the customer finds the answers they need through the content, and comes to trust the brand, a sale is more likely. Explain how you can measure engagement with your content by analyzing sales, conversion, and overall awareness of your organization.

- *Chief Marketing Officer.* Marketing is more measurable thanks to new technology. Because buyers can learn a lot about your company before they choose to contact you, the buyer expects to have a great deal of information. The CMO needs to understand what it takes to have and implement great content. You need to show the CMO the daily, weekly, and monthly tasks and overall workflow associated with running your content projects. Include time and budget estimates for planning content, assigning content to writers, editing articles and blog posts, publishing posts, promoting posts to social media sites, and repurposing content in other channels, such as email. CMOs also want to keep their internal customers happy (all the other members of the C-suite), so demonstrate a direct link between the departments and how information flows back and forth. Capture your CMOs attention by showing you understand her concerns for both internal stakeholders and external prospective customers.

- *Chief Financial Officer.* Finance is concerned with how to grow the business while controlling expenses. Good content becomes more valuable year after year and can generate more leads at lower cost. A recent McKinsey study found that prices drop by 10% or more when buyers do online research, and do not see a meaningful difference between options. Help your CFO understand how strong content can help differentiate your product from the competition. By doing so, you can command higher prices for your goods and services. In turn, profits go up (Dale, 2012).

- *Chief Information Officer.* It's not hard to understand how the IT teams are often wary of new ideas about how to produce and regulate content—they know that most of the implementation and running of this will probably fall on them. Therefore, it is important to get the CIO on board early in the process, be prepared with details about hosting, data, and back-ups, and let her know what kind of support you will need over time (Dale, 2012).

HOW TO EXPLAIN CONTENT STRATEGY AND CUSTOMER ENGAGEMENT (FOR B2B AND B2C)

What follows is a table of the stages of customer engagement. Use this to guide your executives about how content drives your achievement threshold by engaging customers. You can use the Customer Loop in Figure 2.3 to map the process visually.

Customer Engagement				
Stage	**Goal**	**B2C**	**B2B**	**User Action**
I	Get their attention (engaged contact with the brand)	Acquisition	Lead generation	• Watch video • Download whitepaper • Sign up for email newsletter
II	Active consumption of content	Engagement	Lead nurturing	• Read newsletter • Read and share Facebook post • Repin infographic
III	Identification of lead		Lead scoring	
IV	Bought something; donated money; cited research	Conversion	Conversion	• Generated revenue • Pushed the needle on the achievement threshold
V	Continue to consume content	Retention	Re-engagement	• Provide product support • Provide service or consultation
VI	Brand audience	Buy more products or services	Buy more products or services	• Share your name with their networks

CONTENT CHEAT SHEET TO CONVINCE THE C-SUITE

Here are some approaches you can use to help convince and prepare executives to sign off on content projects:

- *Set expectations*: Clearly explain that establishing a content strategy (online publishing cycle) will take 6–9 months to show true results. However, you would like to try it as a small pilot content project so the company can examine if it will work.

- *Include them*: Ask them if they would like to "write" one blog post a month. This will raise their visibility—and they do not have to do anything as your team will write it for them (if they so choose).

- *Keep them informed*: Provide regular updates on a bi-monthly basis. This way they will have all the facts.

- *Publicly celebrate the wins*: Make sure you tell them about the wins!

OVERRIDING THE OBJECTIONS

Sometimes executives need to warm to the idea of using content to drive revenue. The concepts of traditional advertising are familiar, but they may not want to devote a huge portion of their budget to this new-ish enterprise of communicating with people through digital content. Here's a list of typical objections and possible responses:

Objection	Your Response
It won't work	Business is about creating relationships. We do this through a series of conversations. Content allows us to do this in a smooth and efficient manner.
We don't have the time or resources	I've actually mapped each person's time in the editorial department. These are the three people I'd like to select for this project. Looking at their time, I think we can redistribute their efforts, so that they can find time to devote to this project. Obviously, their core competencies will remain priorities.
How will it affect the bottom line?	Our goal is to drive revenue by using content and a systematic publishing system. Therefore we believe we can significantly drive revenue. What we'd like to suggest is that we begin with a small pilot project and see what results we gain before moving on to larger content projects.
How can you be sure we will say the right thing?	By creating customer personas and understanding the types of conversations our customers want to have with us, we will have the opportunity to talk to them directly.
What will legal say?	We're going to use a content strategy—an efficient online publishing system that includes legal in the editorial process. We will consult with them about content that is potentially litigious.

SUMMARY

Every business or organization has an achievement threshold. Make sure you understand what it is before moving forward with any content projects.

1. Understand your sales cycle, lead generation tactics, and your current state of content affairs. Perform research to find out what you might want to change before you approach your C-suite for executive buy-in.

2. Walk into the C-suite prepared to answer their questions.

3. Be prepared for objections.

4. Prepare your executives and stakeholders to understand that this effort takes time to be successful. Ask them to define what success looks like to them so you can set expectations.

Now that we've learned about making the business case for content, we're going to talk about how to get the crucial buy-in you need from stakeholders—the people inside and outside your organization who understand the information you need to create great content. Rule #2 will teach you how to do just that.

REFERENCES

Dale, F. (2012, November 8). *Selling content marketing to the C-suite*. Retrieved from http://www.demandgenreport.com/industry-topics/demanding-views/1808-selling-content-marketing-to-the-C-Suite.html.

Gogo, B. (2012, June 19). *Convince the C-Suite an enterprise social network makes sense*. Retrieved from http://www.tibbr.com/blog/topics/enterprise-2-0/convince-the-C-Suite-an-enterprise-social-network-makes-good-business-sense/.

Harris, J. (2012, May 25). *How to explain content marketing to the C-suite*. Retrieved from http://contentmarketinginstitute.com/2012/05/explaining-content-marketing-to-C-Suite/.

Knudson, L. (2012). *Generating leaders GE style*. Retrieved from http://www.hrmreport.com/article/Generating-leaders-GE-style/.

Leibtag, A. (2013, January). Personal conversation with author.

Pisello, T. (2011, June 23). *Selling to Mahogany Row? Roll out the web carpet*. Retrieved from http://contentmarketinginstitute.com/2011/06/selling-to-mahogany-row-roll-out-the-web-carpet/.

Smith, R., & Leibtag, A. (2012). *6 secrets of social media superstars in healthcare*. Retrieved from http://unbouncepages.com/6-secrets-of-social-media-superstars/; Ebook published 2012, November 19.

INVOLVE STAKEHOLDERS EARLY AND OFTEN

RULE 2

Last year, I worked with a company on three projects: a core messaging strategy, a new design for their website, and content. About six months into the project, just as we were getting ready to approve the final content, the person who originally hired me to consult—we'll call him Jeremy—suggested we talk to a new set of stakeholders. This was a group I had never met or interviewed. Jeremy and his team had omitted them from our initial discussions, thinking they would get buy-in at the end of the process.

Sure enough, even though Jeremy thought that this particular group of stakeholders was not important enough to include in the initial go-round, they did have vital input. More important, they had political clout. Because they were unhappy with certain parts of the messaging strategy and content, we needed to go back to the drawing board to develop a different strategy and information architecture. This delayed the project by another six months and cost the company hundreds of thousands of dollars.

Lesson learned: *all* of the stakeholders matter.

WHO ARE STAKEHOLDERS?

We've already explored two types of stakeholders: your audience and the C-suite. In this rule, we are going to:

- Define internal and external stakeholders
- Identify and prioritize stakeholders
- Understand the importance of stakeholders to content
- Learn how to talk to stakeholders
- Achieve stakeholder buy-in
- Set up a roadmap for stakeholders
- Learn to assign stakeholder tasks

As we learned in the story of Jeremy, we need to include stakeholders in the process as often as possible because they affect and sometimes even control the outcome. Learning to manage stakeholders is an artful process, but one that will result in a better end content product.

DEFINING STAKEHOLDERS

Stakeholders are people who really care about the product or service and have a "stake" in the outcome. As Tomer Sharon, a usability expert, says, "Stakeholders are our clients, whether internal or external to our organization. These are people who need to believe in what we do so they will act …" (Sharon, 2012).

Stakeholders are the people who have vital information about everything in the organization that affects content management and production. They are the people who can provide vital information that you can turn into content; they are also the people who can describe current content workflow and challenges.

When managed properly, stakeholders will help you create the detailed, robust content your audience craves. They may be the people who set the strategy for the business overall, or they may be the data czars. In journalism lingo, stakeholders are the "sources."

In other words, stakeholders give you the critical information you need to help you be successful with your content endeavors. So pay careful attention to them—they can make or break your content process.

In Chapter 2, we talked about the C-suite and ensuring that you have senior executive buy-in for content. Sometimes stakeholders are your C-suite, or a part of your C-suite. Other stakeholders may be elsewhere in the company's hierarchy. For the sake of getting the information you need, a stakeholder does not necessarily have a high pay grade or power. In most cases, the closer a stakeholder is to the front line, the more they can tell you what you really need to know.

CONTENT IS A SHARED ASSET

When you look at the content lifecycle, what you see is a continuous system of planning, creating, delivering, and governing content. As a content professional, you interface with other professionals with a large and varied set of skills, all of whom have a stake in the content because it supports the organization's goals and objectives. *Content is a shared asset within an organization.*

As the person responsible for content within your organization, you "govern" or lead the effort. That doesn't mean that you make all of the decisions or tell everyone what to do and how to do it. It means that you are the guide: You know what matters, how to build consensus, inspire ideas, and encourage information flow in order to create content that works. (Leibtag, 2011; Sharon, 2012).

Because content is a shared asset, it is important to talk to all stakeholders on a project before you begin planning. This helps you know you are on the right track. It also keeps your stakeholders confident because they feel

Stakeholders are all of the people who are involved in all parts of the content lifecycle and have vital information that makes your content robust, detailed, and engaging.

involved. You also build relationships, which is invaluable later when they communicate to you about content that is old, stale, or in need of revision.

As we've discussed already, content is a piece of information distilled into a format that is easily recognizable for your audience. (We're going to talk about content formats in Chapter 3.) Stakeholders possess information. That is the central reason to involve them in content development early and often.

INTERNAL VERSUS EXTERNAL—STAKEHOLDERS VERSUS YOUR AUDIENCE

The external stakeholders are the members of your intended audience(s)—your customers. Internal stakeholders are your clients: bosses, executives, content creators, and anyone who touches content during its lifecycle. In the case of internal stakeholders, you have their attention and interest, and you actually can interview them.

We have already talked about how to learn more about your external stakeholders, that is, your audience in Rule #1. In this rule, we're going to focus on how to work with your internal stakeholders.

Internal Stakeholders

Very often, there's a vast difference between content the audience wants to consume and the content your stakeholders want to create. I call this the internal versus external push-pull. The only way to win this argument is to have strong market research to back up your claims about what types of information and content your customers want.

Your clients may tell you to create content that you know from experience your audience will not read, consume, or share. That's a sign that your stakeholders do not really know their audience and what types of information they crave. That is why Rule #1 about starting with your audience is so important. That is why it is the first step in creating meaningful, valuable content.

You will probably need to educate stakeholders about what types of information are truly important to external customers, and which content they are simply producing (or asking you to produce) to satisfy what *they* think is important to the audience.

When presented with research that shows what customers want to consume, many stakeholders are willing to listen. When stakeholders give me their observations about customers, I ask them, "How do you know that?" If they answer, "We just know," you can introduce them to the data and research you have accumulated. If you are well prepared, your case against "we just know" thinking will be rock-solid.

As a content professional, you must challenge your organization to move away from a culture of assumption to a culture of data. Basing your decisions on things you know and can know is far better than guessing. In a famous scene from the movie *Top Gun*, Kelly McGillis, a flight instructor named Charlie, is analyzing a contentious interaction between two fighter jets, one flown by a Russian pilot and the other by Maverick, an American fighter pilot, played by Tom Cruise.

> *Charlie*: The MIG has you in his gun site, what were you thinking at this point?

> *Maverick:* You don't have time to think up there. If you think, you're dead.

> *Charlie:* Well that's a big gamble with a 30 million dollar plane, Lieutenant.

Convince your stakeholders to take their time to think, and more importantly, *know* what information your audience truly craves. Don't gamble with content decisions.

Build Personas of Your Internal Stakeholders

If you are going to get buy-in from stakeholders, you need to know whom they are and what they care about. Prepare to meet them by building personas of who they are. For example, you and your team might build a persona of an orthopedic surgeon. That persona might tell you that the stakeholder (the physician) is:

- Extremely busy
- Intelligent
- Concerned about his or her patient's expectations for surgery
- Unconvinced of how a website matters for his or her practice

When I first interview this orthopedic surgeon, I'd show him what the competitors have on their websites and blogs in order prove that his potential patients need and want to know how long it takes to, for example, recover from joint surgery. In fact, one thing I always tell writers I train is to be on the lookout for the information the stakeholder *doesn't* want to include in the content. This is usually because he or she thinks it will turn people off or make them hesitant to follow through on the call to action.

Hiding vital information is a bad idea for your audience—the more transparent you are with the facts, the more you will convince potential customers to do business with you.

By giving people information up front, and not making them hunt for it, you let them know that their interests are at the heart of your organization—not your own. This makes for a better relationship. The goal of content is to build better relationships through stronger conversations.

PRIORITIZING STAKEHOLDERS

Your task is to identify the appropriate stakeholders and decide who is central to the project, and who may have secondary information that is important, but not vital. As I demonstrated in the Jeremy story, when we don't identify and prioritize stakeholders, we run into trouble.

Stakeholders will tell you what you need to know about your customer audience, types of content needed, what hinges on content performance, and so much more. Content is a shared asset within the organization—its main purpose is to drive business objectives. Therefore, the information you can glean from your stakeholders is vital to content success.

As we'll learn in Rule #4, when you create and publish content, you need different, overlapping talents to create the best possible product. In the same vein, stakeholders should be a mix of different people within an organization: subject matter experts, executives, content creators, salespeople, and so on.

When I create content for a department within a hospital, my primary stakeholders are the physicians and staff who run the department. They have the deepest insider knowledge—it is my job to translate that information so I can create the best content for their defined target audiences.

However, there are other stakeholders as well—marketing managers, executives running the overall marketing strategy, and the hospital's web team. So, do I need to talk to each stakeholder? Do I even have time to do that? Will they make time for me?

In an ideal world, you should talk to each and every stakeholder. In reality, this is not always possible. Realistically, a large hospital's VP of Marketing will not have time to sit down and talk about the web content of one of the hospital's dozens of departments.

So, where to start? Your main source, the person who recruited you for this project, or who requested you internally, is your starting point. In the Jeremy story, Jeremy was the main client, as he was the one who brought me in as an external consultant.

What can your main client tell you?

- *The basic sketch of the project*: This is probably the most important part of those initial conversations.

- *Some important details:* Your main client will also fill in some important details, but remember, they are her observations. When content is a shared asset within an organization, it is important not to derive conclusions based on one person's opinion. Act like a journalist and gather others' opinions before you make decisions based on that information.

- *Who the stakeholders are:* Determining the identity of these stakeholders usually comes from an in-depth conversation with the main client, listening, and asking tons of questions. You should ask for an org chart—either for the entire organization or for the department you are working with directly. The org chart should give you a sense of how they internally organize their people, leading to a sharper understanding of whom you should contact. Ask the main client to make introductions, so when you contact stakeholders, they recognize your name and the role you play. I've learned that I won't always talk to the senior players (depending on the type of project), but my main client can give me a lot of that information—as long as I know to ask for it.

- *Prioritizing stakeholders:* The central objective you have when identifying and prioritizing stakeholders is to ensure that any individual with a decision-making or supervisory role is involved in the group you engage. Your job is to connect the dots, to listen carefully and jump, like a frog, from one lily pad to the next. Using this approach, I always feel that I am getting as much information as I can from the people to whom I have easy access.

- *Additional internal or external resources:* Your main client will also provide additional resources to help you, as long as you can identify why you need them and how they will help the project. Don't be afraid to ask to talk to more people. Just run it by the main client to ensure you don't step on any toes or ignite some political wildfires without realizing it.

By listening carefully and fitting the puzzle pieces together, you will create the fullest picture you can of what is happening on the ground as it relates to the content you must shape.

WHAT YOU NEED FROM STAKEHOLDERS

Stakeholders are critical for creating a successful digital strategy roadmap for content. By following the rules in this book, you will create content that will drive sales or propel you toward your achievement threshold. Identifying and interviewing stakeholders and negotiating for their buy-in is the only road to creating and publishing better content. There are two parts to interviewing stakeholders:

1. *Gather information* that comprises the building blocks of your content
2. *Understand their part* in the content lifecycle

Stakeholders as Information Sources

Stakeholders possess valuable information about their area of expertise within the organization. Therefore, you need to position yourself as a researcher and investigative journalist to find out everything they know. Doctors can give prospective patients information about new technologies or techniques for treatment not available elsewhere. Government employees can explain what people receiving social security claims can do if their payments stop coming. Engineers can explain how to troubleshoot when something goes wrong with their products. The list is endless and the information infinite.

Understand Stakeholders as Part of the Publishing Lifecycle

Corey Vilhauer, a content strategist, explains: "Content strategy and UX (user experience) are dedicated to enriching the experience and understanding of the people who will come in contact with our web properties, but those web properties are run by professionals who are deeply affected by the changes and shifts we put in place.

Our job is to help make useful, usable web things. Our job is also to ensure that the passion is passed along to the next in line—that we provide some level of empathy and empowerment for the people who will work the content long after we're gone" (Vilhauer, 2012).

Your job is to ensure that content management efforts continue longer after the initial development of content. You also need to see yourself as a champion for your stakeholders; you help them achieve success with their content. And, as Vilhauer so aptly puts it, you need to empower them to feel ownership of the process, so they feel compelled to continue to engage with content throughout its lifecycle.

So, how do you capture the information you need to create great content? And, how do you talk to stakeholders to understand their unique place in relation to the production and management of content within the organization?

Your Job Is to Gather the Facts

You do not want to come to interviews with preconceived notions. When you ask stakeholders for their input, you need to let them know you are really listening. Be sure to listen for the information they want to give, not the information *you think you need.* That means listening carefully, not interrupting, asking tons of questions, and absorbing all of the information. When you introduce bias into this process, you will erode results.

You job at this point is to gather the facts. As Sharon says, "Don't think too much. You are in information-gathering mode. Think army intelligence. You don't plan your moves now. You don't think about the data in front of you. All you do now is collect and gather. Later on, you'll think about it. If you think too much, you don't listen."

Melissa Rach, a well-known content strategist, uses a slightly different approach:

"During the first conversation I have with a client, I go over vocabulary. I ask the client things like: What does 'content' mean to you? What does 'strategy' mean? I share my definitions, too. Then, we work together to define what key terms mean for the purpose of this engagement" (Vilhauer).

Villhauer points out, "I'm also there to listen. To listen to workflow issues that have become so common at the company that they're ignored. To listen for cues as to who is going to spearhead this project. To listen for politics, for under-the-breath backbiting, to the people who are clearly afraid they're going to feel the brunt of

Preparation for Interviewing Stakeholders:

1. *See yourself as an investigative journalist:* Your job is to build a narrative of what's going on now.

2. *Define vocabularies:* So you understand and set expectations.

3. *Prepare a script:* Ask as many questions as it takes to get a full picture of the current state of content management and creation. Avoid asking questions that may put stakeholders into a defensive posture. For example, I once spoke to the editor of a print magazine and asked her how long she thought it would take before her magazine became 100% digital. As you may imagine, the rest of the interview didn't go too well.

the added workload. And they'll say this out loud because I am non-threatening and because I'm listening" (Vilhauer).

Anytime you meet with a new stakeholder you should have a set of questions you are prepared to ask. Having said that, *don't be afraid to depart from your script*. Most important is to ask detailed questions and read between the lines.

Here is a great stakeholder story: My client, an orthopedic surgeon, wanted to tell patients how long after a joint replacement surgery they had to wait until they could resume having sex. He explained, "They are too shy to ask. I'm a doctor! I know people have sex. But, they can really damage their new joints if they have sex too soon after surgery. So I'd rather put it on the website. I'd rather they know than risk that they won't listen when I tell them at the pre-surgical evaluation or that they'll be too shy to ask. Also, their wives read those websites and will tell them."

He chuckled as he said it, but I took the point to heart. Here's a stakeholder who truly knows and understands his audience. Creating that type of content will go a long way for both him and his patients.

Great Relationships Begin with Great Conversations

We cannot underestimate the value of conversations in creating content. Here are some guidelines for engaging in useful and productive conversations:

- *The art of conversation begins with the art of listening.* You may have opinions and thoughts when you talk to stakeholders, but you need to ignore them and get the stakeholder to talk. This may sound simple, but as we all know simple is not necessarily easy. Think of it like this—if I don't listen, I can't create good content.

- *Learn to listen between the lines.* Also not easy. When a stakeholder says, "Well, that's what I think about the situation," your next question should be, "So what do you think *other* people think?" Sometimes, actually quite often, it is what goes unsaid that is so important.

- *Make eye contact.* The stakeholder will know you are listening and you care when you stop taking notes and look them in the eye. Making eye contact should motivate them to keep talking.

- *Don't fill the empty space.* When the stakeholder stops talking for a second, let him or her have time to think. Don't jump in with your next question or comment.

- *Put yourself in the stakeholder's shoes.* Always important in any stakeholder interaction—ask yourself what you would want if you were this person.

- *Determine success for that person.* I find when I ask, "What will success look like to you at the end of this project?" I can uncover unrealistic expectations. So, for example, when a stakeholder says, "At the end of this project, I want our organization to be number one on Google for all of our main keywords," I know I need to do some serious educating about search engine optimization.

Interviewing skills take time to develop. Be patient and remember you will get better with practice.

Uncovering Group Dynamics

Part of what you want to understand when you interview stakeholders about content is how they work together. Another excellent piece of advice from Sharon regarding talking to stakeholders is to uncover group dynamics: "Encourage a conversation. When there are several stakeholders present, it's a golden opportunity for co-discovery. When you ask a question, try facilitating a conversation between stakeholders. It will help you understand the many aspects and layers behind answers. It might also uncover hidden political forces and tensions you were not aware of that might affect the future of the study and its impact."

Those hidden political forces and tensions are critical to any content project, as we will see in the next section.

OWNERSHIP: SETTING UP A ROADMAP FOR STAKEHOLDERS

In order to ensure stakeholders feel they own the content, you need to create a roadmap for them—a plan for how you are going to take them from where they are now to where they want to be. Then you will all feel confident (Figure R2.1).

Figure R2.1 Setting up a roadmap requires mapping your current position and then understanding what you need to do to get to where you want to go.

Make sure it is a roadmap ordinary people can follow. Try not to show them one of those fancy project plans with graphs and bars and dates and timelines. Just make it simple, on a spreadsheet or in a Word table—clearly describing each step. You might even consider using a shared document system. Every line should have a due date, the responsible member, and the goal.

Often a calendar works well in these situations, with simple dates and deliverables listed. People appreciate simplicity: Their lives are already complicated by overflowing streams of information. Make sure that they understand the process. If you expect anything from them, make that very clear on the roadmap you give them—double underline their part, highlight it, send them reminder emails—whatever it takes.

QUESTIONS YOU MIGHT ASK

The questions about information you need to glean from your stakeholders will depend on the facts you need to gather to help shape the actual content.

The following questions are about the content lifecycle: how the organization plans, creates, publishes, and manages content. Designed to uncover the content lifecycle workflow and current processes, their answers will help you build that roadmap.

Roadmap Step #1: Where Are We Now?

You must describe where the organization is now in relation to content creation before describing how you're going to change it.

- What are the data and analytics that describe where we are? How is content currently performing?
- What are the business objectives surrounding this project? Why are we currently not meeting them? What business case do we have that makes us think content will help us? Where are our pain points, i.e., our real or perceived problems?
- Do all stakeholders and content creators within the organization understand the overall business strategy?
- Who are the stakeholders? Who are the content creators? Who gives input to the content creators?

Roadmap Step #2—Where Are We Going?

Make it clear that this process has direction.

- What is the business case for creating content?
- Does this content align with our brand?
- How do we want our customers to feel about us?
- Is our messaging and branding strategy well mapped? If not, who is in charge of that process?

- How does our audience interface with our content? Which devices do they use?

- Which content types are most popular?

- What is the average cost of producing said content type?

Roadmap Step #3—How Will We Get There?

This step puts everyone on the same page regarding the process.

- Do we have the right talent filling the proper roles within the organization to create the content we need?

- Do we have the budget to produce the content we need?

- Do we have the right technology and platform to create the content?

- With whom can we partner to help us get there faster or better?

FOLLOW-THROUGH: KEEPING THE STAKEHOLDERS INVOLVED

Once your roadmap is set, and the process of content creation begins, don't forget your original stakeholders. Make it a priority to keep them in the loop, sharing milestones, and asking them for input along the way.

It's time consuming, I know, but I have used this approach, and I'm convinced of its tremendous value. Stakeholders have a deep investment in content, feel great about being asked for their opinions, and will provide viewpoints you very well may have ignored or brushed aside.

It's not just worth the time—it's essential. Your worst nightmare would be to complete the project and present it as a *fait accompli*, only to have the stakeholders ask why you didn't tell them how it was going and then demand changes.

Let's remember Jeremy—he and his group didn't put the time into identifying crucial stakeholders, and they paid the price.

STAKEHOLDER TASKS FOR CONTENT EDITING AND DEVELOPMENT

There is one other important part of identifying stakeholders and including them in the content process. At some point, they will need to take an active part in content editing and development. As Karen McGrane, a web and usability expert, points out, your stakeholders will need to make conscious decisions about content, including:

- Keep as is

- Revise

- Delete

- Create new content (McGrane, 2012)

So, at some point, let your stakeholders know that they will have to do something with the content. You may want to consider creating a two-page document about:

- Readability online
- How people use mobile devices
- How people use social media to find and share content

This is a leave-behind document they can use when thinking about which actions they should take with their content.

SUMMARY

When creating content, it is vital to include the project's stakeholders in the process. Get input from people for whom the content is important, and who have the necessary information you need to build great content.

Rule #2 includes the following actions:

- Find out who the stakeholders are
- Find out what is important to them
- Bring them into the process during the early stages
- Create a roadmap so that they can see where the process is taking them
- Keep them in the loop during the process
- Assign them certain tasks

Most importantly—have great conversations with them all along the way—this will lead to great relationships with them and by extension, great content.

Now you are going to meet Paige, who followed both of our first two rules to create content for her organization that produced results.

REFERENCES

Leibtag, A. (2011, March 14) *Getting started with analytics: How to get buy-in from your team*. Retrieved from http://contentmarketinginstitute.com/2011/03/getting-started-with-analytics/.

McGrane, K. (2012). *Content strategy for mobile*. New York: A Book Apart.

Sharon, T. (2012, November 30). *Listen to your stakeholders: Sowing seeds for future research*. Retrieved from http://uxmag.com/articles/listen-to-your-stakeholders.

Vilhauer, C. (2012, October 11). *Empathy and content strategy: On teaching, listening and affecting change*. Retrieved from http://eatingelephant.com/2012/10/empathy/.

CASE STUDY: XONEX (HOLDEN, 2012)

Imagine a richly appointed restaurant with blood-red carpeting, mahogany dining tables, steak knives that could slice through fabric, and wine glasses designed for celebration. In an industry where deals are handshakes made over a three-martini lunch and sales pitch, how does content become king? When traditional sales methods stop working, what does a company that wants to win need to do?

XONEX, a B2B corporate relocation company, found major success with content when their old sales approach of lunches and courting stopped working as well. XONEX administers relocation services on a global level, but sales are focused nationally in the Northeast, Southeast, and Southwest. They have an extremely long sales cycle of 3–5 years.

BREATHING NEW LIFE INTO AN OLD SALES APPROACH

Paige Holden began working as Director of Communications at XONEX in 2010 and immediately identified some major marketing challenges. Holden explains, "There were no marketing goals; marketing wasn't clearly defined. We were limited to doing some events around the country with trade association groups. We had a booth, but barely had a corporate brochure. We had ads in our trade association publication, called *Mobility*, but it was expensive, and we couldn't track what type of return we were getting from buying that advertising space."

Further, they lacked an effective email distribution plan. Anything XONEX sent out was incredibly sales-y and did not seem to satisfy the needs of the target audience.

Before she started implementing any solutions, Holden interviewed all of the key people within the organization: the CEO, CFO, head of operations, and some central sales people. She asked them to define the target audiences in their minds, as well as what they thought the company's greatest assets were.

DOING RESEARCH TO GET ANSWERS

After those interviews, Holden was a woman with a mission—she needed to understand the content "holes" within the organization. After a month of research, which included digging online to understand XONEX's brand equity, Holden examined the online competitors to gauge the industry conversation.

After investigating her top five competitors to see their digital marketing objectives, Holden breathed a sigh of relief. "One of the comforting things I found was that they weren't much farther than we were—it was a great feeling to know we could still do something. I realized I was not playing catch up as much as I thought I would be."

Holden knew she needed to begin with defining her target audience so she could determine how to better attract and track leads (Rule #1: *Start with Your Audience*). All of her research pointed to the following business objectives:

1. Create awareness of the brand
2. Generate leads
3. Modernize the IT system and build a new relocation product—a cutting-edge mobile app that would revolutionize the industry

ORGANIZING THE CONTENT AROUND BUSINESS OBJECTIVES

Holden knew that the first step in a successful digital strategy required that she define her customer personas. She continued on her quest to define her target audiences. By the end of 2010, she determined there were four:

1. Human resources professionals, as they define relocation benefit packages
2. Industry peers in relocation and housing
3. Employees who are relocating (transferees)
4. Procurement, as more companies tighten the purse strings

Her next step was to involve stakeholders early in the process and to keep them involved (Rule #2: *Involve Stakeholders Early and Often*).

Part of the surprise in the project was that the XONEX sales force disregarded transferees as a target group and could not prioritize between HR and procurement. Further, and perhaps more puzzling, the majority of the marketing investment went to support industry groups, as opposed to buyer events and publications.

After lengthy discussions of business objectives and several group brainstorming sessions, the sales force realized that they needed to reach HR professionals first and foremost, as they were still the lead buyers. They did not feel they needed to reach industry peers, because they felt that "the person(s) using the product are the ones we need to concentrate on."

However, Holden decided to keep the transferees as a target audience within her persona development. She felt eventually her teams would realize that XONEX's end users could have a great impact on the company's reputation in the long run, especially in the digital, social world.

Once Holden understood her audience—her potential leads—she needed to find a way to attract them. From her understanding of business objectives, as well as her research about the media mix, content holes, and competitors, she knew content was the answer.

After Holden received executive buy-in to move ahead with content, as well as her sales force buy-in (the internal stakeholders) around February 2011, she started to put together a content marketing strategy, based on Joe Pulizzi's system (Pulizzi, 2013). This includes:

- Tweet daily
- Blog weekly
- Distribute a newsletter monthly
- Create a whitepaper or eBook quarterly
- Develop a bi-annual event program

Holden focused on creating a relevant blog and publishing it with five posts so it would immediately look robust. As soon as they launched in August 2011, the XONEX team received very strong feedback from industry peers. "Competitors' ears perked up and they started asking 'who is this XONEX—what are they doing?'"

As Holden explains, "No one wants to be sold anymore unless there's a hook that's really interesting. So we give our target audiences content they care about. For example, in March we release blogs and white papers about corporate tax issues, which are the pressing issues on their minds then. In May, we publish about relocation challenges, because it's the beginning of the relocation busy season."

WHAT WORKED?

Holden followed a system to create change, both at the marketing level and the organizational level. She:

1. Understood and defined her business objectives
2. Defined her sales cycle, as well as the lead generation process
3. Thoroughly researched the marketplace, as well as her competitors
4. Sought stakeholder involvement and executive buy-in
5. Launched a smart content marketing program using a strategy that tied directly to her business objectives

Holden comments, "Your goal as a marketer is to gain the respect of the sales team by showing your efforts can produce changes. It took a year for them to really feel like we were making an impact, but we're about to close a major piece of business we can tie directly back to our content marketing, including our white papers" (Holden, 2012).

Holden also acknowledges an early win in the process that helped convince internal stakeholders this was going to work. About four months into the content marketing program, the sales team was at a relocation event, and the keynote speaker used their blog as a shining example of a leading blog in the relocation industry. "That was a huge victory and an early win," Holden remarks. (Remember, it's important to share wins with the C-suite, so they understand where those budget dollars are going and, more importantly, that they are working!)

CONTINUING THE SUCCESS

Holden continues to work with the sales team regularly to continue the success of the content marketing program. She commented: "For example, I've encouraged the sales team to specifically ask to sign people up for the blog in order to keep in touch with them. We also have an editorial calendar that we plan at quarterly sales meetings. I rely on my sales force to bring me back intelligence from the field—what are people talking about? What blog posts might resonate with our audiences? It was a huge challenge to get them thinking that way, but now they're turning into journalists in front of my eyes."

Now XONEX is working on a mobile app for the transferee group—that very same group her sales force rejected at the beginning. As Holden explains, "We've identified that target audience needs content, but delivered in a different way. When we reach that business objective, we will need a whole new content line for them."

XONEX's story demonstrates the critical aspects of digital strategy that we have addressed:

- Define your customer personas
- Tie content development to business objectives
- Involve stakeholders early and often in your content development and management

WHAT'S NEXT

Now that we understand why and how content drives the sales process as well as how to unearth the valuable information within an organization that shapes the content, we are going to discuss how to design your content so that it floats. How do you spark, conduct, and continue a conversation with your target audiences in this vast digital ocean?

In Part 2 of *The Digital Crown*, we will learn about constructing the conversation, preparing your content for multi-channel publishing, and engaging your audiences on different channels. We'll also talk about why it's so important to have a variety of talented individuals involved in creating and managing your digital content.

REFERENCES

Holden, P. (October 31, 2012). Interview by Ahava Leibtag.

Pulizzi, J. (2013). Content marketing strategy: how to engage influencers in your industry. Retrieved from: http://contentmarketinginstitute.com/2013/03/content-marketing-strategy-engage-influencers/.

Consumers want to have a conversation with your organization. In traditional media, we used to start the conversation with our target audiences via billboards, ads, direct mail, and so on. *In digital media, our target audiences start the conversation with us.*

TECHNOLOGY MEDIATES THE CONVERSATION

Your digital properties, like websites, blogs, and social media channels, are "open" 24/7. Customers are interacting with your content around the globe at any hour of any day. Further complicating matters, the technology they use to access that content changes their experiences. Think about viewing a website on a laptop, or a blog on a mobile phone, or a Facebook page on a tablet. The conversation changes as the format and context shift.

CONTENT MUST FLOAT

If the web is an endless source of waves of information, then our customers are surfers on these waves. Our content needs to float right along with them, no matter what the technology or display format.

Customers need to be able to converse with you using one device, save the content, and consume it on a different device later. It needs to float, unencumbered by the design surrounding it or the "page" it lives on. Your customers should find it when and where they want, how they want, and on the devices they own and prefer to use.

In Part 2, we're going to discuss how to:

- Create great content so it aligns with your business objectives.
- Publish content so it can go everywhere and anywhere.
- Distribute content in a way that makes you part of a conversational marketplace.

Before we begin, let's define three terms: channels, platforms, and formats, using definitions from Halvorson and Rach (2012):

- *Channel* is the place or service through which you are communicating with your users. Examples: email, websites, SMS.

- *Platform* is the technology upon which you build your content or service in order to deliver or exchange content. Examples: content management system, mobile technology.

- *Format* is the way in which information is presented. Examples, text, audio, video, or images. (Halvorson & Rach, 2012).

While format is tied to channel and platform, we must learn to separate them—because we want to create content that can float everywhere. Of course, the content needs to be strong; if you start with poor content, it will not matter how well you present and distribute it.

BUILDING GREAT CONTENT PROGRAMS

In the next three chapters, we will talk about creating content; how content formats change the conversations you have with your customers. We are going to discuss how to structure your content so it can float along the World Wide Web and reach your intended audiences regardless of the channel. We're going to learn to think in terms of content modeling and adaptive content. And, by discussing different publishing formats and social media channels, we'll learn how to extend the life and reach of your content.

To keep your content fresh and your audience engaged, we'll also learn about the next two rules:

- Rule #3: *Keep It Iterative*
- Rule #4: *Create Multidisciplinary Content Teams*

We are going to review some technical issues in these chapters, but as a content and digital marketing professional, you must understand them.

This is a new age, where technology is changing the way we talk to our customers. In these chapters, you will gain the vocabulary you need to talk to programmers, developers, and designers, making you a more effective digital communications professional.

REFERENCE

Halvorson, K., & Rach, M. (2012). *Content strategy for the Web* (2nd ed.). Berkeley, CA: New Riders.

The web is a magical place filled with interactions previously thought impossible. It has changed our daily lives: We can find almost anything we need online: products, services, movie times, the weather, and even human companionship.

Need to know what type of smoothie maker to buy? You can read 47 reviews from others who have bought that smoothie maker or one made by a different manufacturer. Want to find out if a furniture store is reputable? Read about the store on Yelp. Want to learn about almost every possible topic in a multitude of languages? Check out Wikipedia.

THE INTERNET IS THE ROOM OF REQUIREMENT

In this wonderful place, the amount of information flowing around us can feel overwhelming. It feels like the Room of Requirement at Hogwarts from the Harry Potter series: It can be a wonderful safe haven when you need to hide and practice Defense against the Dark Arts. Or it can feel like a room that is a garbage dump for every student who has ever needed a secret place to stash dangerous, magical objects.

In *Harry Potter and the Half-Blood Prince*, Harry needed a place to hide his book of potions from his teacher, Professor Snape. He began to pace in the passageway and imagined a door magically opening so he could hide his book. A door appeared and Harry walked into the Room of Requirements. The room was huge and had "thousands and thousands of books, no doubt banned or graffitied or stolen. There were winged catapults and Fanged Frisbees, some still with enough life in them to hover halfheartedly over the mountains of other forbidden items; there were chipped bottles of congealed potions, hats, jewels, cloaks; there were what looked like dragon eggshells, corked bottles whose contents still shimmered evilly, several rusting swords, and a heavy, bloodstained axe" (Rowling & GrandPre, 2005).

What Harry found is what the Internet truly is: a room that has, essentially, whatever we need at any given moment. But let's be honest; it is also a city-size garbage dump of outdated, old, expired, messy, unorganized piles of junk. Think about when we sift through all of that rubbish to find the piece of information we really need; it can feel like searching for the proverbial needle in the haystack. But, when we find it, the Internet transforms into an enchanted place for us because it fulfills a need—immediately. Magic.

MAGIC CONTENT: MAKING DIAMONDS OUT OF COAL

From your perspective as a content professional, you know you need to develop content that performs just like magic for your audiences. It needs to satisfy a particular need and enchant—and no waiting, please.

At its basic unit of construction, content is a piece of information. Once you decide on the *format for the content* you choose to hold that information in (press release, advertisement, Tweet, blog post, website article, and so on), there are two more building blocks:

1. *Substance*: What formats will we use (text, audio, video)? What messages does the content need to communicate to our audience?

2. *Structure*: How is content prioritized, organized, formatted, and displayed? (Structure includes information architecture, metadata, data modeling, linking strategies, and so on.) (Halvorson & Rach, 2012)

UNDERSTANDING SUBSTANCE AND STRUCTURE

You might compare information to the subject of a picture and substance to the medium the artist used: oil on canvas, digital photograph, or watercolor. Think of a photograph of a person versus an oil painting of that same person. We should see exactly the same picture no matter what the medium. But the medium changes details slightly so that the entire whole feels different. This happens when we change the format of content we use to embed information. Think of a press release versus a blog post. The information might be the same but because of the format the meaning shifts.

1. Information: subject of the picture
2. Substance: medium of the picture
3. Structure: frame and display location of the picture

We can compare structure to the size of the portrait and where we choose to display it. In a gallery, framed in a heavy gold frame, it looks quite different than it does when the picture is posted on Instagram and we see it on the small screen of our smartphone.

The above metaphor demonstrates how much information can flex once it becomes content.

In the next chapter, Chapter 4, we will discuss content *structure*. But in this chapter, we talk about content *substance*, including:

- Creating a content framework
- Controlling the content experience
- Creating different content formats

CREATING A CONTENT FRAMEWORK

From an internal business perspective, content needs to align with the organization's achievement objectives. With all the junk that's out there—the piles of unorganized, messy, complicated rubbish stacked in teetering piles—how do you create content that sparkles and catches the eyes, ears, and interest of your target audience?

You need a content framework—a way to think about building and creating your content—guided by these questions:

1. How and when does the content support the sales cycle or help you achieve your achievement threshold?

2. How do the different formats of content relate to each other? Do they help support the story you want to tell?

3. How will this content float along the web, facilitating conversations?

Content is all of the information and factual assets of your company or organization—connected to one another for the customer to access. This is called an "interconnected system of assets" (Wachter-Boettcher, 2012). Captured inside your content are all of the knowledge assets of your organization; they all relate to and depend on one another. Further, depending on the quality of the content, these assets support your audience and help facilitate interactions—both good and bad.

THE CONTENT FRAMEWORK

We're ready to build a content framework in order to build great content for your organization. This will help guide you in creating the right content formats to drive your sales process. We also need to support the audience in accomplishing *their* tasks. To do this, we need to have the right types of conversations with them, in the right way, at the right time.

CONTENT IS WHERE INFORMATION LIVES AND THRIVES

We're going to learn how to break down the three questions above within your content framework, but first let's review what content truly is.

Content is a piece of information, a kernel embedded in a content format that your audience seeks to find. Content is a way for your information to come alive. Figure 3.1 shows that we begin with information. We then select the appropriate content format to set, or highlight, the piece of information; then we distribute the content. Deciding on the delivery method of content will make all the difference in funneling the information to the appropriate customers, at the right time, effectively.

1. How and when does the content support the sales cycle or help you achieve your achievement threshold?
2. How do the different content formats relate to each other? Do they help support the story you want to tell?
3. How will this content float along the web, facilitating conversations?

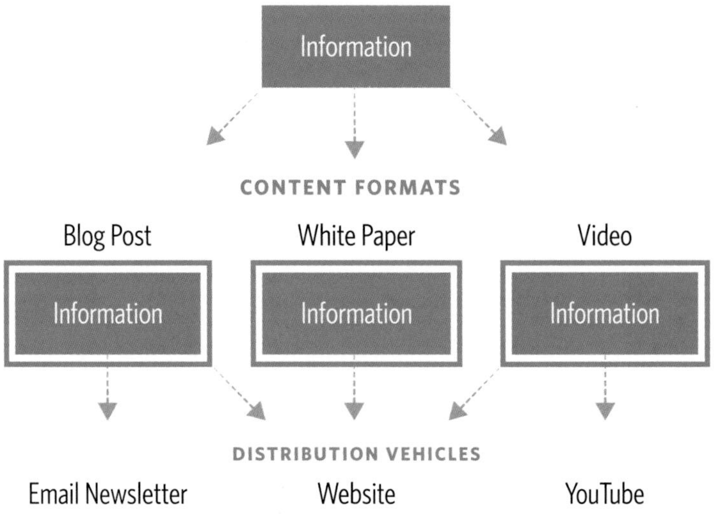

Figure 3.1 Content: From Information to Distribution. Ahava Leibtag. All Rights Reserved.

THE THREE PARTS OF CONTENT

It is critical to understand the difference between information, content format, and distribution because each one needs to stand on its own: all of them need to work together to satisfy your audience.

- *Information*: What you want to communicate
- *Content format*: The way you present, or showcase, the information
- *Distribution*: The channels and platforms you choose to float the content out onto the web

CONTENT FORMATS THAT FLEX

We choose content formats in our own lives, often without thinking about it. Let's say you receive an email from a colleague. You read it, realize it's a sensitive or complicated issue, and think, "I should really call this person back, not email

---

Channel, Platform, Format

This is a good place to review the following concepts:

- *Channel* is the place or service through which you are communicating with your users. Examples: email, websites, social media channels, print, and broadcast
- *Platform* is the technology upon which you build your content or service to deliver or exchange content. Examples: content management system and social media websites
- *Format* is the way in which information is presented. Examples: text, audio, video, print, or images

him." You realize that the information you need to communicate may not be appropriate for an email.

That is an automatic, gut response; you probably don't realize how you are flexing from one mode of communication to another, even as you are doing it. We choose which platform of technology is best to communicate our message; in other words, which content format works best—in this case written versus verbal.

Do you text or call a friend to let him or her know what time you will be at the restaurant? Think about it—you could call, but you know that will take longer than texting. The "Hi, how are you?" turns into a longer, perhaps unnecessary, conversation when all you really want to do is convey the information that you will be there at 6:00 p.m.

Recognizable Formats Attract Attention

We also exercise this flexibility when we choose, for example, to write a press release rather than a blog post. You write a press release because you know journalists *immediately recognize a press release as a content format designed just for them.* The format of the content communicates whom it is for immediately.

Our audience has thousands of immediately recognizable content formats to look for/recognize/react to: Stop signs, customer reviews, prescription pads, report cards, medical forms, applications, and so on. Designed so we immediately recognize them and take certain actions, these content formats facilitate crisper interactions. Imagine the Internet without content formats? Overwhelming as it is now, it would be totally unnavigable.

THAT is our goal: We want our audience to immediately recognize the content, know it is for them, know what to do, and do it.

We don't want our content and our conversations to feel like the Room of Requirement. We want the very opposite, in fact. We want them to feel like controlled experiences that help customers make decisions.

CONTENT: FORMATS, PLATFORMS, AND CHANNELS

There are probably hundreds of formats for content—there is no way we could list them all here. For the purposes of your content framework, however, I think we can look at the following divisions:

- Text
- Audio
- Visual

In the following table, we differentiate information from content format, platform, and channel:

Content	Information	Format	Platform or Channel
Text	[Whatever you are trying to communicate]	• Written text	• Website • Blog • White paper • SMS • Print newsletter • Enewsletter • Email • Twitter • Facebook
Audio	[Whatever you are trying to communicate]	• Podcast • Radio program • Music • Webinar	• Website • iTunes or other audio distribution site • Blog
Visual	[Whatever you are trying to communicate]	• Video • Infographic • Pictures • Webinar • Interviews • Commercials	• YouTube • Pinterest • Video on your website • Vimeo • Facebook • Flickr • Instagram • Vine

Content is not the same as the way it's delivered to you, in the same way that your print newspaper is not the same as the newspaper delivery person.

When you talk to people about content, they think you mean their website, as in *the entire thing*. But, as we know, content is not the website, it is what is ON the website, or in the book, or the subject of the video. You need to disassociate this idea that *content* is the same as the *way* it's delivered to you. Content is not a magazine, or a TV program, or the mail. Rather, those are the channels through which you receive the content.

Your customers can encounter your content anywhere on the World Wide Web. You must divorce yourself from the idea that your content is tied to its point of origin—like your website—and instead think of your content as floating throughout the Internet, just waiting to fulfill a need for your target audience.

SUPPORTING THE SALES AND BUYING PROCESS CYCLE

In Chapter 2, we talked about the business of content creation and about the sales cycle. (We also talked about the achievement threshold, which is how not-for-profit, government agencies, and others measure their success.) Content—its creation and its distribution—must support that sales cycle or achievement threshold. In the next chapter, we will discuss production, publication, and distribution of content. But for now, let's focus on creating content and supporting the sales cycle.

To be successful with our content, we must tie our content development to our business objectives. Before you begin to create content, you need to understand your sales cycle as well as the business objectives. If you recall, "leads" are prospects—people who could eventually convert to customers, donors, or advocates. The sales cycle is the amount of time from when your lead learns of your services to the time that person converts and becomes a buyer.

Most companies illustrate their lead "funnels" in a framework based on the shape of a funnel (Figure 3.2).

I prefer the term "customer loop," which we illustrated in Chapter 2. Think loop because it accurately represents how companies would like to continue relationships with customers (Figure 3.3).

By examining where your lead currently is in his buying process, that is, the person's location in the loop, you can determine the right formats of content, or "content mix" to create for that potential customer. Some like to call this supporting the decision journey. You want to build a content framework that supports the consumer's decision journey. So, how do you create content that supports the sales cycle?

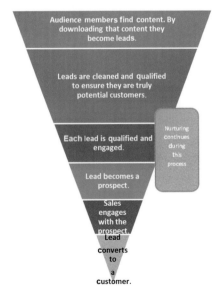

Figure 3.2 Sales leads funnel.

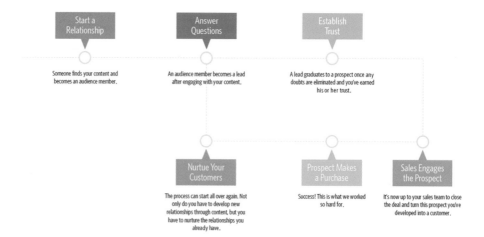

Figure 3.3 Customer loop: Continue relationships with your customers. Ahava Leibtag. All Rights Reserved.

Here's another way to think about it: Let's say you want to grow a vegetable garden. You choose to plant watermelon, zucchini, and tomatoes. Each of those vegetables needs to be planted at a different time, have a different amount of water and sunlight, and be picked from the plant at varying points of ripeness.

Customers are the same way—they need to be nurtured at different points in their own decision making process. Knowing where they are in that buying process will help you create content that nurtures your sales in a supportive, strategic manner. But, before we talk about where your leads are in their buying processes, let's talk about the process for using content to support the sales and buying process cycle. Content needs to:

- Inform
- Persuade
- Convert

The reason you produce content is to *convert prospects to customers or to support the customers you already have.* Developing content is the primary tactic we use to inform, persuade, and convert. The primary goal of content is to keep people moving through your loop—therefore; you must control their content experience to keep up that forward momentum. *Controlling the experience comes from truly understanding the value content can provide for customers, as well as understanding the customer's journey.*

UNDERSTANDING THE BUYING PROCESS

Let's go back now to where your leads are in the buying process. "Every decision to purchase a product or service is an attempt to satisfy a need or relieve a dissatisfaction of some kind" (Tracy, 2000). People tend to follow this process when they are in a buying decision mindset (Sandler):

- *Appear interested*: They identify a need

- *Act motivated*: They decide they are going to pursue a solution to that need

- *Get information*: Begin to learn more about a service or product that fills that need

- *Avoid commitment*: May take a long time to decide whether they want to commit

- *Disappear*: May decide they are not going to buy or that they will wait for a sale or a better deal

Brian Tracy, a well-known sales expert, explains, "Every buying decision is an attempt to solve a problem or achieve a goal. One of the most important things you do in successful selling is put yourself in the shoes of your prospects and see the offering through his or her eyes. You must determine what this product or service means to your prospect in terms of his or her goals or problems before you can offer it or sell it effectively" (Tracy, 2000).

What Tracy is describing is the process of understanding your audience and where they are *now* in the buying process—just like Rule #1. He's also describing understanding everything you can about your product so you can provide information that will answer your audience's questions.

In an article about how to build a blog following, Karlee Weinmann quotes the well-known sales guru Marcus Sheridan, and explains his method, "Be an active listener, and encourage your team to do the same. Go over commonly asked questions, review customer inquiries and brainstorm topics that people might not fully grasp right away. Each of these is a totally useful, readable blog post" (Weinmann, 2012).

In the several times Sheridan has worked through that process with companies, he says the team usually comes up with about 100 questions in 15 minutes. Yet even beyond answering people's questions about the product, you also need to understand the product fully before you create content that explains its benefit to the buyer. That's why you need to follow Rule #2.

This is true for any organization, institution, business, and not-for-profit or government organization. A university needs to convince students that it is the right place for them. Government agencies need to answer people's questions about how to interact with them (file forms, apply for assistance, and download information). Hospitals need to provide important, detailed information about the advanced technologies or treatments they offer.

Charities may need to convince donors why their donations do more good with them than with a different charity.

As Kristina Halvorson and Melissa Rach point out, "No matter how they find you, your users almost always have very specific goals and expectations. And if your content doesn't meet their expectations—and quickly—they will leave. Period" (Halvorson & Rach, 2012).

Know who your customer is by knowing what segment of the customer loop she is going through *right now.*

THE LAW OF TRUST

Even if you know everything you can about your audience, you can't win a sale or convert a prospect to a buyer if they don't trust you. More than anything, content needs to forge a connection between you and your prospects.

How can you do this? With transparency and trust.

> The trust bond between the salesperson and the customer is the foundation of the successful sale. Trust is everything, especially in a large or complex sale. The higher the level of trust between you and your customer, the lower his or her fear of failure and perception of risk. When the level of trust is high enough, the sale will take place (Tracy, 2000).

When we think of content as a conversation, we understand the following two points as well:

- Successful salespeople listen twice as much as they talk.
- No one ever listened themselves out of a sale (Tracy, 2000).

So how do you listen and create trust when you create content? Well, first you use all the feedback channels you have: Social media channels, comments, emails, customer service information, and so on. More importantly, when you encounter places where your content was confusing, you go back to clarify it.

Even more, "Customers look upon top salespeople as friends who are trying to help them solve their problems or achieve their goals. They look upon those salespeople as partners and advisors. The customers do not perceive them as salespeople and they do not see themselves as being 'sold' to. They see them more as teachers and helpers" (Tracy, 2000).

Content should be there to answer anticipated questions and provide clarity for your customers. That is always your goal. You are a teacher and a helper when you create content.

BUSINESS IS ABOUT RELATIONSHIPS

Fundamentally, people crave relationships and connections. They buy from and commit to people they trust and like because they believe they have a relationship with that person.

"All selling is ultimately relationship selling. People don't buy products or services. They 'buy' the people who are selling the products or services." Therefore, "Develop a process for relationship management. Maintain regular contact with your customers and your good prospects. Show them that you appreciate them by developing various ways to say, 'Thank you'" (Tracy, 2000). Thinking about nurturing customers in a loop, rather than a funnel, is so vital to finding success when using content to build relationships.

Content Supports the Loop

Content can move your audience through the customer loop. When executed properly, content can persuade, inform, validate, instruct, and entertain your prospects (Halvorson & Rach, 2012). Good content can:

- Create a relationship
- Provide answers to questions
- Eliminate doubt
- Establish trust
- Educate and help
- Nurture the relationship
- Support the sales and buying process

As we discussed earlier, content is an interconnected set of assets. You need to understand how all of these assets relate to each other, how they support the buying process, and how they move customers through your pipeline.

We're going to focus next on the different formats of content and how they relate to each other in order to create a strong content framework. This is how we control the content—and the conversation—as we listen to customer needs.

CONTROLLING THE CONTENT EXPERIENCE

Most of the time, it takes repeated exposure to your content before someone will decide to buy. Google calls this the Zero Moment of Truth (Google), the moment when your prospect makes that online decision to

The Hallmarks of a Controlled Content Experience

We need to control the content experience in order to ensure that our audience moves through the customer loop and becomes a buyer. When this happens, we can be almost certain that our audience has found content that has done the following:

1. *Corresponded to real-life needs*: "I want to find a charity I connect with so I can donate. Reading about all the wonderful work this charity does with developmentally disabled adults inspired me to give."

2. *Educated*: "My father is elderly and has started to forget things. Is this a normal sign of aging or do I need to consider the possibility that he may be developing dementia or Alzheimer's? Is there a geriatric practice at my community's hospital? Do they have someone I can talk to about this? Looking at their website and their checklist of normal signs of aging made me realize we need an appointment."

3. *Entertained and told a story*: "I've been looking at several universities and I know I want to study accounting and business. Watching the video the accounting principles class made with their professor about understanding the difference between cash basis accounting vs. accrual basis accounting made me want to attend that program."

When you produce content with the goal of moving customers through your customer loop, you ease the challenges inherent in creating valuable content. Connect with your customers' needs so you produce content that informs and educates. Don't forget to entertain prospects with great stories—it's almost always the emotional connection they need to move them across the line to customers that, yes, drive revenue.

buy. According to Google's research, the average user needs to *digest ten pieces of content* before making a purchasing decision.

In other words, you need ten conversations or interactions with your prospects before they buy. This suggests we must develop different formats of content, or a content mix, in order to engage our prospects and keep them moving through our loop toward conversion into customers.

UNDERSTANDING AND CREATING A CONTENT MIX

We need to understand how all of our chunks of content—our organization's assets—relate to one another, so we can create the right mix of content formats, channels, and platforms to move our prospects through our customer loop.

You want to have many different formats of content on your website that represent your brand and the information you want to communicate. Remember, the goal of the loop is to drive demand for your product or service—if consumers need ten pieces of content to drive a decision, then you need to have ten pieces of content for them.

The table explains the loop stage, the activity, and which content formats you may want to use to keep them moving through the loop.

Loop Stage	Loop Activity	Content Formats
Lead finds content (awareness)	This is how the leads come into the loop	Anything could attract them to you at this point. But knowing who you are targeting and where they spend their time will help you narrow the possibilities. For example, if you're marketing B2B, you might want to consider white papers or eBooks to begin the conversation. Other formats include: • Webinars • Request for Information (Lead Generation Forms) • Events • Website Content
Lead is engaged (consideration)	Typically, the lead will download something from your website, comment on a blog, follow you on Twitter or Like you on Facebook	This is where you can use the different questions people have about your products and services. What would work best here? A how-to piece of content? Something about your products or services? A video that demonstrates the product?
Lead becomes a prospect	This is where you need to score the leads to find out exactly where they are in the buying process. Perhaps they are interested in following your content, but not ready to buy	You may need to send content directly—an email, phone call or some other personal contact. Maybe the salesperson needs to talk directly to the customer, sharing different content formats, likes sales decks or product demonstrations, developed specifically for this purpose
Lead becomes a sales lead (possible customer)	Once the prospect expresses an interest in actually converting to a customer, you know they are probably going to buy	You may need to continue to nurture your lead. Email newsletters, direct mail, and phone calls might work during this period. That's why it's so important to capture their attention on channels where they spend their time, so you continue to be top of mind for them
Conversion (customer)	They've become a customer, donor, patient, etc.	At this point, they've made the buying decision. But that doesn't mean you should stop nurturing them, as they may become repeat customers. That's why it's a customer loop, not a funnel. In a funnel, the process actually ends; in a loop, it just keeps going

Create the Content Mix

Here is a good matrix to hold up against your customer loop to decide *which content formats* to use at each stage of the sales process.

Kathy Hanbury, a content strategist, suggests, "Define the purpose of your content: Refer to your brand focus and your audience's goals to identify the right mix of content purposes. *Each piece of content should have one clearly defined purpose—no more, no less* [emphasis mine]. Sure, you may argue that you want to both entertain AND inform, but unless you clarify which purpose trumps the other in this particular piece of content, you're likely to fail. Some common purposes include to:

- Inform (conceptual knowledge)
- Teach (how to)
- Inspire
- Entertain
- Persuade
- Start a conversation
- Spark a controversy
- Express an opinion
- Share industry knowledge or resources" (Hanbury, 2011).

Let's take a simple example: Your client has a dog walking service and you want to communicate that he is on time, responsible, good with dogs, and affordable. He also needs to communicate in which neighborhoods he walks dogs. You want to create one piece of content that supports *each* of those facts or pieces of information.

For example, he may want to make a video of himself interacting with some dogs to demonstrate that he's a careful and loving caretaker. You would use customer testimonials to communicate that he's responsible and on-time. He may write some articles to talk about how he got started in dog walking to demonstrate he's passionate about taking care of dogs. If you publish his fees on the site or blog, you'll be able to show that his fees are affordable.

Each content format communicates a certain piece of information. Choosing the right content mix means truly thinking about your audience—some people are visual learners, some auditory learners, some are readers. You can't know—unless you do extensive content testing—which ones your audiences are. Because most of us do not have the budget to do extensive content testing, it's best to have a mix to make sure that you engage every kind of learner.

Your goal is to have the most successful conversation possible with your intended audience. The most successful conversation means they get enough answers to their questions so that they move along the customer loop until they convert. Demonstrate to them, through an effective mix of written, visual, and auditory content formats, why you are the right entity for them to engage and do business with.

Planning the Content Mix

Information	Content Format	Distribution (Channel)
Location: Where the dog walking takes place	• Text • Map	• Website • Enewsletter • Print newsletter
Testimonials: How great he is at walking the dogs	• Text • Video	• Website • Facebook • Twitter • Video on website
Products: • Dog walking • Dog sitting • Taking dog to vet when it is sick	• Text • Video	• Website • Ecatalog • Pinterest • Print newsletter • Facebook • Twitter • Email
Expertise: His experience with dogs	• Written text • Articles • Videos	• Blog • Ebook • Print newsletter • Email • Twitter • Vimeo • Videos on website
Fees: How much it costs for him to walk the dog, or provide the other services	• Written text	• Facebook • Website • Print newsletter
Contact information: How to get in touch	• Written text • Form	• Website • Print newsletter • Enewsletter • Email

Because relationships are typically built over time, you will need many conversations before your prospects convert to customers. If people have more conversations and interactions with your brand via the various forms of content you offer them, they may need to have fewer conversations with your sales team. Or, they will come to your sales team with a very direct set of questions, helping to facilitate the sale in a more efficient manner. Either way, you have increased efficiency by providing excellent content—a nice business goal to reach. And, one you should absolutely share with your C-suite. As the now defunct Syms clothing retailer used to say, "An educated consumer is our best customer." That is true for all businesses that want to make efficient sales.

As Joe Pulizzi, the author of *Get Content, Get Customers* says, "There are a number of content products to choose from; and this list is growing longer every day. By mixing your knowledge of the customer, your organizational objectives, and frankly, your budget, you should able to determine an appropriate content mix of products … Make sure all touch points speak to each other" (Pulizzi & Barrett, 2009).

TYPES OF CONTENT

You are now ready to create content—the framework is developed, you have decided on your content formats and your content mix, and it's time to put it all into practice.

From creating fresh content to using what's already out there on the Internet, content creation can take several forms, and for each there are pros and cons. In later chapters, we'll discuss issues like voice and tone, but for now let's concentrate on the content formats you can create.

Here is a list of types of content you may want to consider using, particularly if you don't have the budget to always create your own custom content, followed by a table comparing them:

- Original content
- Co-created content
- Aggregated content
- Curated content
- Licensed content
- User-generated content

Pros and Cons of Content Formats (Halvorson & Rach, 2012)

Format	Description	Pros	Cons
Original content	• Created by and for your organization	• Unique to you • Total control	• Most expensive • Doesn't involve audience
Co-created content	• Created by someone outside your organization whom you partner with or hire	• Gain built-in audiences because the person may bring his own built-in audience • Unique perspectives • Allows you to experiment with a wide range of content formats for less money • Creates a bit of competition between contributors, which can be a good thing (Chernov, 2011)	• You give up some control

Format	Description	Pros	Cons
Aggregated content	• Created by gathering from other sources (RSS feed, search algorithms)	• Least expensive	• Can dump too much content • Unknowingly publishing something that can get your company in trouble • No qualitative review • Minimal value added
Curated content	• Collect content and have someone curate/edit it	• Most control	• Can be time consuming for the editor • Must be very careful about credit, linking
Licensed content	• Content created by a third-party publisher	• Content is already reviewed	• Risk brand dilution • Still requires oversight and curation • May affect your search engine optimization (SEO)
User-generated content	• Invite audience to create content, e.g., via a forum	• Works beautifully for some brands • Engages consumers	• Can be messy as you can't control what the users submit

SUMMARY

Your audience is somewhere in the buying process. It is up to you to provide them with the content mix that will lead them through the customer loop, all the way to the sale. The mix needs to meet all of their needs, make them feel as if they can easily have a conversation with your brand, and engage them in conversation long enough that they remain interested and want to become a paying customer.

Now that we've learned about how to construct your conversation, we're going to learn Rule #3 about keeping your process iterative. There's always new information, which means content is always going to need updating. That doesn't mean you will have to redo all your work; on the contrary, by following the lessons in this chapter, you begin on firm ground.

REFERENCES

Chernov, J. (2011). *The fourth type of content marketing – Co-creation*. Retrieved from http://www.marketingautomationinstitute.com/mai-blog/2011/12/the-fourth-type-of-content-marketing-co-creation/.

Google. *Zero moment of truth*. Retrieved from http://www.zeromomentoftruth. com/.

Halvorson, K., & Rach, M. (2012). *Content strategy for the Web* (2nd ed.). Berkeley, CA: New Riders.

Hanbury, K. (2011). *5 Steps to creating an effective content mix*. Retrieved from http://contentmarketinginstitute.com/2011/02/content-mix/.

Pulizzi, J., & Barrett, N. (2009). *Get content, get customers: Turn prospects into buyers with content marketing*. New York: McGraw-Hill, p. 47.

Rowling, J. K., & GrandPre, M. (2005). *Harry Potter and the Half-Blood Prince*. New York: Arthur A. Levine Books, p. 526.

Sandler Sales Training.

Tracy, B. (2000). *The 100 absolutely unbreakable laws of business success*. San Francisco: Berrett-Koehler, pp. 199–200.

Wachter-Boettcher, S. (2012). *Content everywhere*. New York: Rosenfeld Media.

Weinmann, K. (2012). *How to build a blog following*. Retrieved from http://www.openforum.com/articles/social-media-for-business-2012-how-to-build-a-blog-following-a-small-business-guide/.

KEEP IT ITERATIVE

RULE 3

So far, we have learned about the vital connection between content and branding, as well as how to make a business case for content.

We're now at Rule #3 of the seven rules you need to master to ensure the success of your content. The first rule was about getting to know your audience, including how to talk and listen to them. The second rule was about identifying the appropriate stakeholders in your organization and involving them in content creation and management.

We've also learned about building strong content frameworks in Chapter 3. In Chapter 4, we're going to learn how to structure and code your content so it can float on the World Wide Web and be picked up by your target audiences no matter where they are, or what device they are using.

Now let's discuss a way to think about the state of your content and how you structure your content programs for effective management.

GETTING TO WEAR THE DIGITAL CROWN— ITERATE FOR GREATNESS

"Good is the enemy of great. And that is one of the key reasons why we have so little that becomes great." These are the famous first starting lines of *Good to Great*, a business book by Jim Collins (2001) that changed the way millions of people thought about organizations.

Why is good the enemy of great? Because most companies see themselves as *good enough*. They never make the leap to great because they don't have the ambition to do so. Collins and his research team did a thorough analysis of how companies get from good to great; one of the main ways they do this is through an iterative process. They figure out what they can be great at, and then they put systems in place to become great at the thing that separates them from the pack.

As an organization, you need to become great at lots of types of conversations internally and externally. Remember, there are two parts to managing content in an organization:

1. Bubbling the information you need to create content to the right content creators (external)

2. Creating an solid process to manage and publish content (internal)

The Art of Practice

Justin Timberlake is an American recording artist who began his career as a member of *The New Mickey Mouse Club*, which also launched the careers of Britney Spears and Christina Aguilera. In 1995, Timberlake joined 'N Sync, a boy band that sold more than 50 million albums worldwide, becoming the third-best-selling boy band in history (Wikipedia) (Justin, 2013).

In an interview with the writer David Hochman, Timberlake talks about refining his dance and practicing instead of partying with his bandmates:

> *Hochman:* What was it like being 17, 18 and having 400 girls chasing you?
>
> *Timberlake:* I hate to disappoint you, but I was the youngest one in the group, so the other guys were getting more of that action, and they were protective of me. I think I was the one who cared about what we were doing onstage. My role was, we'd come offstage every night and get a DVD of the show, just like an athlete watching tape from a game. We'd get on the bus, and I'd go, 'Okay, here's what we did right; here's what we did wrong,' and we'd fix it for the next day (Hochman, 2012).

Timberlake has the most successful solo career of all of the members of "N Sync," selling more than 14 million albums worldwide and winning six Grammy awards to date.

Timberlake understood that the art of getting better means work. It means critically viewing what you did, where you need to be, and how to get there. Every night, he would direct his bandmates on how to iterate their performance so they would get better each time. In the same way, you need to demonstrate to your team how your content performs so you can continue to iterate and improve your content. Become content rockstars through iteration.

Iteration is important in getting at the information you need, as well as to the content process itself. Iteration does not come naturally; in fact, many professionals would rather just have a flat plan to follow from point A to point B. That approach does not make for something great—great comes from practice, from iteration. That means trying and trying and trying again.

CONTENT ITERATION: THE KEY TO GREAT

Why is iteration so critical to producing a great content program?

Approaching your content process as an iterative process requires an understanding that many things keep shifting, whether they are:

- Outside your organization
- Within your organization
- Within your digital team

The following three criteria are always true in every organization:

1. Digital is always a moving target as technologies change
2. Business objectives shift
3. Processes change as staff changes

Routine Creates Success

Greg Starrick, a basketball player for Southern Illinois University in the 1970s, was the best free-throw shooter in the country during the 1970–1971 season, when he made 92% of all his free throws. Starrick explains that his father, the late Wendell Starrick, was a basketball coach who would challenge his son to make as many free throws in a row as he could, before leaving the gym after practice.

"We just spent a heck of lot of time shooting free-throws. This was back when I was in the fourth and fifth grade and I would have to make 10 in a row before we could leave and then we got it up to 15 and then 20 in row," said Starrick. "We knew what time dinner was going to be ready and there were a lot of times when dinner had to wait because I didn't leave the gym until I made 20 free-throws in a row."

Starrick said he took a lot of "pride" in becoming a great free-throw shooter.

"I don't see that same pride today from young people who want to spend the time to become a good free-throw shooter," Starrick said. "Good shooting fundamentals aren't stressed enough. Repetition is the key and I don't think players get enough shots to become good at free-throws."

Starrick said his dad helped him at an early age to develop a routine and that routine didn't change from grade school until he led the nation in free-throw shooting (Muir, 2012).

Let's break each of these down to understand how to move toward an iterative approach with our content.

DIGITAL IS ALWAYS A MOVING TARGET AS TECHNOLOGIES CHANGE

When I first started in the web business, we were right at the beginning of Web 2.0 and people were just starting to create their own blogs. There was no Twitter and no Facebook. Content distribution happened through RSS (Real Simple Syndication) and emails.

Guess who said the following? "Every day, there is more and more to manage and get right and learn."

I bet you think it is a digital professional, or someone involved in information technology, right? Nope.

Atul Gawande, MD, a surgeon who wrote a supremely useful and convincing book, *The Checklist Manifesto: How to Get Things Right* (Gawande, 2010) said the above, which holds true for any complex and evolving industry. We'll talk about checklists later in the book, but for now it's important to talk about how consistently iterating on our process is an imperative because of how consistently our digital content process will insist on iterating on its own.

Technologies seem to change almost every day. Companies introduce new devices and applications to the market on a constant basis. As soon as a new app comes out, our audience downloads it and starts using it. They want the content we offer to move with them. And get this—Google, the world's most popular search engine, re-analyzes its search algorithm on a daily basis and makes at least one change per day—500–600 changes to their algorithm each year (iGoogle). Everyone is iterating, trying to find the jump from good to great. It is time to join the party!

BUSINESS OBJECTIVES SHIFT

We've spent a lot of time talking about aligning content creation and management to business objectives. Whether we like it or not, businesses sometimes have to shift—for good reasons and bad. Think of a business that's growing quickly because its product is taking off in the marketplace, or organizations that need to change course because they are not hitting their achievement thresholds.

Whatever the reasons, sometimes businesses need to change their strategies. Hopefully, it's not their core strategies, but there may be ancillary products or services they want to offer. That means that you need to create new content to support those conversations.

Again, take Google. To the dismay of many, Google decided that as of November 2013, it would discontinue the iGoogle service, which allows you to shape your own home page with your favorite links, weather, news, etc. They made this decision based on how technology has changed. In their opinion, their audience no longer wants or needs a "home page": "We originally launched iGoogle in 2005 before anyone could fully imagine the ways that today's web and mobile apps would put personalized, real-time information at your fingertips. With modern apps that run on platforms like Chrome and Android, the need for something like iGoogle has eroded over time …" (iGoogle).

So when change happens, we need to create conversations around that change. That's where iterating on content comes into play.

PROCESS CHANGES AS STAFF CHANGES

Here's one thing you know for sure: a year from now your team will not look the way it looks now. It's the nature of business that people leave companies and move on to other opportunities; or, they stay within the organization, but the nature of their role changes.

If your talent is moving, then your process is going to need to move with it. For example, let's say you have an amazingly talented editor who is in charge of all written content and follows all content governance standards. When he leaves, you need to find someone else to fill that role. You will need to iterate on your process—even if you don't really want to.

There's one more reason you'll always have to iterate in terms of your content process, and that has to do with conversations. If you are building relationships with your target audiences, those audiences are going to change as your business grows and changes. You will need to iterate on your content, as well as your content process.

And with content it's all about practice, iteration, and getting great, as we'll learn in this rule.

UNDERSTANDING THE GROWTH MINDSET

Chip and Dan Heath, authors of the book *Switch: How to Change when Change Is Hard* (Heath & Heath, 2010) explain the growth mindset (Dweck, 2006). They write, "People who have a growth mindset believe that abilities are like muscles—they can be built up with practice. That is, with concerted effort you can make yourself better at writing or managing or listening to your spouse" (Heath & Heath, 2010).

The Heath brothers explain: "In the business world, we implicitly reject the growth mindset. Businesspeople think in terms of two stages: You plan, and then you execute. There's no 'learning stage' or 'practice stage' in the middle. From the business perspective, practice looks like poor execution. Results are the thing: *We don't care how ya do it, just get it done!*"

To create and sustain change, you must act more like a coach and less like a scorekeeper. You need to embrace a growth mindset and instill it in your team. Why is that so critical? Because, as Harvard Business School professor Rosabeth Moss Kanter observes in studying large organizations, "Everything can look like failure in the middle" (Heath & Heath, 2010). Let's see why with content, failure is absolutely necessary.

FAILURE IS A NECESSARY STEP TO SUCCESS

It's exactly that failure in the middle where the richness and depth of practice pays off in the digital world. The leaders at IDEO, the world's preeminent product design firm, understand that the way we look at failure is critical to how we eventually see success.

As they've learned, "the project often feels like a failure in the middle. But, if the team persists through this valley of angst and doubt, it eventually emerges with a growing sense of momentum. Team members begin to test out their new designs, they realize the improvements they have made, and they keep tweaking the design to make it better. And they come to realize, *we've cracked this problem.* That's when the team reaches the peak of confidence" (Heath & Heath, 2010).

This is something I truly believe from my work with implementing systems: You must embrace failure as a necessary step to success. "I've had the privilege of hearing two content strategists at Facebook describe the hacker mindset as central to the social media giant's corporate culture. Many of the programmers are former hackers who used to break into computer systems in order to control them. Hackers are often thwarted time and again until they find the way in through a secure system. So they embrace failure as a natural step to success" (Leibtag, 2012).

Joe Flacco, the Baltimore Ravens quarterback who led his team to victory in Super Bowl XLVII, once tried to characterize what made him great and answered, "I'm not afraid to fail" (Svrluga, 2013). That fear of failure often freezes content creators and digital marketers. But, that is exactly the mindset that's stopping you from developing amazing content experiences. Creating content is like anything—you have to keep trying until you get it right. Embrace an iterative mindset and you will always be improving. If you think you can just publish content and leave it alone, you are wrong. Would you end a conversation with a customer right before he was going to buy? So why are we so afraid to keep changing and improving our content?

WHAT IS AN ITERATIVE APPROACH?

Iteration means that we need to try many different paths, until we find the way that works for our target audience. We must embrace the fact that as content professionals we always approach our craft with constant change and improvement in mind. We only get better at doing something by practicing—something we saw with Justin Timberlake and Greg Starrick. In order to improve, you also need to analyze *how* to improve, which we'll talk about at the end of this rule.

An iterative approach means keeping your organization and your content teams open to change. Instead of moving along a flat, predetermined path to an end goal, be flexible and sensitive to changes so you can move from one point to the next. You also need clear timelines and metrics for measurement to guide your movement forward.

Everyone iterates, probably without realizing it most of the time. Think of people you know who like to cook. They are always "tinkering" with a recipe. Or people who are training for a marathon; they consistently change their workout routine to challenge their bodies so they are ready on marathon day.

Think of your own work that you do every day. You create something for your company, but after getting to the first step and receiving input; your next step may be completely different from you thought at first. In a sense, you are practicing, and anything you practice to get better at is a form of iteration. Content within your organization is no different.

The Iterative Process (Figure R3.1)

Figure R3.1 The iterative process. Ahava Leibtag. All Rights Reserved.

In web design culture, iteration is a well-established approach. That is why you will see many versions of different design deliverables with version numbers after the name of the file (or the iterative process, as you see in Figure R3.1). That is because designers sketch a design, show it to the working group, make changes, move things around, and begin to iterate from that next version.

We see this with writing as well, but there is a big difference. If you've ever edited any document, you know that you will track changes, or make editorial marks, in the hope of improving the written text. At some point, the written version reaches a point where the team agrees it can be published. It's done. With our web content, can we get to a point where we can say we're done?

No, and all of us working in web content understand this. It has to do with thinking about digital content as part of a lifecycle and framework for publishing *that never really ends*. With each change, no matter how slight, we feed information into the next phase. Defining "done" is vital.

But it's even more than that. It's about thinking of your content as an asset, like a product, in and of itself.

CONTENT AS A PRODUCT

As we have discussed, content drives the sales cycle and is a shared asset in an organization. If it does not help your business communicate with your target audiences and have great conversations, then it fails, just like any of your company's assets. (Again, assuming the aim of your site is to sell—if not, we call that the achievement threshold, which we discussed in Chapter 2.)

As Erin Scime, a content strategist, says, "Dealing with content is actually no different than any other product. It needs a business strategy followed by a lot of coordinating and socializing to people so they execute on one strategy rather than resisting change and producing a poorly performing product" (Scime, 2012).

Imagine if Apple had stopped with the iPod, or the iPhone 1, or never introduced the iPad. What if Apple had said: "You know what? This is good enough. We're not going to strive for greatness?" Imagine how different the world would have been. Maybe it wouldn't have been different at all, because if Apple hadn't

Apple: How Do They Do It?

How does Apple keep innovating? Vince Crew, in a 2010 piece, analyzes how Apple "does it." Much of his answer to this question is based on what we are talking about—they use an iterative process. He explains, "[Apple developers] think strategically, think simply, and as Apple said in its infamous advertising campaign, 'think differently.'" He lists these as the "considerations" in thinking differently:

1. Connect the dots—solve the problems of the audience.

2. Ask "What if"?

3. Go smaller or bigger

4. Risk failure

5. Go younger or older

6. Elegance is in simplicity (Crew, 2010)

In each of these, there is an element of an iterative process, a "let's keep working on this until we get it right, until we solve the problem, until we have something amazing."

done it, the talent at Google and Amazon were already considering changing modes of content consumption. They knew there needed to be more than just smartphones, laptops, and desktops to access content.

Apple didn't stop with good enough. They are still going. As of April 2013, the iPhone 5 is one of the three best-selling smartphones in the world (Faas, 2012). What will be next in their iterative process? Companies who fail to make an investment in learning to fail, ironically, do just that. Mistakes need to be built into the timeline on the way to great.

MANAGING CONTENT WITHIN THE ORGANIZATION: SETTING UP THE ROADMAP

As we discussed in Rule #2, when we set up a roadmap for our stakeholders, we first need to show them where we are before we show them how we're going to get to where we need to be. Before we begin to talk about getting to an iterative process, let's describe how content is typically managed (or not managed) within an organization.

What typically happens at a company when they decide they want to redesign or repurpose one of their digital properties—typically, for most organizations, their website? The list below is oversimplified but describes what happens in the majority of cases:

- *Make a business case*: Someone decides there is a business reason to create or redesign a site. Typically it's because the site "looks old."

- *Perform a content audit*: If you have an existing site, this step is critical but often skipped. You must capture the content that is viable, as well as what is out of date. If your site contains thousands of pages, you may need to figure out a technical, automated solution to this problem, but there's nothing like actually "touching" each and every page.

- *Develop an information architecture (IA)*: IA is not visual design—it is the guts of the website, the spine. Information flow as well as how users will interact with the website are diagrammed in information architectures.

- *Create a visual design:* Visual designers decorate and cue the user with visuals.

- *Create or migrate content:* This comes in many forms—text, video, audio, slideshows, PDFs, etc.

- *Production time!* This is where templates are built, content is slid into place, and quality assurance is performed.

DON'T FOCUS ON DESIGN RIGHT AWAY (IT EATS UP TOO MUCH TIME)

Unfortunately, during this process most clients are imagining a gorgeous site with all kinds of bells and whistles, beautiful colors, and sliding home page pictures. This moves them to spend a tremendous amount of time on design and neglect content creation and migration.

While design is incredibly important to a site, people can't and won't have a conversation with a design. They can and will have a conversation with content.

Design supports the conversation. We will talk more about design in Chapter 11. Until then, think of design as one part of a website project.

As Scime says, "Not accounting for content unfortunately results in surprise due to a naiveté of the accountability needed and organizational change that will inevitably occur due to post-launch ongoing content production and strategy. After designs are set, it is time to create—which means roles, responsibilities, and ownership of content will change. New titles will be introduced and new ways of distributing content across platforms and integrating into a larger partner/advertising ecosystem will be established. Someone will need to captain this effort" (Scime, 2010).

Karen McGrane, a web and usability expert, has a great term for what happens when organizations realize they should have been paying more attention to their content. She calls it "the 11th hour shitstorm" (McGrane & Eaton, 2010). That's the moment when everyone suddenly says, "Oh, whoops, maybe we should have some content to fill in these pretty templates." You do not want to be there. *Like ever*.

The way to avoid that storm is to be constantly improving your content. That means you must focus on it—like you do on any asset in your organization. If you are going to focus on an asset, you need someone to lead that charge.

CAPTAIN CONTENT (AHOY!)

So who will captain this huge ship? Such a tremendous effort that cuts across so many different parts of an organization requires someone who can direct the entire process. Who should that person be? If you are reading this book, chances are YOU might be that person. Or maybe you are trying to decide how to manage content within your organization in an efficient, streamlined manner, even without the lofty title (or cool cap).

Scime explains: "You likely have someone who owns the digital product from a brand or functional standpoint, but not in terms of content operations and strategy. Not having a content czar means that teams run the high risk of reactive and ad hoc operations, with little focus on where to prioritize efforts."

When you are in reactive mode, with no focus and priority, I call this a content spaghetti strategy: "Let's just throw content up on the wall and see what sticks." That's definitely one way to do it—but it's a bad way—and it won't work—trust me, I've been called in after the spaghetti has hardened onto the wall, and it isn't pretty.

The point of having an iterative approach is to avoid reactive and ad hoc operations. Instead, you need to establish a strategy in which you prioritize your efforts so that you are supporting customers and the business objectives of your organization. Being reactive versus proactive is the difference between anticipating customers' needs and being too late to the game.

Back to Captain Content. To avoid an ad hoc atmosphere, the person who leads the content effort should ideally have the following qualifications:

- Understands how to manage an iterative process
- A great communicator
- Savvy about web technology (or curious enough to learn)
- Able to talk to staff members at all levels
- A solid familiarity with the company's digital personas

If you are a small business owner, you may end up being Captain Content—I know, I know—you already have a long to-do list. Later, in Chapter 10, we're going to talk about the different people you need in order to create great content; you can outsource a lot of that work.

But, at the end of the day, someone in the company needs to be in charge of the content. Your content is floating out there, and you need a cruise director—particularly when you learn to set up your social media channels and content distribution activities, as we will learn to do in Chapter 5.

WHAT DOES A GREAT ITERATIVE PROCESS LOOK LIKE?

Now that we know that iteration is the key to survival in the digital and content age, how does a great team iterate?

We know that people usually fail without a system that works, and systems fail without the right people in place to manage them. Therefore, if we want great iterative processes in place we need to place people at the center of the process. Process on its own is nothing. People make process happen.

The one potential danger of an iterative mindset is that you can always be iterating and therefore never go to market. As Andrew Chen, an information technology journalist, points out, "Anyone working on getting their first product out to market will often have the feeling that their product isn't quite ready. Or even once it's out and being used, nothing will seem as perfect as they could be, and if you only did X, Y, and Z, then it would be a little better. In a functional case, this leads to a great roadmap of potential improvements, and in a dysfunctional case, it leads to unlaunched products that are endlessly iterated upon without a conclusion" (Chen, 2012).

So you need to set up a workflow where iteration is part of the process but not the end game. At some point, someone has to yell "No Whammy, No Whammy, Stop!" (That's a joke from the 1980s. Yup, I just dated myself.)

THE ITERATION ROADMAP

Setting up a good roadmap for improving your process starts with three things:

1. Process evaluation
2. Review of past projects (This means you are actually publishing content and using data to improve your process.)
3. Incorporation of what you've learned

PROCESS EVALUATION: "IS THIS WORKING?"

Your iterative process should revolve around a clear system of evaluating your process. The very nature of iteration means constant review and rethinking. On the practical side, that means scheduling review meetings often to see how things are going.

Don't underestimate the value of the conversations you have in these meetings— even though everyone groans at the thought of *another meeting*, nothing can substitute for a good old brainstorm/discussion. Let the conversation flow and let people churn, compliment, or just plain talk. If you are a good listener, you will gather important information from your teams.

On the theoretical side, that means that review and evaluation is as much a part of the process as writing and designing. Everyone needs to keep asking, "Is this working?"

REVIEW PAST PROJECTS ON A REGULAR BASIS

Doctors hold morbidity and mortality conferences once a month to review what happened in various patient cases. The goal is that other doctors can learn lessons and not repeat any of the same mistakes.

Aside from regular evaluation meetings, have your team review one specific project a month—oh, and remember to pay for lunch to make sure everyone comes. Quarterly, you should go off-site and spend some of that time reviewing several key content projects. The main lead on the project should present the story behind the project. Then let the other members of the team pick it apart. This exercise will teach your team to anticipate project needs and avoid costly content mistakes (Leibtag, 2011).

Evaluation Questions You Should Ask

1. *Goals*

   - Was everyone on the team aware of the goals for the project?

   - Were the goals clearly defined in a written project brief?

   - Did everyone understand the goals the same way?

   - Was the project brief followed?

2. *Content Formats*

   - Did we pick the right content format?

   - Did we choose the right content creators to create this content?

   - How did the approval and revision process go?

   - Did we check in with stakeholders at the appropriate times?

   - Could we improve on that process in the future?

3. *Channels and Distribution*

   - Did we pick the right channel(s) to distribute the content?

   - Was the content shared by our target audiences and prospective customers?

   - Were we able to engage in conversations around this piece of content?

4. *Measurement*

   - Were timelines clearly communicated to both the client and the content creators?

   - Did we set the right Key Performance Indicators (KPIs) at the beginning?

   - Are our analytics telling us the full story?

5. *Return on Investment*

- Where was this content intended to live, within the decision journey of the audience?
- Did this content drive sales or the achievement threshold?

INCORPORATE LESSONS LEARNED

Now that you know what you did right, as well as where you could have improved, make sure the entire team understands how to avoid those pitfalls in the future. Also point out where projects have gone well and reward those good decisions. Teams, in general, will develop good habits when:

- Their work is consistently reviewed
- Mistakes are pointed out and discussed
- Decisions about how to manage things in a positive manner moving forward are collective

SUMMARY

Iteration is a critical part of running anything successful, but sometimes it is a difficult concept to operationalize. Knowing you consistently have to shift and grow can feel overwhelming.

As the Heath brothers remind us, "That's the paradox of the growth mindset. Although it seems to draw attention to failure, and in fact encourages us *to seek out failure*, it is unflaggingly optimistic. *We will struggle, we will fail, we will be knocked down—but throughout, we'll get better, and we'll succeed in the end*" (Heath & Heath, 2010).

Learning to create and manage great content within any organization requires assessing what worked and what did not in any given project. Using that information gives you valuable data you need to iterate and create a better product the next time.

Train your team to do a regular review of content creation projects to improve managing them in the future.

You can never feel that you've actually finished and created a final content product, but that's a state of being you MUST accept to ascend the throne and wear the digital crown. Content is never finished—your teams and your content are always growing, changing, and iterating, and that makes your work fun and consistently interesting and challenging.

Ready to learn how to prepare your content for multichannel publishing? In Chapter 4, we will learn how to do exactly that.

REFERENCES

Chen, A. (2012). *Why you'll always think your product is shit*. Retrieved from http://andrewchen.co/2012/03/02/why-your-product-will-never-seem-like-its-good-enough/.

Collins, J. C. (2001). *Good to great: Why some companies make the leap–and others don't*. New York, NY: HarperBusiness.

Crew, V. (2010). *How does Apple do it? The innovators*. Retrieved from http://www.thestreet.com/story/10682745/1/how-does-apple-do-it-the-innovators.html.

Dweck, C. (2006). *Mindset: The new psychology of success*. New York: Random House.

Faas, R. (2012). *iPhone sales accounted for 8% of all mobile phone sales worldwide last quarter*. Retrieved from http://www.cultofmac.com/167439/iphone-sales-accounted-for-8-of-all-mobile-phone-sales-worldwide-last-quarter/.

Gawande, A. (2010). *The checklist manifesto: How to get things right*. New York: Metropolitan Books.

Google algorithm change history. (2000–2013). Retrieved from http://www.seomoz.org/google-algorithm-change.

Heath, C., & Heath, D. (2010). *Switch: How to change things when change is hard*. New York: Broadway Books.

Hochman, D. (2012). *Playboy interview: Justin timberlake*. Retrieved from http://www.davidhochman.com/wp-content/uploads/2012/05/JUL-INT-Timberlake6.pdf.

Justin, T. (2013). In: *Wikipedia*. Retrieved from http://en.wikipedia.org/wiki/Timberlake_Timberlake#1995.E2.80.932002:_27N_Sync.

Leibtag, A. (2011). *5 ideas to help communications teams prioritize marketing activities*. Retrieved from http://contentmarketinginstitute.com/2011/01/prioritize-marketing-activities/.

Leibtag, A.(2012). From one professional mom to another: 7 pieces of advice for Marissa Mayer. *Retrieved from* http://onlineitallmatters.blogspot.co.il/2012/07/from-one-professional-mom-to-another-7.html.

McGrane, K., & Eaton, J. (2010, November 14). Content strategy will make or break your process [Web video]. Retrieved from http://blog.duoconsulting.com/2010/11/14/content-strategy-process-karen-mcgrane-jeff-eaton-video/.

Muir, J. (2012). *The vanishing art of free throw shooting*. Retrieved from http://www.sisportsconnection.com/the-vanishing-art-of-free-throw-shooting/.

Scime, E. (2012). *Your content is giving you a people problem*. Retrieved from http://www.forbes.com/sites/ciocentral/2012/12/10/your-content-is-giving-you-a-people-problem/.

Svrluga, B. (2013). *NFL playoffs: Baltimore's Joe Flacco brings more to the table than meets the eye*. Retrieved from http://articles.washingtonpost.com/2013-01-19/sports/36473978_1_joe-flacco-keeler-baltimore-ravens.

What's happening to iGoogle? Retrieved from http://support.google.com/websearch/bin/answer.py?hl=en&answer=2664197.

PUBLISHING CONTENT FOR EVERYWHERE

In the film *The Empire Strikes Back*, Luke Skywalker lands on the planet Dagobah in search of the great Jedi master, Yoda. He crashes his ship into a swamp, trapping it in the muck. Later, after being trained in the great ways of the Force, Luke is unable to use his new skills to lift his ship from the marsh. He believes the ship is too great a mass for him to move with his mind. Yoda responds, "You must unlearn what you have learned." Then Yoda uses the Force to lift Luke's ship safely to dry land.

UNLEARN WHAT YOU HAVE LEARNED

Get ready to challenge your assumptions about content creation and publishing. If you want your digital properties to wear the digital crown, your thoughts around creating and publishing content need to change. Many of us learned about the editorial and publication process in a print environment. Many of us are still stuck thinking about digital content as *printing* a publication.

Digital technologies have changed the process of publication. Producing content is now an instantaneous, easily editable endeavor. This means you and your digital teams need to rethink publishing content as divorced from a print publication.

This chapter helps you navigate the world of multichannel publishing, creating content that is ready for display on any device: smartphones, tablets, traditional desktops, and other technologies we haven't even thought of yet.

Like Luke, we must unlearn what we have learned—the legacy days of print publishing are over. The speed at which modern business moves means there is no time to edit a document that lives in 18 different places; there are no more pages, no more versions. Instead, we begin a new journey today. May the Force be with us.

CONTENT AS A CONCEPT

In the last chapter we introduced the concept that there are three parts to content: information, substance, and structure.

- *Information* is the main fact or idea we want to communicate.

- *Substance* is how we typically think of content—how it is presented—also known as its format.

- *Structure* is how we code our content for distribution on different channels.

Information is not messaging. Messaging is how we shape the information to suit our brand. Information is simply a clear fact, such as "this is a phone number you can use to get in touch with us."

Do not confuse structure with distribution. Structure is how we package our content so it can be viewed, seen, and shared on the web. Distribution is about the channels we use to talk to our audiences. We will talk more about distribution in Chapter 5.

Customers surf web channels on myriad devices: desktop computers, laptops, smartphones, and tablets. Our content needs to float right along with them, regardless of the technology or display format they use to converse with us.

ATTRACTING SURFERS

We used to have two ways to talk to our audiences: print and broadcast. Print channels are newspapers, magazines, circular ads, billboards, and so on. Broadcast channels include television and radio. Now, on the web, we have myriad distribution channels available to us: social media channels, websites or blogs, ads, and so on.

Customers surf these channels on a wide-range of devices: desktop computers, laptops, smartphones, and tablets. Our content needs to float right along with them, no matter what the technology or display format they use to converse with us.

INTERSECTION OF PEOPLE, PROCESS, AND TECHNOLOGY

Content stands at the intersection of people, process, and technology. We will revisit this idea many times, but I bring it up now because this chapter addresses the challenges we all have around publishing content.

Publishing content means interfacing with *technology* and using a *process* to push content out onto the web so others can consume it. Much of this is transparent to us until something goes wrong. Then we notice that something doesn't look right, like content hovering over the menu or a set of links that are floating in the middle of the page when they should be flush to the left or right.

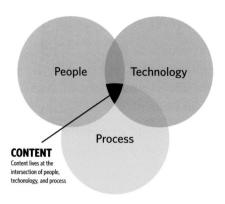

Figure 4.1 Content stands at the intersection of people, technology, and process. Ahava Leibtag. All Rights Reserved.

When your digital content publishing efforts go awry, typically the problem is with people, process, or technology (Figure 4.1). How do we get every person in one organization to follow the same standards and guidelines for publishing content *every single time*? Multichannel publishing and structured content is one way to solve this challenge.

WHAT IS MULTICHANNEL PUBLISHING?

Multichannel publishing is the ability to publish your content on any device and any channel. People access your content from the device of their choice: desktop computers, laptops, tablets, smartphones, video game consoles, and so on. Even trickier, these devices evolve on a frequent basis, leading to disparities in size, power, and operating systems.

As a content professional and publisher, you need to adapt and change your publishing process. You can no longer count on a customer accessing any of your digital properties from a traditional desktop computer. The technology that runs behind these other devices is different and varied. You need to change your publishing mindset to suit a universe of devices.

Charles Darwin said it best: "It is not the strongest of the species that survives, nor the most intelligent, but the one most responsive to change." If you want to keep engaging with your customers, and having smart, intelligent, task-focused conversations with them, then you need to adapt to multichannel publishing.

We use a multitude of devices these days, as customers and as content creators. Is there a day that goes by when you don't check your phone countless times for email, update your Facebook status, write or check Tweets, then go on your laptop or tablet and watch a video or check the price of a product? It seems second nature to us now.

MAKING YOUR CONTENT ACCESSIBLE ON ANY DEVICE

Simply put, your content needs to be displayed on the device of *your customer's* choosing, not your own. This is called being platform-agnostic, meaning that no matter what type of platform or technology your audience uses, they can still view and interact with your content.

Therefore, your content needs to be accessible on a desktop browser, tablet, smartphone, or laptop. And if that doesn't freak you out, these statistics should:

- By 2015, more US Internet users will access the Internet through mobile devices than through PCs or other wireline devices (International Data Corporation, 2011).
- Global mobile data traffic grew 70% in 2012 (Cisco, 2011).
- The number of mobile-connected devices will exceed the world's population in 2013 (Cisco).
- Global mobile data traffic will increase 13-fold between 2012 and 2017 (Cisco).

These numbers are a wake-up call. Whatever content you create will need to float, meaning it will need to be available on multiple channels, immediately, without you or your team having to spend all night repurposing it. This is the goal of efficient content creation, and it is critical to organizations as they move toward publishing more content.

The traditional framework we use to think about this is "mobile" versus "traditional." You need to unlearn this fallacy—like Luke—because your customers want to talk to you, and they don't care if you think about it in terms of mobile first or content first. You need to be ready to respond on any device because they say how and when.

THEY SAY HOW AND WHEN

Our audiences, particularly those who have grown up using these mobile devices (called digital natives), don't think about which device they are going to use based on the type of content they want. They simply engage on a device—usually the one that's closest. It's all about what's fast, easy, and immediately available.

Without sounding like my grandmother, I would say that a degree of impatience exists in today's audience that is new. If the information isn't there, doesn't load fast enough on whatever device they're using, or doesn't give answers right away, they move on and never come back. In fact, 75% of people would not return to websites that took longer than *four seconds* to load (Munchweb). The phrase "you never get a second chance to make a first impression" was never truer than it is today. Can't give me the information I want NOW? No? Then I'll be over here, talking to one of your competitors.

CHANGING PATTERNS OF CONTENT CONSUMPTION

These changing patterns of content consumption challenge the way you organize and publish your content. You can no longer afford to think of your desktop website as the "mothership" of your content. R. S. Gracey explains this well when he speaks about abandoning the primary platform: "Historically, all content has been designed and created for a 'primary platform' whose format is well understood. After its initial publication, it must then be reformatted to meet the design realities of any contexts in which it is to appear" (Gracey, 2012).

He expounds by describing a situation we are all familiar with: A marketing department creates a sales brochure and then posts it on the web as a PDF. But now that content is trapped inside the PDF and not easily available for consumption by your audience, who might not have the software necessary to download it on one of their devices.

The PDF is handed back to the designers, who have to redesign the print piece to fit on the web. Who has time for all of this? It's a complete waste of business resources, especially when there is a way to create content once, and then publish it everywhere you want it to be (like Visa).

The content of the conversation with the audience matters most because the device will change for each audience member, several times each day, if not each hour—making their context shift. If technology mediates the conversation, then each device they use to interact with your content changes that context.

When you think about the way customers use technology, you should realize they don't want it to mediate the conversation. They just want to *have* the conversation they want to have. They assume that if you want to have that conversation with them, you will deliver it in any way they want.

If you don't deliver in the way they expect, they will end the conversation.

PAGES ARE DEAD

I used to tell my writing team to look at the website of the organization before they begin writing content. Why? Because they could see how the content will display when published—this helped them envision the reading experience for the audience.

Tasks Versus Information: Forget "Pages"

Gerry McGovern, a noted content expert (who said we should stop calling customers "users" back in Rule #1), says that we need to stop thinking about *pages* as units of content, and start thinking of *tasks* as units of content (Snare, 2011). Therefore, customers come to websites (or applications) to accomplish tasks, and the content should support them in completing those tasks.

However, I would argue that getting a piece of information is also accomplishing a task. You need to answer a question; the task is done when you find the answer. Tasks raise the question of developing a mobile application or mobile website—which one will help our customers accomplish their tasks faster and more easily? You will have to answer many questions before you make this decision; know that whichever direction you go in, information is the starting point of content.

However, that's over, folks. We no longer have the liberty to think in terms of pages, which is really a framework created by print publishing. Instead, we must divorce the way the content may appear to our audience, in the same way that we need to divorce how they may find us from our own website, blog, or social media channel. Content floats now—untethered to design or location.

> While many things need to change before organizations can start creating reusable content, the most fundamental challenge is a change in mindset. Content creators need to break free of imagining a single context where their content is going to 'live' and instead plan for content reuse.
>
> (McGrane, 2012)

If content is floating, waiting to be interacted with, it may be in the form of a phone number, a blog post, a link to a product offering, a coupon code for a sale, and so on. We have no idea which device our audiences are using to look for and pick up that content.

STRIP CONTENT FROM DISPLAY

So we cannot think about the *way* they will see it—known as the display. Instead, we need to think about the *information* they need and the best content format to use to communicate that information.

In *Content Everywhere*, Sara Wachter-Boettcher explains, "As connected devices continue to multiply, and as users continue to expect to access your content in more and more places, the less you can afford to be rigid, manually applying content to each and every page. Instead, you need to create content in chunks, giving it the fluidity and flexibility for it to travel—across devices, sites and channels—so users can experience it in whatever context they choose" (Wachter-Boettcher, 2012).

We need to unlearn what we've learned about print publishing, like Luke in *The Empire Strikes Back*. We need to strip content from display, so that it can travel where we need it to go. We need to rethink the concept of a "page" on a website in the same way that electronic readers changed the way we thought about pages in books. We need to think about *future-ready* content.

SO IF IT'S NOT ABOUT PAGES, THEN WHAT?

So if it's not about pages anymore, then what is it about? Well, this is where it gets a bit complex. You may be thinking to yourself, "I'm going to skip this part and move on to the chapter about social media." Trust me, hang in there. Because the rest of this chapter teaches you the technical details you really need to know to manage content and distribute it effectively. The knowledge of these technical details will also shape your vocabulary, so you can talk to your programmers and developers in an intelligent, informed fashion. And who doesn't want more respect at work?

Here's a quick example. Let's say you make televisions in China. You need to think about getting those televisions from China to the rest of the world so consumers can buy them. Would you think to yourself, "I've made the televisions, so who cares how they get to the consumer?" No way. You would figure out the logistics of getting those televisions to the marketplaces where you could make the most profit.

Using that same mindset, you need to think about how to publish the content you have worked so hard to create; the two processes are intimately intertwined. Content is a shared system of assets within your organization: How it ends up distributed and consumed is very much your business. Therefore, learning about publishing content is important for you as a content professional or as someone who is responsible for the content professionals within your organization.

Think about it this way—you're spending so much time trying to fix content, keep it consistent, merge it from other websites, and have your teams think about how to repurpose it. What if there was an easier way?

WHERE WE FIX YOUR PROBLEM

Multi-channel publishing is the reality of content creation and publishing today. In a way, you can think of it as "chunking" content—breaking it apart into small bite-size pieces, each being told where and how to appear, depending on a device's template. We need to think about the material in terms of *chunks of content*, otherwise known as *structured content*. Think of this as breaking up any blob of content into smaller parts, so it can float.

Remember the televisions we were selling? If we were creating content about the televisions, we would need to create one piece, or chunk, of content about each component: a picture of the TV, the price, the specs, reviews, and the stores where they are sold. Each of those chunks must float separately because they will display differently on different devices. When we structure our content properly, we can deliver the best possible digital interaction. Our end goal is to deliver the most user-friendly experience (one day we shall call it customer-friendly, but for now we will bow to the industry-friendly term).

DEFINING SOME TERMS

Before we dive in, let's define some terms around content so we are all on the same page (but remember, no more "pages"):

- *Content formats*: A type of content the audience consumes. For the sake of this list, let's talk about a news article
- *Content attributes*: The modules and chunks that make up that content type: title, author name, date published, headings

Explaining a Bit About Format and Display

Let's understand this better:

When we type something into Microsoft Word, and we highlight it and bold it, Microsoft Word makes it stand out next to "lighter" text. Called "applying a style," it tells the highlighted piece to display a certain way on our screen and when we print the document (Figure 4.2).

Most websites are published using WYSIWYG-enabled (pronounced Wiz-ee-wig) interfaces. WYSIWYG stands for What You See Is What You Get. It's a program that allows people who are unfamiliar with html (hypertext markup language) to post content without (hopefully) having to look at the back-end code. With WYISWYG, you "get" or "see" the content you input the way it will look on the web. So content authors put content they've written, or someone else has written, into the WYSIWYG part of a content management system (CMS) without having to manipulate any back-end code.

CMS use templates to control the structure of information across different pages and views. Those templates are then formatted (typography, color, white space) with Cascading Style Sheets (CSS). But let's say the content author wants to change a format. She probably can override the style sheet and change formatting. However, when the content is published to a different template, like a smartphone page, the style changes, or worse the style messes up, the *intended display format*.

Problems!

Let's understand this better:

When we type something into Microsoft Word, and we highlight it and bold it,

Microsoft Word makes it standout next to "lighter" text. Called "applying a style" it tells the

highlighted piece to display a certain way on our screen and when we print the document.

Figure 4.2 Sample of text with applied styles in MS Word.

- *Content model*: How these different elements coexist so they display in different relationships within a certain preprogrammed format
- *Content Management Systems*: CMS is software that manages publishing, editing, and changing content as well as maintenance, all from a central interface

Now we're going to talk about how you can structure your content so it can publish to all the different devices your audience uses to have a conversation with you.

WHY DESIGN ISN'T ALWAYS THE ANSWER

You may have heard of responsive design, a format that allows for the display of a website to shift depending on the width of the screen, or the size of the customer's viewing area. "Responsive design calls for building sites using flexible grid layouts, flexible images and media, and CSS3 media queries. Together, this allows the site's layout to shift on the fly, based on the display size of a user's device. The result is a single website that responds to the device you're on, delivering the same content in a way that's optimized for that device's display" (Wachter-Boettcher, 2012).

While this solves many of the design issues of mobile, it doesn't solve *content* issues regarding different devices because as the design "reads" the size of your viewing area, it serves up certain types of templates designed for the dimensions of your screen. In most cases, responsive design uses this pattern of grids to take horizontal layouts and turn them vertical for easier viewing on mobile devices. Responsive design can substantially alter a template based on the screen width (Figure 4.3).

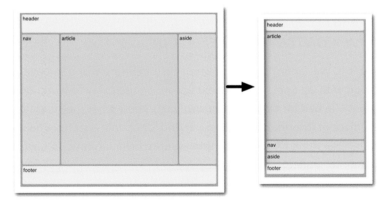

Figure 4.3 Horizontal versus vertical formatting: Mozilla-provided instructions about how to transform a horizontal layout to a vertical one (Mozilla).

Template Talk

Templates are the designs created for different viewing situations. There is a different template for each: smartphones, desktops, tablets. However, unless the developers or designers specify, these templates don't prioritize content—they just prioritize layout depending on the screen size of the device (Figure 4.4).

This provides a challenge. If the digital team has not thought through which types of content are important to the person accessing the content, important content may be buried, according to the way the template is structured. For example, when you access a recipe from a mobile device, you may want to know how long prep time will take. If the template shows that piece of content all the way at the end of a long scroll, customers may jump off the mobile page in frustration, because that piece of information was under a long, heavy pile of ingredients.

Therefore, instead of a normal conversation flow, technology impedes the conversation. It's mediating the conversation in a way that's unsatisfying to the customer. Bad.

Figure 4.4 The same content as seen on a desktop computer, tablet, and smartphone.

ADAPTIVE CONTENT TO THE RESCUE

So we admit it. We cannot predict how our customers are trying to have a conversation with us: a small screen, big screen, on their way to work, on their way to a date, in bed, or on the couch. We don't know what they want to do: Acquire a piece of information, talk to a friend, or update a status. Their task is unknown. One thing we do know: they want to communicate, to have a conversation, to connect.

As Gracey reminds us, "It's time to admit we're powerless over technology and its users. We can never know enough about our users, their needs, or their devices—let alone how devices will have changed by next year—to teach our content how to adapt to them. Instead, we must build into the content solid

What Makes Content Adaptive?

According to Karen McGrane, author of *Content Strategy for Mobile*, "there are five elements that make content adaptive (McGrane, 2012):

1. *Reusable content*: content has been developed to maximize reuse across platforms; where that's impossible, different formats or types of content are available.

2. *Structured content*: discrete content chunks can be combined in different ways for different platforms.

3. *Presentation-independent content*: design decisions can be made by the platform, rather than having style and format imposed on the content.

4. *Meaningful metadata*: category, tag, author, and date information can be used to filter or highlight content, and metadata can be used to help platforms decide which content to display.

5. *Usable CMS interfaces*: content management UI and workflow encourages people to create well-structured and metadata-enhanced content, without letting them fall back on making styling choices."

information about its structure and meaning, so that we can allow others to make decisions about how it should look and behave" (Gracey, 2012).

Adaptive content is a methodology that prepares your content for repurposing. Think of the relationship between content and design for multi-channel publishing like this:

$$\frac{\text{Design}}{\text{Content}} = \frac{\text{Responsive Design}}{\text{Adaptive Content}}$$

Reusable Content

Now we understand reusable content. We want our content to go everywhere it needs to go. We want it to float. We don't want to have to edit and change it every time we invent a new technology or device. We don't have the time to update or edit 18 different documents. Reusable means we can use content for multiple purposes and in multiple places without worrying how it will display. This is called *content parity*—we want content to be separate from its formatting so we don't worry about how it will look on every single display and device known to humankind.

Structured Content

For content to be adaptive, and "fit into" the different templates that have been created on all of our different devices, we need to "structure" the content. This means we use metadata (information about the chunk of content) to tell the content what it is—to give it a designation that later will be interpreted by a web browser.

Markup is one way we tell content how to behave—it's snippets of code wrapped around the text—that direct how a program will interpret it. For

NPR's COPE

Daniel Jacobson, former Director of Application Development for NPR, recognized the need for flexibility in content creation several years ago when he wrote a piece about COPE: Create Once, Publish Everywhere, NPR's content management system. As he describes it, "The basic principle is to have content producers and ingestion scripts funnel content into a single system (or series of closely tied systems). Once there, the distribution of all content can be handled identically, regardless of content type or its destinations."

NPR's development of this system is based on several basic philosophies:

- Build content management systems (CMS), not web publishing tools (WPT)
- Separate content from display
- Ensure content modularity
- Ensure content portability

In a presentation about COPE in 2011, Zach Brand, Senior Director of Technology and Strategy at NPR, summarized the company's experience with COPE (Jacobson, 2009) that "to be findable, your content should be flexible" (Brand, 2011).

example, if you were reading the following sentence on a website it would look like this:

"Markup labels content so it behaves the same way every time depending on the code."

It looks bold to you because on the back-end of the code, there is markup around the sentence that says . Markup labels content so that it behaves the same way every time depending on the code . (Strong in markup means bold.)

So how else do we tell content how to behave? Well, we don't just need it to appear in a certain style, like bold or italicized. We also need it to separate itself into fields of meaning, otherwise known as content attributes, so it can display on different devices the way it is supposed *to look*.

HOW TO STRUCTURE YOUR CONTENT

Structuring your content means *de*constructing it—breaking it down into pieces of information that relate to each other, but don't have to be together to create meaning. For example, you can read an article without knowing the author. But you can't read an article without the main body copy of the article.

Here's an example from a popular website, HipHopDX.com. You'll find a case study about their content strategy project at the end of Part 3.

WELCOME TO THE WORLD OF HIP HOP

As one of the most visited hip hop sites on the web, HipHopDX attracts traffic to its traditional website, as well as to its mobile site. To avoid having to change articles depending on how their audience will access the content, the developers created a custom Content Management System (CMS) with structured content. Much like Jay-Z, they wanted to avoid having 99 problems.

A news article on HipHopDX first has a piece of content: the article. Now we break out the different chunks of the article into content attributes (Figure 4.5):

- Headline
- Summary
- Author's name
- Date published
- Photograph
- Body of the article
- Related articles
- Social media connection portals

When you look for the article on a mobile device, the summary appears in the menu to give you more information to decide whether to click on that link and read the article. However, it doesn't appear on the mobile article page, because the designers and developers probably decided you didn't need a summary (that content attribute) on the actual mobile article page. The video also doesn't appear on the mobile page (Figures 4.6 and 4.7).

Figure 4.5 Traditional website page of HipHopDX.com. All content attributes boxed in green show up on the mobile menu (Figure 4.6) and article page template (Figure 4.7). The purple boxes show up on the article page template, but do not show up on the mobile menu. The red boxes do not appear on the mobile versions. By telling the content how to behave on different devices using structured content, a better user experience emerges.

Figure 4.6 Content on the mobile menu. The headline, subheading, and picture from the desktop site are displayed.

Figure 4.7 Content on the article page template. All of the elements from the desktop version are transferred to the mobile template.

Without the markup around the content attributes telling them how to behave, the content would just appear the way it wanted, probably breaking the design on a mobile site.

Now look at the content in the back end of the CMS (Figure 4.8).

The content could have appeared in a big blob (not a technical term), with all of the information coded into the same big blobby field: Headline, name of the author, article text, etc. Instead, the developers, designers, and content authors thought through how the content should appear on different displays, and they created different attributes for each piece of content. What they did is

Figure 4.8 The back end of the CMS, where CMS authors input the content into fields, allowing for multi-channel publishing based on responsive design.

called content modeling—they plotted the relationships between each piece of content to determine their importance to each other.

Now instead of a huge blob appearing on your screen, and scaring you with its blobbing out of the frame, there are precise chunks of content. A field for the:

- *Author's name*: one content element.

- *Date published*: another content element.

- *Headline*: another content element.

By assigning metadata to these fields and telling them how to behave on different displays, the content doesn't become unruly and unfit for any display. In fact, it can float right along, showing up wherever and whenever it is called for duty.

Pull information out of content. Pull content away from design. Float.

CONTENT MODELING

Content modeling involves understanding the relationship each content attribute has to every other content attribute. No runways are required.

The developers at HipHopDX asked themselves:

- For this news article, what is each piece of information that is important to the central news story? They are the content attributes: author's name, date published, accompanying photo, accompanying video, related content, etc.

- How important is it for the audience to see each content attribute on every display type they may use? For example: Does someone on the mobile site need to see the summary on the article page? Maybe the summary functions better to help them decide if they want to click on the article.

- What other pieces of information relate to this main chunk of content that we may need to repurpose or use later?

Then, to make content authoring an easier task, they input meaningful metadata (or markup) into their CMS so it would be easy to enter the right pieces of information into each field. By doing it this way, content authors don't need a PhD in computer science, and HipHopDX content floats in cyberspace without hurting any other content or display.

CONTENT MANAGEMENT SYSTEMS (CMS)

Anyone who has ever worked with a CMS will laugh at the following quote from Karen McGrane: "Many content management systems look like a database got drunk and vomited all over the interface" (McGrane, 2012).

As defined earlier, a content management system (CMS) is software that is supposed to help organizations manage the publishing, editing, and changing of content, all from a central interface. First, you enter the article's title, its author, its publication date, and so on, into the system as separate attributes. Then, you can use the CMS to program exactly how each of those attributes will look to the audience, depending on what device the audience is using to access the content. So, yes, it is a lot of pieces of information, but it is all well organized, accessible, and manageable.

IT COMES DOWN TO PEOPLE, YET AGAIN

Another joy of our world is that structured content doesn't solve all your content problems, in the same way responsive design doesn't solve all your design problems. As Sally Bagshaw, a content strategist with expertise in content authoring, explains, "Content will turn to crap if the people putting it into the CMS don't care" (Bagshaw, 2012).

Bagshaw describes one of her clients who operates like most large enterprise systems: They have a distributed content workforce of about 400 people. She explains, "There are quite a few CMS authors (people who put the content inside of the CMS) who are enthusiastic and motivated and want to create great content. The majority of the 400 just need to update lists and put in driving and parking directions. Yet, all 400 people have the exact same training and support, when in reality their needs are very different."

I call the parking directions type of content "assembly line content," and there are all types of it out there:

- Maps and directions
- Bios
- Rosters
- Event calendars

- Payment information
- ... and so on

Assembly line content just needs *to get up and out there*, but that does not change how *valuable that information is for the audience*. These types of content need to live on your digital properties—in fact many times, they are the only conversation our audiences want to have with us at that moment.

However, to get that content out there correctly requires our content authors to understand structured content. They need to know how to input content into the CMS so that it retains meaning across different templates, devices, user settings, syndications, and more. In other words, we need to think about hardcoding our content's end behavior while we are creating it. That way it is programmed to display appropriately on varied devices and within different templates when it shows up on our end customers' screens.

That's a massive technology, process, and people challenge. Welcome to the sweet spot of content!

The Challenge of Content Authoring

It used to be that writers would write their stories and then "content producers" would upload the content into the system. However, as we move toward a multi-channel publishing world, it's going to be increasingly harder for us to separate authors from workflow. Therefore, we need to create content authoring teams who can create content directly in the CMS.

This has several advantages:

1. *Governance*: The CMS can provide content governance rules to the authors so that they follow guidelines like naming conventions and security standards.

2. *Ready to float*: Content can be structured and packaged correctly so that it's ready to float on the web.

3. *Workflow*: The creation and publishing of content is streamlined and efficient.

There are also some challenges to a content authoring team:

1. *Hard to find talent:* You need a group of people with a very complex skill set—excellent writers who understand the technical backend and who also have marketing and branding experience—these people are hard to find.

2. *Broken content:* Without proper training and support, content authors will make errors, so there is increased chance of mistakes showing up on your site.

3. *Killing creativity:* If we take away autonomy from our content authors by enforcing all of the rules of a CMS upon them, are we killing storytelling?

You're Authors, Not Designers

Content authoring means writing content directly into your CMS. There are myriad reasons for doing this: It saves time, it gives authors the ability to separate attributes, and it creates workflow efficiency. However, problems arise when authors want to also influence the design of the content, or the way it looks.

For example, they may want to apply bold markup to certain sentences, just as they would if they were working in a word processor like Microsoft Word. However, CMS are not word processors and markup isn't just bolding. As Michael Hogenmiller, the visual designer and CMS developer for HipHopDX, says, "It's not your job to design this content; it's your job to author it."

The new world of multi-channel content authoring within a CMS makes it necessary for authors to divorce whatever influence they want to have over the visual display and design of their content. That is hard for authors and content creators. They know that design can help highlight and support certain concepts.

But, if we are going to move toward successful multi-channel publishing, content authors need to learn to use markup to designate their content, NOT how it's supposed to look. Then designers can assign design styles to that markup so that content appears in the proper style within each template.

Of course, as Kevin Potts (Leibtag, 2013), a developer, points out, "The most successful web projects are not only ones where responsibilities between parties are respected, but where writers, designers and programmers are operating TOGETHER from the beginning. Upfront communication between these skills provides exponentially higher benefits to the user experience downstream." We'll learn more about working together in Rule #4.

Content Authoring and Creativity

We all must adapt. Right now, most online authors use some sort of CMS to publish to the web. And, as Bagshaw points out, when they can't find a way to get the CMS to do what they want it to do, they circumvent the process, leaving us with a whole other world of pain. So, first, we need to accept that content authorship inside of a CMS is where we're headed.

However, as Bagshaw also points out, "Content is still allowed to have a soul. We don't have to let the machines do all the work." That is the critical piece here. Assembly line content will always exist and needs to exist—in many cases, it too pushes the sales cycle forward. Creative content is what keeps our audiences hooked and consistently returning, reading, consuming, sharing, and saving our content. How do we keep creativity flowing in the face of rigid publishing structures like CMS?

Usable CMS

What would you do if your star reporter came to you and said, "I need a new computer because the b, c and ? keys on my keyboard don't work anymore." You'd buy that man a new computer, correct?

Well CMS are not so easy to buy as a new laptop preloaded with software, but at the end of the day, when your company does buy one, or update the one you have, you need to ensure that it makes the experience of content authorship as easy as possible for your publishing teams. Potts says, "In my opinion, writers are indispensable in the evaluation of a CMS, and should be actively involved in requirements gathering and the decision-making process" (Leibtag, 2013).

There is a strong business case for having the best CMS tools. If your content teams have easy-to-use publishing tools that make assigning markup easy and structured, your content publishes effortlessly wherever it needs to go. You've saved yourself and your business a lot of resources, talent, and time. That translates to bottom line profits.

A NEW TYPE OF CONTENT CONSUMPTION

There is another massive change in content consumption, known by a few terms: content transportation, time-shifted content, portable content, and orbital content. This means saving your content for later, in apps like Pocket or Evernote or on the Reading List in your mobile browser.

As Wachter-Boettcher says, "While your users may want your content, they don't necessarily want to get it on your website … In all likelihood, your users are feeling overwhelmed, and they're looking for a way to keep up with the flow and sense of the things that are important to them. These services can help them easily save the interesting bits that would otherwise flit by, avoiding the painful experience of trying to recollect who shared which link and then searching through pages of updates to find it again" (Wachter-Boettcher, 2012).

Apps like Evernote or Pocket are what I like to call a Digital Video Recorder for content. Just as DVRs changed content consumption for broadcast, apps like Pocket are changing online content consumption.

Of course, there are pros and cons to this new reality in content consumption. On the good side, in the same way that DVRs let you speed through commercials, apps like Pocket and Evernote strip out the annoying ads on some websites and deliver just the text and pictures associated with a particular article. But, if your content isn't structured and encoded for this to happen, your audience won't be able to save it and read it later. They suffer. And so will you, because they will not engage with your content.

Now for the bad news: In the same way that technologies like DVRs created challenges for network TV and broadcast rating measurements, so too do these apps create challenges for you, the publishers of content. How do you know people are saving or shifting your content? Can they experience it the way you intended when it is shifted so far away from its original format—like the page of your website?

Well in truth, if your content is great, then yes, they will. Because it is about the conversation you would like to have. If you structure your content in a way that is easy for them to read and enjoy wherever they are, then they're more likely to continue that conversation.

ARE YOU PLANNING FOR CONTENT PROPERLY?

Look at your content with your digital team and determine whether you're publishing content that is future-ready. While this year we're worried about multi-screened and multi-threaded conversations, in the coming decade your content may be used in everything from voice-activated technology to user manuals that are easily searchable.

You need to free your content from its "containers," whether those are pages, PDF documents, or press releases. Content will only be able to travel across the web and other places (but not galaxies far, far away) if we divorce it from display.

After Yoda pulls Luke's ship from the muck, Luke turns to him and says, "I didn't believe it was possible." Yoda replies, "That is why you fail." The only way to learn how to multi-channel publish is to accept that we need to think differently.

SUMMARY

No matter where your audience is when they consume your content—on a street corner, in bed, at an airport—and no matter how they consume it—on their laptop, tablet, or smartphone—there are critical things you must do for your content so it can live anywhere online and resonate with your target audiences.

Now that we understand how to plan for content, how to create content, and how to publish it so it can float, breathe, move, and engage, we need to understand how to distribute it. Understanding multi-channel publishing is a critical part of understanding distribution strategies. If you're going to use all of your channels properly, you need to understand how to structure your content to appear the way you want, where you want, and when you want.

So now, the chapter we've all been waiting for Chapter 5, or the chapter in which we finally cover social media.

REFERENCES

Bagshaw, S. (2012, December 31). Interview with author.

Brand, Z. (2011). *NPR's API: Create once, publish everywhere*. Retrieved from http://www.slideshare.net/zachbrand/npr-api-create-once-publish-everywhere.

Cisco Visual Networking Index: Global Mobile Data Traffic Forecast Update. (2012–2017). Retrieved from http://www.cisco.com/en/US/solutions/collateral/ns341/ns525/ns537/ns705/ns827/white_paper_c11-520862.html.

Effect of website speed on users. (2010, September 29). Retrieved from http://munchweb.com/effect-of-website-speed.

Gracey, R. S. (2012). *Adaptive content: Our primary platform is burning; Time to jump*. Retrieved from http://contentstrategy.rsgracey.com/adaptive-content-our-primary-platform-is-burning-time-to-jump/.

International Data Corporation. (2011). *More mobile internet users than wireline users in the U.S. by 2014* [Press release]. Retrieved from http://www.idc.com/getdoc.jsp?containerId=prUS23028711#.UNysm2871v4.

Jacobson, D. (2009). *COPE: Create once, publish everywhere*. Retrieved from http://blog.programmableweb.com/2009/10/13/cope-create-once-publish-everywhere/.

Leibtag, A. (2013, February 20). Personal interview with the author and Kevin Potts.

McGrane, K. (2012). Content strategy for mobile. New York: A Book Apart, p. 53.

Mozilla. *Using CSS flexible boxes*. Retrieved from https://developer.mozilla.org/en-US/docs/CSS/Using_CSS_flexible_boxes.

Snare, R. (2011). *Gerry McGovern: CS Forum Podcast Episode 1*. Retrieved from http://blog.csforum.eu/articles/gerry-mcgovern-cs-forum-podcast-episode-1.

Wachter-Boettcher, S. (2012). Content everywhere. New York: Rosenfeld Media.

ENGAGEMENT STRATEGIES

Now that we understand how to create a content framework to ensure that our content supports the sales cycle and we know how different types of content are interrelated, we need to answer the last of our three questions. Remember, the questions were:

1. How and when does the content support the sales cycle or help you achieve your achievement threshold?

2. How do the different formats of content relate to each other? Do they help support the story you want to tell?

3. How will this content float along the web, facilitating conversations?

So, how will this content float along the web and facilitate conversations?

In Chapter 4, we learned about multichannel publishing, which is one way we can ensure that our content is ready to publish across the web. But that's just the *structure* of the content. *Distribution* is the interplay between structure and substance, and it's where platforms and channels sometimes seem to merge.

Let's review quickly:

- *Format* is the way in which information is presented. Examples include text, audio, video, or images.

- *Substance* is the formats of content you have and your messages.

- *Structure* is the way the content is encoded for publication.

- *Channels* are how you communicate with your audience, for example, email, websites, SMS, broadcast, direct mail.

- *Platforms* are the technologies you use to deliver the content, for example, content management system, mobile technology.

THE MEDIUM (CHANNEL) IS THE MESSAGE

If you've studied communications, chances are you've come upon this famous phrase by Marshall McLuhan, "The medium is the message." What he meant by this is that the medium in which a message is encoded affects the quality, substance, and perception of a message. So, we perceive messages differently based on the format and channel in which we encounter them. For example, a newspaper article about a fancy resort in the Caribbean will resonate differently than a commercial because the visual encodes different pieces of information than text. We talked about content flexing in Chapter 3; how we may pick up the phone instead of responding to an email. The medium encodes the message—it mediates the conversation on some level. That matters when you're talking about distributing your content—a piece of information embedded in a recognizable format.

That's why so many of us think of the broad term "Facebook status" as a piece of content. But, it's not really; if you break it apart, you realize that yes, the information is the sentences of the status, but the status box is the format—the information encoded in a way you recognize. The status box is distributed through Facebook's news feed, which is a platform, a set of technologies that allows for sharing and interaction (Figure 5.1).

Facebook Status as a Piece of Content	
Sentences	Information
Status box	Format
News feed	Channel
Facebook	Platform for distribution

Facebook is a platform for distributing and sharing content. Your status update begins as a piece of information you embed in a status box. Then you share it on the news feed, which is the channel upon which others receive it.

DECIDING ON THE RIGHT CHANNELS TO DISTRIBUTE CONTENT

In Chapter 3, we learned about which formats of content you need to create to support your customers during the buying process. You also know that you need to structure content to float along the web (Chapter 4). How do you decide which channels are best to send your bottle out to sea? We want those channels to support our messages and not change them, and we certainly don't want our message to sink to the bottom and disappear. Yet according to Mr. McLuhan, that's not possible.

Let's find out if he's right.

INFORMATION

"Content is king."

FORMAT

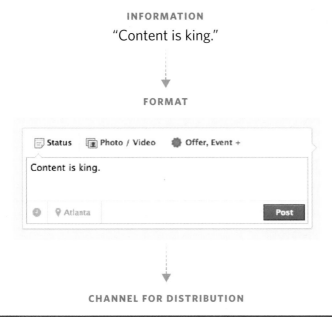

CHANNEL FOR DISTRIBUTION

Facebook is a platform for distributing and sharing content.

Figure 5.1 Separate format from channel and platform, Ahava Leibtag, All Rights Reserved.

DEFINING CHANNELS

First, let's define the number of channels you could use to distribute your content:

In Person	Print	Broadcast	Digital
• In-person sales • Phone* • Product demonstration	• Newspapers • Newsletters • Direct mail • Printed books • Flyers • Billboards • Print advertising	• Television • Radio	• Emails • Social media channels • Digital ads • Blogs • SMS • Ebooks • Websites

* Might count as its own category.

Is it really possible that there are only four major ways to reach people? Well, basically, there are, unless you've mastered Jedi mind tricks. And, if you recall, even Harry Potter wasn't too successful in reading someone else's thoughts.

However, within each of these four categories there are numerous channels. In social media alone, I can count at least six major ones (as of this writing):

- Facebook
- Twitter
- LinkedIn
- Pinterest
- YouTube
- Foursquare

So, how do you decide the best distribution channels for your content? You think about it like a conversation—a delicate interaction with an intended goal.

What are we really trying to do when we're creating content? We're trying to have a conversation with the audience to tell them about our brand, so we can build rapport with them. We aren't just trying to sell one product or service and have them move on; we usually want to sell many, over time.

Even if the customer will only use us once—like, for instance, a wedding planner—we still want that customer to tell others how wonderful we are. Like the conversations we have in our daily lives, the ones we have with our customers build relationships—hopefully long-term and mutually beneficial ones. Many of those conversations happen on social media, which we're going to talk about next.

THE RISE OF SOCIAL MEDIA, DIGITAL CHANNELS, AND THE MULTI-SCREEN WORLD

Our lives have changed so rapidly because of the communication technologies we now have in the palm of our hands. How are we using those technologies to communicate with our customers? We know they must want more than pictures of cats (Figure 5.2).

If content is king, then according to Google, multi-screen experiences are queen. In August 2012, Google released research showing that more and more US consumers were using multi-screen experiences to consume content. In fact, on average, each day 4.4 h of our time is spent spread across four devices (Figure 5.3):

- Phones
- Tablets
- Computers
- TVs (Leibtag, 2012)

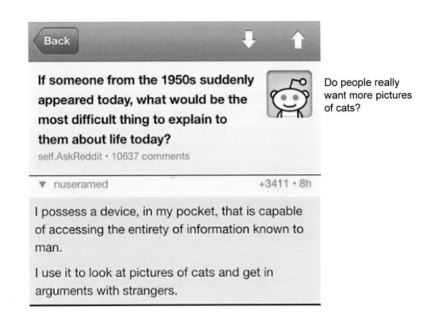

Figure 5.2 Separate content from channel and platform, Ahava Leibtag, All Rights Reserved.

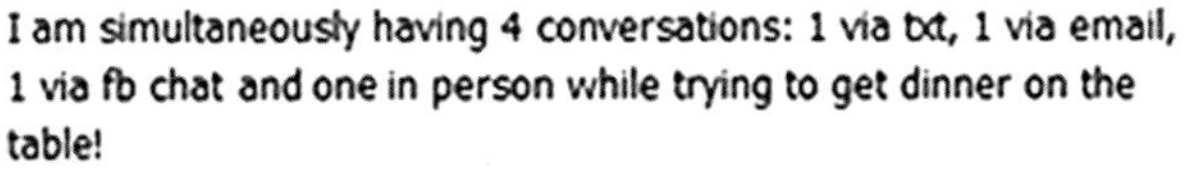

I am simultaneously having 4 conversations: 1 via txt, 1 via email, 1 via fb chat and one in person while trying to get dinner on the table!

Figure 5.3 My friend from elementary school's status says it best: Life is busy and my attention is fractured.

The challenge for digital marketers and content professionals is maintaining customers' focus on their content and goals. Delivering a fabulous content experience to an audience that is continuously shifting its attention is what makes managing content complex.

So as audiences engage in multi-screen experiences and multi-threaded conversations, constantly moving and consuming information, the content moves too. If you buy a product and post the purchase to your Facebook account, that item has now shown up on Facebook with an endorsement (we hope.) That makes content "slippery" in that it doesn't stay in one place, it moves and morphs all the time—without your control. The other consideration is that consumers are hungry for content but their attention span is short.

So here's the problem, which we all struggle with: how do you get your content in front of your target audiences? More importantly, how do you get them to engage with it long enough to connect?

Multi-Screen, Multi-Threaded

Multi-screen experiences happen like this: We split our attention between different screens to consume content in different ways. Think about it—do you watch a TV show with your smartphone or tablet in hand to talk to "friends" about the happenings on the show? We split our attention between the action on the screen and the reactions of our Twitter or Facebook friends.

These multi-screen experiences lead to multi-threaded conversations.

Multi-threaded conversations are conversations happening with multiple people at once, usually around different topics and on different devices. We might pick up our smartphone to answer a message, and then use our tablet to continue the conversation. Our attention is divided and we can wrap our thoughts around multiple topics.

THINK ENGAGEMENT—THINK COMMUNITY

We can't possibly expect ourselves to create the ultimate interactive experience for every single audience member. So, instead of thinking solely about content distribution, we need to shift our focus to something else (which is actually more interesting)—increasing and encouraging engagement and trust by building a brand community (Smith & Leibtag, 2012).

Facebook, Twitter, Pinterest, and all similar channels are so popular because it gives us a chance to talk. Did you ever think you'd spend hours reading and commenting about your friend's cousin's trip to Mexico? When you do it, doesn't it make you feel connected? Being part of a community is fun, energizing, and comforting. It also creates what we need most in marketing—trust.

We build trust over time, over a number of conversations between consumer and consumer, and between consumer and company. As the authors of The Cluetrain Manifesto describe, "The Net invites your customers in to talk, to laugh with each other, and to learn from each other. Connected, they reclaim their voice in the market, but this time with more reach and wider influence than ever" (Levine, 2009). This means we need to respect those conversations more than ever, as they do have such a wide reach.

To build a brand community, we need to understand the community. One of the oldest marketing phrases still in play is "audience segmentation." Today we can add the phrase "channel participation." We need to understand both of these factors to build a brand community. When we think about channel distribution, we need to focus on:

- When?
- How?

Let's keep that in mind as we talk about audience and channel selection.

Audience Segmentation: Does the World Still Belong to the 18-34 Age Group?

Reaching 18-34-year-olds is the Holy Grail of audience reach. The reason for that is simple—sales. As Robin Oatley states, "You must have noticed that Adults 18-49 (or A18-49) is a very important demographic. But why is that? The answer is advertisers (surprising, right?). Because most commercials are aimed at those people between 18 and 49, the broadcast networks only get paid for impressions by that target audience. Now, to get to the bottom of this all: Why are the commercials aimed at 18-49-year-olds? Traditionally, those were the people that had the most money to spare. They were the ones with the high paying jobs. People over 50 were considered poor old pensioners (*slight exaggeration*), and were less influenced by commercials. Therefore, they were not interesting to advertisers."

Today, as Oatley states, "… people over 50 are not all poor pensioners. During the second half of the 20th century, people have been living longer and longer. As a result, they have been working until they are way over 50 years old. Also, people have been saving for their pensions more than they have before, so even if they have retired, they are not automatically poor" (Oatley, 2012).

In fact, many of them have lots of money to spend and find that ads are not directed to them. The 18-34-year-olds will only be knocked off their pedestals, however, when tons of research shows marketing professionals that more than advertising is at play now. Digital engagement can drive demand and increase sales—for all ages.

IDENTIFYING THE COMMUNITY AND ITS CHANNELS

Different types of people hang out in different types of places. I remember when I was a teenager, the mall was fun. Now, as a mom with three young children, it's a place with stuff I need, and all I want to do is get in and get out. When I was in college, I wanted to hang out with my friends at bars and coffee houses and talk about existential issues. Now, I want to hang out at home on the couch with my husband and watch our favorite programs—*on demand*.

My life has changed, as have my interests and focus. Having an effective and memorable conversation with me now is different than at other stages in my life. Our audience is the same. If you want to engage with your target audiences, you need to:

1. Find them on the right channels
2. Engage them with content which is entertaining and/or relevant to their lives
3. Build a relationship with them through consistent conversations
4. Invite them to engage further

Let's break down those four elements because your job is to know who is spending time engaging with your content and on which channels. Even more than that, you need to understand how the medium changes the message, so you can understand how it may shift the conversation you are having with your potential customer.

How One Team Does It—Identifying the Community by Channel

A prestigious medical school staff and cool social media gurus are not two groups that would naturally seem to go together. Enter Albert Einstein College of Medicine. As a result of a Twitter chat, I chanced upon their posts and was intrigued by their engaging manner. It was clear some very fun and smart people were behind this. I interviewed them and found them to be a truly creative team. They were kind enough to let me ask them some questions—here is their answer to my question of why they divide content efforts by channel.

The team explained: "We figured out persona development over time. What sells on Facebook is different from what sells on YouTube. Because of this, we decided to figure out content by channel." For example, the entire editorial team works on an email newsletter that is published two times a month. Sent to the extended Einstein community—researchers, students, alumni, and donors—the content includes subjects that resonate well with those audiences, as well as a wrap up of what's going on at Einstein. After the newsletter is completed, the editorial team eyes the content critically and decides what belongs on which channel. That way they ensure, "all the content we're spending time creating works for a different platform and has a shelf life; meaning it's not going to die in a week. We've iterated constantly to figure out which platforms which content belongs on." "This helps to keep the content fresh, by extending the content on different platforms," they explained.

Note: In this story, the Einstein team is using the words platform and channel interchangeably, and when talking about Twitter and Facebook, they are correct. However, you can distribute a commercial on different television channels, and still be using one platform: broadcast television.

FIND YOUR AUDIENCE ON THE RIGHT CHANNELS

Michael Hogenmiller, a media professional, compares media channels to TV channels: "To build our audience, our job is to consider the interplay between content and distribution, and then marry them together. Today's Internet is built around a group of channels, just like cable television. Each of these channels is more than a dumping ground for posts—it's a pipeline that, if well-optimized, can deliver compounding growth results. TV shows on Lifetime or Bravo are radically different from the programming on Spike, FX, or HBO. We need to shift our thinking so that it revolves around channels of the Internet. When our creators sit down to pen an article, they need to understand which distribution channels they're writing for" (Hogenmiller, 2013).

You have to identify your audience, which is why personas and audience segmentation are so important. Every business is marketing to a variety of customers with different:

- Ages
- Income levels
- Educations
- Interests
- Geographical areas

How to Identify Communities of Interest

Understanding how, where, and when to use different social media channels should be your number one priority when developing a strategy to connect. Here are some examples of finding communities of interest across some of the major platforms:

- *Twitter*: Hashtag communities and chats are quick and easy ways to get involved in social media. You can also take advantage of promoted Tweets as a form of advertising to increase content consumption and brand awareness.

- *LinkedIn™*: Use LinkedIn to search for organizations within your expertise or interest. Another way to find valuable groups is to search the "Answers" portion of LinkedIn; find those individuals who have provided the most "best answers" within a category. You can also follow those people, and backtrack to find other groups these potential contacts belong to as members. LinkedIn advertising can also be a powerful channel to distribute whitepapers and other B2B marketing collateral.

- *Facebook*: Facebook is a wonderful channel for sharing content. Facebook also runs ads so that you can capitalize on people's interests because of certain words they use in their status updates. Take advantage of that kind of consumer targeting.

Through interacting on these platforms, you will start to make connections and shape your understanding of who is hanging out on different social media channels. From there you can examine where and how they spend their time. Use that information to shape your online engagement into your own voice (Smith and Leibtag, 2012).

"Your choice of channel should depend on who your customers are and what interests they have expressed. Content that speaks to them as individuals and relates to their everyday interests will keep them engaged and encourage them to participate in conversations."

(Liberman, 2013)

So how do you find your audience on the right channels?

ENGAGING THE COMMUNITY

Engaging a brand community takes three steps:

1. *Listen*: Go out there and spend time listening to your customers. What are they talking about on different social media channels? What are their comments on YouTube videos? What types of emails do you get from other entrenched members of that community? Which of your email lists do they show interest in, subscribe to, or unsubscribe from? If there are books in your space, look at the comments on Amazon. Get a feeling for audience interaction in different spaces.

2. *Test*: Try different types of content to see what response you get. I'm not advocating for a spaghetti content strategy (putting up content to see what sticks)—I'm simply saying, try different content formats—videos, pictures, articles, and polls—and see how your audience reacts.

3. *Measure engagement*: You can draw certain conclusions if you carefully follow your measurement analytics for engagement. Deciding on what those analytics are is a very important part of the process. Don't look at how many followers you have; look at your engagement with those followers. If you are looking at the wrong metrics, you're making bad decisions.

Use what you know about different consumer segments. Based on that segmentation, you should be able to tell which channels they frequent and how often. If your target audience spends more time on Facebook and likes or shares certain types of posts, you now hold important information about what works for *your* brand community on Facebook.

ENTERTAIN AND BE RELEVANT!

When I read a magazine article with pictures of food, smiling children, and a woman wearing a suit, I know I'm probably reading about working moms and quick recipes. But when I come across a link on Facebook from someone within my network that shows a steaming loaf of coconut banana bread straight out of the oven and she says it took her 20 min to make it—well then, I'm more engaged. There's an added layer of communication embedded within the channel: I encountered the recipe from someone I know and trust. Plus, she confirms it's delicious, and even more important to me, it wasn't difficult to make.

This is where the medium shaping the message gets complicated. Figuring out what formats of content are going to keep prospects moving through your customer loop (sales funnel) and engaged with your brand requires testing and iteration. Knowing which channel is best is going to change all the time, so you may need to resign yourself to exploiting the strengths of each channel. Also remember Rule #3. Keep testing what works on different channels and what you can change to improve your engagement metrics.

One approach is to focus on the inherent strength of each channel. Pinterest is a way to distribute visual content. If you don't have visual content to accompany other types of textual content, you may want to consider distributing it on Twitter, where you have 140 characters to communicate why people should read your article. On Facebook, you can post almost any type of content, so you may want to use the advertising functionality on Facebook to increase your reach to consumers who might not otherwise find you.

KEEP THE CONVERSATION GOING

How should you enter into the social media space, if you haven't already? First, you need to know what people want to talk about. If you've been listening, then you probably have a good idea.

Facebook Advertising

Just do a search on "Advertising on Facebook" and you'll find hundreds of articles—both for and against. There are both stories of huge successes and horror stories from business owners about their experiences.

There are thousands and thousands of businesses advertising on Facebook. Even Hollywood, who creates a new page for every new movie, wonders about the value of advertising on the social media giant. In a recent article about Hollywood's criticism of its Facebook advertising, the author notes, "That doesn't mean Facebook is an ineffective channel; it means Hollywood isn't using it in the best way for its business. Movie marketers are emphasizing Likes at the wrong point in the funnel, and they're not using the right ad formats for their goals" (Darwell, 2012).

Here are some basic guidelines about how to advertise on FB (Black, 2011):

1. Carefully set your goals and plan your approach: understand what you want to achieve and make sure you are set up to measure success.

2. Get creative with targeting—zero in on a very specific audience—less is more.

3. Choose text and images that pop.

4. Create and test multiple ads.

5. Be ready to capitalize on the traffic.

Dip one toe in at a time—take it slowly. Provide rich, valuable content people can use. Guide them to it by using links, pins, and videos. Make yourself a go-to resource for things that interest them. Make sure you use an editorial calendar to plan your consistent conversations. We'll talk about this later, in Chapter 8, but it's an absolute must when creating, publishing, and distributing content.

So, how do you keep the conversation alive and lively?

1. *Measure*: Many of the platforms have powerful analytics packages you can use to measure your reach on different channels (or you can buy third party packages specifically designed to monitor your analytics and reach on the web). You can find out how many people have seen a post, how many have commented, liked, or shared. This will help you determine if you are creating content that people find timely, relevant, and shareable. Or, you will realize that you need to change course.

2. *Respond*: Your audience wants to engage—now more than ever before, when social engagement has become a way of life. A 2012 study found that 58% of its respondents were more likely to interact with brands that integrate social media, while only 16% are not. In addition, 62% of those surveyed said that they are more likely to stay engaged with brands that integrate social media (Griggs, 2012).

3. *Ask*: There's nothing wrong with asking your brand audience what they'd like to hear about or what might be interesting to them. In good conversations, we encourage give and take. If you're always publishing links to your content, then you're only talking about yourself. Give them opportunities to ask you things they want to know.

Follow the Rule of 70 Listen/20 Share/10 Self-Promote

Spend 70% of your time listening, 20% sharing, and 10% of your time promoting your brand and/or products and services. The initial course of action for social media newcomers is to talk about what they know. This seems innocent enough, but it quickly turns to self-promotion. *Nothing stunts your growth in the social media world like focusing on yourself.* Find a way to identify communities of interest and participate; do not promote yourself. Think of the overeager student who always raises her hand first. Don't fall into the trap of thinking that raising your hand again and again will garner positive attention. It won't (Smith and Leibtag).

INVITE THEM TO ENGAGE FURTHER

One of the reasons that social media is so exciting for marketers is that it gives them the ability to increase their reach exponentially—meaning that because people see content on their Facebook and Twitter feeds from their "friends," they'll aggregate content they wouldn't normally see.

I like to read *The New Yorker* and *Entertainment Weekly* every week, but on Facebook and Twitter, I see content from publications I might never read or have any interest in purchasing. Because the people I interact with on a daily basis on my social networks are trusted—meaning I follow them or are friends with them—I am more likely to give their content a second look.

If I happen to stumble upon content I like from a brand, I may go ahead and like that brand, sign up for their email newsletter, or engage with them in a way that will make nurturing more possible. That's the goal of channel distribution and that's the power of social media—exponential reach. Many more potential customers may consume your content: you may be able to pull them into your customer loop to keep the conversation going.

> That's the goal of channel distribution and that's the power of social media—exponential reach. Many more potential customers may consume your content: you may be able to pull them into your customer loop to keep the conversation going.

How to keep engaging:

1. *Lead prospects to other avenues of communication* with you: email signups, follows, and likes on different social media networks.

2. *Provide coupons or special offers* to keep them engaged and wanting to hear from you.

3. *Monitor your channels*: There's software you can use to see who is talking about you. Talk back to them or thank them for the compliment. They may not talk about you directly on your Facebook page or write to you via Twitter, but that doesn't mean the conversation isn't happening. Make sure you're a part of it.

WHAT TO DO IF THE COMMUNITY DOESN'T COMMUNE?

Social engagement is not the be all and end all (see below)—especially if it doesn't link to your carefully crafted business objectives. Apple, currently one of the most valuable brands, has virtually no social media engagement. Dell, on the other hand, is considered a guru of social media and its stock price keeps falling (Worthen & Sherr, 2012). What's the answer?

Mark Schaefer, a well-known marketing consultant, feels that it's the failure of the company to not link its strategy to its business goals—as we said above, to sales, prospects, and leads. He suggests that, "… not all conversation is created equal. A company may drive an artificially high engagement level simply by posting inane polls and cat pictures that don't contribute to business objectives in the least."

So if you're striking out on a new social media strategy, I hope you'll consider these take-always. Engagement:

- *"Should be evaluated and supported* in the context of company objectives. That means picking the right metrics and examining them on a regular basis.
- *Alone is not necessarily* a meaningful indicator of marketing success or financial performance.
- *Comes at a cost* and must be considered as balanced part of an optimized marketing mix." (Schaefer, 2013)

HOW AND WHEN TO BUILD A COMMUNITY

Deciding which channels to use means you must understand who your audience is and if they spend time on that channel. After all, who wants to create content that just sits out there, ignored because no one is interested? Once you know the *who*, you need to know the *how* and *when*.

When to engage your prospects has to do with the particulars of each channel and the engagement your audience demonstrates at each stage of the customer loop (lead funnel). So it's the:

- How (Content format)
- When (Channel)
- Why (Why at this moment are they interested, searching, or engaging? Some content professionals call this the use case or context.)

Be wary of rules about when. Too much is dependent on:

- Who you are
- Who your customers are
- Your content topics

For example, some people claim that email open rates are best on a Tuesday at 8 a.m. Others say their email open rates improve when they send out emails on Saturdays at noon. Well, what type of company are you? Are you international? Who are your customers? Are they B2B emails or B2C emails? Does the one that opens well on Tuesday have important information on how to succeed at some form of investing? Is the email that performs well on Saturday about brunch hours at the neighborhood corner café?

When is really something you have to keep testing—iteration here is key—so you find the right mix of how and when for distributing your content. You already know that from Rule #3.

IT ISN'T SOCIAL MEDIA—IT'S AUDIENCE ENGAGEMENT

We know we need to build a community and engage with it carefully, and we do that through social media. Social media is our daily reality—it is not a fad—it is how people will engage with each other and with the world at large (for now at least, until something else comes along). If you're a content professional, salesperson, or marketer, you should be using this engagement strategy daily. But, the channels are endless, the monitoring tools confusing, and your resources tight.

In 2012, I attended the Health Care Social Media Summit, co-hosted by the Mayo Clinic and Ragan Communications. While the focus was on healthcare, the principles of social media and audience engagement are similar for any industry. One thing I heard in almost every session was that social media is about building communities.

If this is true, then why are we are we still calling it social media?

Social media is simply a set of communication technologies that allow us, as marketers, to interact directly with our customers.

So, even though we've used the phrase in this book, let's stop saying social media and start saying what we're really doing—community or audience engagement.

When you sell a product or service, you are asking people to change their behavior—to choose your product instead of another. Most people find greater success when a community supports their behavioral changes—think Weight Watchers or other types of support groups. So focusing on building a community, rather than on channels, technology, or deployment, is destined to have greater, longer-lasting impact.

THE MIND-SHIFT TO A CULTURE OF COMMUNITY

It's exciting when you start thinking about building a brand community. Because we're not in the era of "Mad Men" anymore, it sounds less manipulative because it is—it's working *with* the audience, not forcing ideas and products *on* them.

Brand communities feel better, and they work better because today it is all about sharing ideas, comments, and experiences. Recognize that when it comes to engagement, the people hold the power.

Here are five ways to transform from a social media culture to an audience engagement culture:

1. *Listen more than you speak*: It's an easy enough adage. Social media is a great monitoring tool. Yes, you should be tweeting and posting relevant important information about your product or service, but remember to listen. Use social media as a way to connect directly to your users—there's nothing between you but a screen.

2. *Have a great story to tell*: You don't always need to have a super fabulous narrative to tell, but have stories in your back pocket to engage people. As human beings, we have an aching need to connect. Don't forget how you learned your earliest lessons about life—from stories. Think about how your own eyes and attention glom onto the human interest story whenever you look at content. Make sure you are using different types of stories as you engage with your communities.

3. *Focus on your content*: Content is a BIG word for a much smaller idea—information. (Yes, I can count the letters.) Think about it. When you hear "content," you probably get nervous. When you hear "information," it's an easy, familiar concept. So remember, your content is simply information molded into a recognizable content type for your users. Ads, direct mail, press releases, tweets, and posts—they are all versions of content that people instantaneously recognize. Choose the right type of content to serve the story best.

4. *Hire an audience engagement manager—NOT a social media person*: What I hear is that most organizations want to hire a social media "guru." What you need is someone who understands how to transform your brand's online social activities into a community. Then the engagement part needs to happen by LISTENING to your customers' wants and needs. They can have social media in their previous title, but change it when they come on board your ship. You're driving engagement—the technologies will continue to morph as you do. The greatest social media managers understand this.

5. *Encourage teamwork*: Audience engagement is really the intersection of several different parts of an organization: marketing, PR, customer service, crisis communication, and emergency response. Work with people in those departments: ensure you are delivering the best possible experience for your customers as they engage with your brand using these technologies.

One of the speakers at Mayo, Dan Hinmon, talked about strategies for audience engagement. He said one woman compared moderating a social media community with hosting a party—don't dominate the situation but make everyone feel good about being there. Don't you think your customers will keep coming back if you make them feel like a beloved member of a community—one where there's always a party?

FIGURING OUT WHAT TO MEASURE

Once you have a clear picture of how your consumers are finding you, then it is time to identify and understand what to measure—to show the C-suite that it has all been worth it. There are a few types of measurement:

- *Return on Investment (ROI)*: ROI is a finance metric only. To accurately state a case of social media ROI, you would track actual dollars coming in or dollars saved. If you cannot show actual money changing hands, then you are not measuring ROI. However, you can demonstrate that social media promotes your brand's products and services.

- *Volume*: Measuring volume helps you shape your C-suite's understanding of how social media promotes your brand online. You are most likely doing this with web analytics; metrics like:

  - Number of visitors

  - Time on site

  - Number of fans

  - Number of followers

  - Page views

  - Impressions

- *Engagement*: This is somewhere between the first two metric categories. A consumer interacts with you but is not yet spending money. This includes numbers like:

  - Retweets

  - Repins

  - Comments

  - Likes on posts

  - Form completion

  - Seminar registration

  - Review submission

SHOWING THE C-SUITE THAT CONTENT IS WORTH IT

Once you have identified how people interact with your brand online and what metrics you can measure, then it is time to show a return. This could be a return on investment or return on your time—for a review of how to state those, see Chapter 2. In either case, be clear about what you are illustrating.

Your goal is to move the needle on the data you share with your C-suite. Right now, you may only be able to demonstrate volume metrics. Your next goal is to incorporate engagement statistics. Once you've conquered those two data points, you want to show the amount of contribution margin you provided via an online effort.

Here are some examples for both return on time and return on investment:

Return on time:

- *Online issue resolution*: Consumers come to your Facebook page to voice a concern and your organization is able to address the issue (online or offline).

- *Increasing engagement*: By consistently engaging as well as creating and sharing relevant meaningful content, you will see your engagement metrics rise.

- *Earned media*: Being active on social media and connecting to local news reporters transforms you into a trusted source for information. You will be the first call when they need content.

Return on investment:

- *Stop printing newsletters (both internal and external)*: Instead, use a blog or eNews to distribute the same information. The cost savings from print and postage provides ample evidence of ROI.

- *Create online signups for seminars*: Track these submissions and procedural conversions from the seminar to show ROI around online visitors. After the potential customers visit the seminars, and convert to customers, you can prove ROI.

- *Use your CRM (customer relationship management) tools*: These are the tools that run on the backend of your website and calculate how your digital marketing efforts convert site visitors to customers. Calculate the value of online visitors by earmarking individual users online. Show downstream revenue from those visitors. These capture points could include:

  - Contact us forms

  - eNews signups

  - Event registration

  - Online seminars

  - Virtual groups (like a Facebook group)

If those people turn into customers, then voilà—a straight line to revenue and true ROI.

JUST TO REITERATE …

Keep in mind that the tools you will need to use social media to distribute content, increase audience engagement, and build a brand community will be the same ones that you use for all of your digital strategy:

- Time

- A commitment to an iterative process

- Learning from experts

- Creating collaborative teams across disciplines

SUMMARY

Our audience uses many channels, often at the same time. It is close to impossible to expect to reach them only with information and content—we also need to engage them in a robust, energetic conversation as a community. First, though, we need to build that community. Once we have done that, we must figure out how to engage and interest its members. Afterwards, we'll need to let the C-suite know that their investment in content was worth it, so we'll need to be able to create meaningful metrics to measure our impact.

Next, in Rule #4, we're going to learn how to use all the talent assets within your organization to create the greatest content experiences for your audiences.

REFERENCES

Black, L.M. (2011). *Facebook ads: 5 tips for success*. Retrieved from http://mashable.com/2011/08/29/facebook-ads-tips/.

Darwell, B. (2012). *What Hollywood gets wrong about Facebook marketing*. Retrieved from http://www.insidefacebook.com/2013/01/08/what-hollywood-gets-wrong-about-facebook-marketing/#more-77576.

Griggs, W. (2012). *Mass relevance releases new research: Social integration drives consumer engagement, trust*. Retrieved from http://www.massrelevance.com/mass-relevance-releases-new-research-social-integration-drives-consumer-engagement-trust/.

Hogenmiller, M. (2013, January). Audience development. Shared with the author.

Leibtag, A. (2012). *Is multi-screen the new content queen?* Retrieved from http://onlineitallmatters.blogspot.com/2012/08/is-multi-screen-new-content-queen.html.

Levine, R. (2009). *The cluetrain manifesto*. New York: Basic Books, p. 84.

Liberman, N. (2013). *Content strategy: 4 tips for communicating at every customer stage*. Retrieved from http://contentmarketinginstitute.com/2013/01/content-strategy-communicate-at-every-customer-stage/.

Oatley, R. (2012). *TV Ratings 101—Why is the adults 18–49 demographic so important and total viewers not?* Retrieved from http://robinoatley.husbpages.com/hub/TV-Ratings-101-Why-is-the-Adults-18-49-demographic-so-important-and-Total-Viewers-not.

Schaefer, M.W. (2013). *Social media "engagement" is not a strategy*. Retrieved from http://www.businessesgrow.com/2013/01/06/social-media-engagement-is-not-a-strategy/.

Smith, R., & Leibtag, A. (2012). *6 Secrets of social media superstars in healthcare: Best practices for your hospital's social media and community engagement programs* [E-book]. Retrieved from http://unbouncepages.com/6-secrets-of-social-media-superstars/.

Worthen, B., & Sherr, I. (2012). *Dell still struggling amid shift in computer market*. Retrieved from http://online.wsj.com/article/SB10001424127887324735104578121390191628634.html.

CREATE MULTIDISCIPLINARY CONTENT TEAMS

RULE 4

So far, we have covered a lot about the philosophy of how to think about content. You now understand the importance of branding so you know who you are and what you're trying to say. We also broke down the building blocks of content: information, substance, and structure.

We have also learned about our first three rules: Start with Your Audience, Involve Stakeholders Early and Often, and Keep It Iterative. Now we are going to talk about who creates content and why it is so important to have a wide variety of different skills and talents.

CONTENT: INFORMATION AND THE PROCESS

As we've already discussed, there are really two parts to getting content right in an organization: *what* you're trying to say (external) and *how* you plan, create, and publish the content (internal). To address both of these, you need the right team working together with a smart process in place. Otherwise, nothing will move forward with purpose and energy.

This rule is not about which people should be on your team; we will cover that in Chapter 10. This rule is about *why* you need a team of people who have overlapping skill sets. We will also discuss why you should recruit subject matter experts within your organization into your teams so that you can ensure you are getting valuable organizational facts that inform your content development.

Let's make note of the fact that we are not calling these teams *web strategy teams* or *user experience teams*. All of our learning together highlights how much we need to turn the focus back to the audience when creating content. Instead we will call them audience engagement teams. Language is constructive; it cements our approach to things without us even realizing it. Therefore, using the term *audience engagement teams* is deliberate on my part, and I hope you'll begin to use it as well.

THINGS HAVE CHANGED

With digital communications, social media, content strategy, content marketing, and digital publishing, the world of information moves at an amazing pace. In fact, many biologists say our brains are rewiring to manage all of this information (Richtel, 2010).

The ever-accelerating flow of communication affects many things, one of which is how we organize our teams and departments. In today's incredibly fast-paced world, the traditional communications firms and advertising agencies are rethinking their models. They know the teams they have in place are not empowered to do everything they need to keep up with digital marketing and communications.

And it's not just the pace of things today, it's also because each individual has so much power, in the palm of his or her hand, that our audience has become the center of focus. Our customers are complex: their ages, locations, levels of education, and interests all whirl around us at breakneck speed. That's why when we talk about who should be involved in audience engagement, we can't just think about marketing specialists or social media gurus. Now we need a true multidisciplinary team of experts who can work together for the customer.

As Jonathan Kahn, a content strategist, comments, "Web content is the one thing you can't touch without involving every part of the organization, which is why most organizations are in denial about it—they'll do anything to avoid talking to each other" (Kahn, 2011). But, as we'll see, talking to each other provides serious valuable benefits.

VALUE IN BREAKING DOWN SILOS

It's not just in digital communications that organizations are thinking about restructuring the way they work. In a 2013 *Time* magazine article, Bill Saporito reports that because of new understanding of how cancer begins and grows, medical science had to mobilize a new research methodology and fight back (Saporito, 2013). "You no longer do science and medicine differently," says Dr. Lynda Chin, director of the Institute for Applied Cancer Science at MD Anderson Cancer Center.

"The team model is also disrupting the normal course of business across the medical research community. For investigators, it means changes in the way careers are developed, the way data—and especially credit for achievement—are shared. For institutions, team research means changes in contracts, compensation, titles, and the path of intellectual property. For pharmaceutical companies, it means restricting the way experimental drugs are allocated and clinical trials are conducted."

In the same article, National Institutes of Health Director Dr. Francis Collins comments, "I am strongly anti-silo, strongly pro-breaking down barriers, bringing disciplines together, building collaborations and building dream teams."

Disruptive mechanisms drive progress. If medicine can break down silos—across different global institutions—then certainly digital teams can find a way to do so in their organizations.

WHAT DO WE MEAN BY MULTIDISCIPLINARY?

Multidisciplinary means using professionals with a variety of different skill sets to solve a problem. Multidisciplinary teams *examine complex problems from multiple angles.* Many industries use this word, as well as interdisciplinary, cross-disciplinary, and cross-functional. Many fields understand the value of working together to solve a problem or reach a goal, using the very different perspectives of talented people.

When it comes to content creation, I have seen that the most effective approach is to work with other web experts who specialize in content strategy, visual design, information architecture, and usability. If you want to create great conversations, and great content, then you need to rethink the way your digital and editorial teams are structured.

Now that we think about content in a different way; meaning, we understand it has three parts—information, substance, and structure—we can use that knowledge to break down organizational barriers and silos that occur when you create and publish content.

Think about it—now that you know content isn't the website, or that social media is simply a channel for distributing content, you are primed to engage with information holders who will help your create outstanding content that drives your sales process. The marketing professionals shouldn't be separate from the digital professionals. There shouldn't be a difference in on-line and off-line tactics. The old ways of organizing talent just don't work, if we want to create satisfying conversations for our target audiences.

ACCESSING TALENT IN THE ORGANIZATION

Great teams are inclusive and invite analysis and observation from all angles of the business to create great content experiences. Even with the greatest team, you still need to challenge yourself and your teammates; you need to step out of your comfort zone and look outside of your digital/marketing/communications world for help. You need to talk to others in the organization who manage audience engagement issues—those in customer service, business development, sales, and so on, on a regular basis. You will be pleasantly surprised at how much you can learn that will help inform your content development.

Audience engagement teams should include designers, writers, IT experts, programmers, developers, project managers, user experience professionals, usability experts, and content strategists. Create this team carefully and empower them with a clear strategy. Then invite subject matter experts from within the organization to help craft bold tactics to meet your overall communications and marketing strategies.

Let's learn *why* you need different skillsets and how to use them to create great content experiences for your customers.

WHY MULTIDISCIPLINARY TEAMS?

We must move toward teams that break down silos and offer all the information an organization can deliver to content consumers. You need multidisciplinary teams to break down silos and adapt to changing technologies. These teams may be a mix of internal and outsourced talent, and for many organizations, that makes the most sense from a resource and project perspective.

ADAPT TO CHANGING TECHNOLOGIES

When you have a team of writers, and a team of developers, and a team of social media professionals, you get into trouble fast. Teams that don't cross-collaborate and share ideas with each other get stuck moving content from one team to the other. Baton-tossing content across teams does not result in better content.

Rather, having people with expertise in different areas—particularly technology, which changes so quickly—will influence not only the quality of your content, but also how you distribute it. Designers and developers who keep up with changing technology norms will inform your editorial and content teams how they need to think about the display and distribution of content, which results in a better end product. We'll discuss an example of this type of cross-pollination in our case study about REI at the end of Part 2.

BREAK DOWN SILOS

Different types of professionals create and manage amazing content by bouncing ideas off of each other and bringing their creativity and specialized talent to the table. You can't afford to limit the team to a few people who are great in one or two areas. When you do that, you end up with content that can't survive when it gets tossed out on the great currents of the web.

As Erin Scime, a content strategist, points out, "You'll need a nimble content team. Unlike traditional media, your team needs to be able to work across multiple channels and think like digital natives. It's no longer possible to be a deep expert

Waterfall or Agile? Or Both?

There has been a great deal written about these two methods of software development. "Waterfall" development is what we think of when considering how software is created—a classic linear approach where each step is assigned to a separate team and the product moves from one team to the next until completion (baton tossing). With "Agile" development, ideas and plans evolve through collaboration between teams; usually teams of people from various disciplines. The term was coined by a group of software developers who met in 2001 and created "The Agile Manifesto" (Wikipedia, 2013). Agile emphasizes the value of sharing and collaboration rather than just moving toward the goal line (Agile Intro, 2008).

Here is a quick comparison of the differences between the two methods (Agile Intro, 2008):

Stage of Development	Agile	Waterfall
A project stage is complete and something needs changing	Changes can be made if necessary without redoing the whole project	The problem can only be fixed by going back and designing a new system
Bug caught during development	The team has a product ready for launch at the end of each tested stage, so a bug can be easily fixed without losing momentum	The product is tested only at the very end, which means any bugs found result in the entire program having to be re-written
Meeting customer specs and timelines	There is always a working model for timely release even when it does not always entirely match customer specifications	There is only one main release and any problems or delays mean highly dissatisfied customers
Spec changes by customer	Allows for specification changes as per end-user's requirements	Cannot accommodate changes, as this would mean that the project has to be started all over again

The two can also co-exist, according to Deepika Ganeshan, "As with most things—the middle ground does most people a world of good. What has been happening recently is a hybrid version of Agile with Waterfall—this requires much more discipline on the project manager's part—but usually the end result is a much more palatable outcome satisfying both the business and the IT organization" (Ganeshan, 2011).

By looking at both approaches, we can see why an agile approach is so important for content development. Content happens at the intersection of people, process, and technology, which necessitates a fluid, nimble environment. However you organize your content teams, be aware of both approaches and which way works best, so that you're meeting the needs of your teams, internal stakeholders, and external audiences.

in one functional area. Digital requires employees that are more cross-disciplinary and able to adapt to the demands and challenges of varying platforms and understand how communication needs shift between channels" (Scime, 2012).

Crossing Organizational Barriers

How often have you heard, "We're not in charge of that," or "We don't own that content" from people within your organization? Attitudes like these harm the customer experience. Can you imagine saying to a customer, "Oh, there's no content that describes what you're looking for because we operate in silos. Sorry." That attitude directly affects your bottom line, as your customers will jump to your competitors' digital properties to have better conversations with them.

As Sara Wachter-Boettcher, a content strategist, says, "Look for opportunities to make it [the team] more cross-functional and interdepartmental, pulling people in from different places" (Wachter-Boettcher, 2012). You absolutely can no longer afford silos around information.

Better Ideas

Who says no to better ideas? But, it's really true—when you get in a room with the right people, and everyone leaves their egos at the door and works in service to the customer, some powerful magic can happen. People usually see the organization best from their own vantage point, but your customer doesn't care about your internal structure, do they? That's *your* problem.

So when you assemble your teams, make sure you are cutting far and wide across the company, so you get a sampling of different areas. This doesn't mean these people are a part of every web or digital discussion, but rather they are part of a broader audience engagement strategy within the organization. We'll talk about how to structure those, but first we must talk about how to find the right people.

FIND THE RIGHT PEOPLE

If you are going to create audience engagement teams that really care about great conversations and developing content within your organization, then you need to find the right people outside of your digital team.

WHO TO LOOK FOR

First, look for people who want to make a difference and are willing to work hard, listen, and iterate. Think about the groups who can give you different perspectives:

- Subject matter experts on your services and products
- The people who designed the products
- Sales
- Customer service
- Teleprospecting, or those who qualify leads

As far as thinking outside your comfort zone when creating the team, according to Michelle Linn, a popular content marketing blogger, you should include people from:

- Technology and operations departments
- Human resources
- Investor relations (Linn, 2010)

The Five Personality Types You Need on Your Web Teams

You need a strong digital communications team who thinks about strategy as well as tactics. Every role may not belong to just one person; some people may wear multiple hats. So, instead of talking about skills, I'm going to describe personality types you need on those teams:

- *The Customer Advocate*: While focusing on the customer should be a personality trait of all members of your team, we are sometimes so close to our work that we fail to see how outsiders may perceive it. On every team I've ever been on, there's always *one person who circles the conversation back to the unique needs of each customer*.

- *The Cheerleader:* Every team needs one person who will cheer the team's efforts. You might hear this person say, "To every problem, there's a solution." Do not underestimate the need for a Julie Andrews-type to continue to *uplift the team and provide encouragement*, even in the face of what seems like an insurmountable problem, or even failure.

- *The Cynic:* Oh, we all know The Cynic: he's the one in the meeting who rolls his eyes, always asks questions, and presses the point. *He's incredibly useful, though, because you'd make mistakes without The Cynic. You'd start living in the clouds, instead of tackling the weeds.* Cynics are good on audience engagement teams because they can project what the future will look like and provide an accurate scenario of how things might go wrong.

- *The Risk-Taker:* This character wants to put it out there before it's tested, *believes more is better, and isn't always thinking about the consequences of major decisions.* The value of The Risk Taker is that she *pushes the team forward.* She lets you see what is possible and is not afraid of iteration.

- *The Analyzer:* Different from The Cynic, The Analyzer *believes in data, statistics, and demonstrated facts*. She'll consistently bring you back to your strategy by looking at proof that you're doing the right thing. Make sure you have at least one person who believes in data, big-picture analysis, and post-game rundowns. She'll help you improve your game, and will advocate for the business (Leibtag, 2010).

MANAGING AUDIENCE ENGAGEMENT TEAMS

Once you've found a great mix of people with different skill sets and professional roles within your organization who care about creating better interactions with your customers, here are ways to make those teams manageable.

Manage in Smaller Teams for Cross Collaboration

You need answers when your audience asks questions. In some cases, you may have thousands of topics to cover. Coordinate smaller teams of four to six people that utilize all the different information creation structures of the organization: marketing, PR, customer service, crisis communications, and emergency response. Work with other people in those departments so that their skills cross cut those of your digital team.

For example, consider teaming up the project manager, the salesperson, one of your content creators, and a developer to work through a certain section of your website that isn't performing well. Each of those people may see the challenge from a different angle. By tackling a smaller project, they may bring important lessons you can use for other sections of the website.

Create Guidelines

Create and distribute guidelines to all the employees involved in touching content. Something short (no more than four pages) that describes some of your digital strategy challenges. You may also want to ask people to volunteer for smaller committees to solve those challenges.

Consider the Committee

Sometimes a great committee can help with content development and governance. Consider creating a larger committee to manage some of the smaller teams. Schedule quarterly meetings for the larger group and monthly meetings for the smaller groups. Ask them to report about successes and describe when and where they are hitting roadblocks. More people in the room doesn't necessarily facilitate a better decision making process, but the more engaged minds you have conversing about the problem should help to uncover the best solution.

SUMMARY

To create great content, find varied talents in your organization and create multidisciplinary audience engagement teams that cut across skill sets and professions to attack your content challenges. Organize these teams and empower them so they can make real progress and deliver feedback on how to move ahead with planning, creating, publishing, and managing fantastic content experiences for your customers.

REFERENCES

Agile introduction for dummies. (2008). Retrieved from http://agileintro.
 wordpress.com/2008/01/04/waterfall-vs-agile-methodology/.
Ganeshan, D. (2011). *Waterfall vs. agile methods: A pros and cons analysis.*
 Retrieved from http://www.theserverside.com/tip/Waterfall-versus-
 Agile-methods-A-pros-and-cons-analysis.
Kahn, J. (2011). *Web governance: Becoming an agent of change.* Retrieved from
 http://alistapart.com/article/web-governance-becoming-an-agent-of-change.
Leibtag, A. (2010). *Five personality types you need on your digital
 communications team.* Retrieved from http://contentmarketinginstitute.
 com/2010/12/digital-communications-team/.
Linn, M. (2010). *How to find internal allies for content marketing.* Retrieved from
 http://contentmarketinginstitute.com/2010/11/content-marketing-allies/.

Richtel, M. (2010). *Attached to technology and paying a price*. Retrieved from http://www.nytimes.com/2010/06/07/technology/07brain. html?src=me&ref=technology&_r=0.

Saporito, B. (2013). *The conspiracy to end cancer*. Retrieved from http://healthland.time.com/2013/04/01/the-conspiracy-to-end-cancer/.

Scime, E. (2012). *Your content is giving you a people problem*. Retrieved from http://www.cmo.com/articles/2012/12/10/your-content-is-giving-you-a-people-problem.frame.html.

Wachter-Boettcher, Sara (2012). *Content everywhere*. Rosenfeld Media.

Agile software development. (n.d.) Retrieved April 30, 2013 from http:// en.wikipedia.org/wiki/Agile_software_development.

We talked about two essential ingredients for creating great content teams in Rule #4. The first task is to staff your digital communications teams (internal or outsourced) with the appropriate professionals: writers, programmers, designers, information architects, project managers, content strategists, user experience professionals, and so on. The second involves creating audience engagement strategy teams built from varied roles across the organization so you can break down organizational silos.

Jonathon Colman, former search engine optimization (SEO) manager and current Principal Experience Architect for REI, an outdoor gear and apparel retailer, describes how great digital teams can accomplish more when they work together and share ideas and expertise. Colman started at REI in December 2008, after managing the Internet marketing team at The Nature Conservancy in Washington, D.C.

REI is a consumer cooperative whose mission is to "inspire, educate and outfit for a lifetime of outdoor adventure and stewardship." Because of this, while REI is engaged in providing top-brand outdoor gear to their audience of customers who enjoy camping, backpacking, snow sports, and cycling, the co-op also embraces the outdoor enthusiast and creates a brand community around these passions. Every year, they donate millions of dollars to conservation efforts in local communities and engage volunteers in keeping these natural areas both accessible and sustainable.

The REI.com website is a huge resource for all outdoor-oriented people, from the beginning camper to the most passionate climber, skier, paddler, or cyclist. They sell thousands of products online and also provide helpful videos and tips on gear and outdoor activities, a global travel program, and a guide on how to create outdoor family fun. REI isn't only selling products—they're selling an outlook, a lifestyle, and a membership community that values connecting through outdoor activities.

Running a massive website like REI's is a formidable task that requires a large technical team, as well as those who understand the marketing side of digital properties. Colman was brought in as an SEO expert to bring an external traffic perspective to an enterprise-wide information architecture (IA) team.

Information architects build the infrastructure of a website and organize information to enhance the user experience. The other two people on this team were a taxonomist and a data architect. Taxonomists organize content around standardized, governed vocabularies of terms, and data architects help to define both data standards and data structures that an organization can use to manage its information.

Bringing an SEO expert into an IA team was a radical idea at the time—it was unheard of to add SEO, which was considered to be a digital marketing skill, into enterprise information architecture activities. Think about it, though: all of these professionals are responsible for the naming conventions, information structures, and links between different pieces of content. The brilliance of bringing them together was their shared experience and knowledge about how customers find the products they want to buy. That's building a direct line between content teams and the bottom line.

As Colman explains, "Information architecture is the pathway to findability, discoverability, and usability [for content] and a great means of introducing SEO to an enterprise." By extension, how you label sections and pages, structure data and content, and create links between them all will impact whether your target audience can find them. By examining organic search data, Colman showed how customers were behaving and introduced those concepts to his team and others. They, in turn, were able to use that information to drive better customer experiences.

Colman describes one of his core accomplishments at REI as building a business case for why REI should speed up its web site to both improve the customer experience as well as drive more inbound search traffic. All other things being equal, the faster a web site loads and performs, the more visibility that site can receive in search engine results when customers search for terms for which that site is relevant. For example, Google uses site speed as an organic search ranking factor for highly competitive user search terms because high speed and performance correlate with higher quality customer experiences.

Various individuals within REI wanted to make their website faster, but they didn't have the data and research to make the project a priority. Colman was able to help them show key REI decision makers that making the website faster would make a measurable difference for the overall customer experience, and would also help drive additional search traffic.

As he explains, "Speed isn't a tactic for SEO...it's a strategy for customer engagement and loyalty." As we have already learned, how fast your website loads is critical to the user experience as well as to customer conversion. Most users expect a website to load in 2 seconds and 40% of customers will abandon any site that takes longer than 3 seconds to load (Colman, 2012). That's not a lot of time.

When the teams optimized REI.com to maximize its performance, they reduced the amount of time that it took Google to crawl a typical web page on the site by 50%. This resulted in a 100% increase in the number of pages that Google crawled each day, which helped REI to earn more traffic from Google searchers. When the teams measured how decreasing their site performance work influenced the overall user experience, they found that they saved customers about 1.5 seconds per page view, on average.

If you multiply that time savings by total page views over the course of a year, it saved their customers almost 22 years of time. That's 22 years that REI's customers would have spent waiting for the site to load; instead, those customers spent that time outside with the gear and apparel they bought, doing the activities they loved.

Colman concludes, "Infrastructure maintenance and support and SEO aren't normally aligned, but by bridging that gap, we were able to align our teams to improve the customer experience while driving more traffic."

What Colman's story proves is that by meshing cross-functional talent, businesses can improve the bottom line in so many ways: customer experience, profits, reputation of an organization, and more. By working together in multidisciplinary teams, you get many different types of heads putting together their best ideas. This can only result in a better, smarter business (Personal interview, 2013).

REFERENCES

Colman, J. (2012). SEO, site performance, Battlestar Gallactica. Retrieved from: http://webcache.googleusercontent.com/search?q=cache:www.slide-share.net%2Fjcolman%2Fseo-site-speed-and-battlestar-galactica-search-fest-2012-11735155.
Personal interview with the author, March 22, 2013.

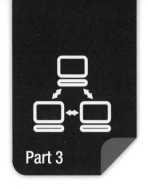
My daughters, who are eight and ten, like to tease me with riddles. They posed the following question: Imagine you're trapped in a black box, underground, with no tools and no way to get out. What do you do? I was stumped, until the eight-year-old grinned and said, "Stop imagining!"

After Parts 1 and 2, you are no longer in your black box of content nightmares. You can see your way out because you have a firm grasp of the philosophy of content. Now that you think about content differently, you can approach it differently from within your organization.

You've learned who you are by exploring branding (Chapter 1). You know how to say what you want to say by exploring the three parts of content: information, structure, and substance (Chapters 3 and 4). We've discussed how to distribute content effectively (Chapter 5).

In Part 3, we're going to roll up our sleeves and explore the "devil is in the details" stages of how to create content that drives the sales process. You are going to learn about the tools that you need to manage your content in a productive, streamlined workflow.

Gerry McGovern, a well-known thought leader on content, says, "Content thinking and technology thinking are classic organization-centric approaches. People don't want a 'book a flight' tool. They want to get to Dublin from London. People don't want the installation manual. They want to install the product. For most people, content or technology is not the end, not the point" (McGovern, 2012).

Content lies at the intersection of people, process, and technology. What it takes to make great content needs to happen without our audiences knowing, as McGovern notes. They don't care how we get it done—*they* just want to *get it done*. In Part 3, we're going to learn how to interpret and communicate your business strategy so you create meaningful, valuable content.

In Chapter 6, we'll talk about creating tools you can use to represent different potential customers. When you create personas and decision journey maps, you suddenly realize that you know whom you want to talk to, which makes your content vibrant and real.

In Chapter 7, we'll talk about identity pillars, messaging architectures, and voice and tone. Knowing what your brand represents matters more than ever online. Because if you don't know who you are, how can you possibly engage in a great conversation?

In Chapter 8, we'll learn about different tools you can use to create an online publishing strategy for your content that works for your organization: people, process, and technologies.

Finally, in Rule #5, we'll talk about how to create consistent content experiences across all the different channels you use to talk to your customers.

REFERENCE

McGovern, G. (2012). *Content is an enabler*. Retrieved from http://www. gerrymcgovern.com/new-thinking/content-enabler.

UNDERSTAND YOUR CUSTOMERS

CHAPTER 6

Are you ready to define who your audience is? To sell/convince/influence/impress our audience, we need to know who they are so we can speak to their interests and in their language. Content is a conversation. We don't want to come across as narcissists, focused only on our own needs and what we want to say. Nobody likes someone who is always talking about herself. It's boring and makes for no interchange; if the other person is always talking, how can there be any exchange of information?

When speaking to your audience, you need to be clear that your content is there to provide the information they need and want. The more we know about our audience, the more effective our content will be. That's why there are a variety of tools you can use to:

- Understand your customers better (personas)
- Sketch how they make decisions and what information they need to do so (decision journey maps)
- Plot what they are doing when they interact with your content (interactive scenarios)

Together we are going to learn how to create and use these tools, which are part of customer identity profiles. These profiles will help you mine and examine your customers in depth, communicate who they are within and among your internal teams, and help align your content with every stage of your audiences' decision-making process.

ABOUT PERSONAS

Personas are tools we use to create composite characters so we have an idea of who is at the other end of the conversation. Personas answer the critical question: To whom are we talking and what should we say to capture their attention?

> The more we know about our audience, the more effective our content will be.

THE ANSWERS YOU NEED

You must be able to answer these four critical questions if you want to create fantastic content for your brand:

1. Who is our audience?
2. What do they care about?
3. Where do they spend their time?
4. How do we get them the information they need?

Back in Rule #1, we talked about a framework you can use to discover and define your audience. Your tools and criteria for defining your audience should include:

1. Customer personas
2. Audience research
3. Understanding how customers access content

We discussed the data you need to create personas in Rule #1. In this chapter, we are going to dive deeper and learn:

- What a persona is
- Why personas should be used

J.C. Penney—We Didn't Understand Our Customers

J.C. Penney, the huge department store chain, hired a new CEO who decided it was time to make the store more hip and modern. Ron Johnson's ambitious changes included getting rid of most sales and bringing in new, hip brands. Some of the other changes he made involved eliminating maternity clothing and some of the larger sizes that Penney's carried. Instead, he introduced slimmer, "skinny jeans" types of clothing in an effort to attract younger, wealthier shoppers. In a bid to reinvent the stodgy retailer, he alienated Penney's loyal customers and caused sales to plummet (Anderson, 2013).

After the retailer fired Johnson, they proceeded to run a campaign to let their customers know they had made some terrible mistakes. One of their ads acknowledges the missteps and asks customers to return to its stores: "Come back to J.C. Penney. We heard you, now we'd love to see you," the voice-over states.

"It's no secret, recently J.C. Penney changed," the ad goes. "Some changes you liked, and some you didn't. But what matters with mistakes is what we learn."

The narrator continues: "We learned a very simple thing: to listen to you, to hear what you need, to make your life beautiful. Come back to J.C. Penney. We heard you. Now we'd love to see you."

What's even worse (cue the sad music for the C-suite), was that Moody's Investors Service downgraded J.C. Penney's rating in the wake of this error (Hsu, 2013).

The lesson is clear: Understand your customers. Know who they are. Don't pretend they are someone else. Because if you abandon them, as Penney's learned, they'll abandon you, too.

- How to create personas
- Types of personas
- The challenges of using personas in large organizations
- Aligning content development with the largest persona group

Then we'll touch on other tools you can use to learn more about your customers and actually put yourself in their shoes as they make decisions based on your content.

WHAT IS A PERSONA?

A persona is a full profile of your customer—everything relevant you could possibly want to know about him or her. A persona is not a real person or someone you know. When you create personas, you want to imagine who these people are, what they care about, and questions they have when they encounter your content.

User experience (UX) professionals use personas to understand how to design, write, and develop interactive applications for people. UX professionals include usability experts, human factor designers, information architects, content strategists, and user interface designers, among others. These professionals need to understand their audience so they can build better digital content and designs.

Marketers also use personas to identify target audiences to understand how to better connect to their customers. When audience engagement teams discover how customers consume content, use interactive applications, and engage with the digital world, they enrich their understanding of the audience they need to reach.

Of course, there is never just one persona—after all, we are trying to reach a world full of people of all shapes, sizes, races, religions, interests, and so on. Particularly in a large global organization, the challenge of creating personas may feel overwhelming. However, it can, should, and must, be done. We'll talk about how to face those challenges at the end of the chapter.

PERSONAS REPRESENT YOUR PEOPLE

According to UX Magazine, "A persona represents a cluster of users who exhibit similar behavioral patterns in their purchasing decisions, use of technology or products, customer service preferences, lifestyle choices, and the like. Behaviors, attitudes, and motivations are common to a 'type' regardless of age, gender, education, and other typical demographics. In fact, personas vastly span demographics" (O'Connor, 2011).

In other words, a grandma who loves computers could be represented by the same persona as a teen who is addicted to texting. This is a critical point because

Personas are shared tools to create composites of the real people who interact with our content on a daily basis.

When audience engagement teams discover how customers consume content, use interactive applications, and engage with the digital world, they enrich their understanding of the audience they need to reach.

when we tend to think about target audiences, we start falling into classic demographic measurements: age, race, geographical location, income, and so on. However, you may be responsible for content that spans a broad variety of people—so much so that it is impossible to categorize them according to those typical measurements.

Instead, you want to look at *how they behave and their motivations*, rather than surface identifying characteristics. Your audience could have hundreds of different personal characteristics: What unites them makes them one persona, or archetype, even though they may share no other demographic identifiers.

We use personas to create relevant content, according to the authors of *Content Rules*: "A buyer persona essentially represents a type of buyer you think will be interested in your product or service, and the idea behind creating buyer personas is to understand customers' specific needs and wants. Knowing your audience is particularly important for creating content and buyer personas can help shape your content to make it more relevant to your prospective buyers, especially if you are using words and phrases your potential customers use" (Handley & Chapman, 2011).

Shaping your content to make it more relevant to your customers is exactly the point of this book. Imagine starting a conversation with someone and having no idea who the person is—nothing about them—not their age, interests, passions, fears—nothing. How would you even begin?

WHY USE PERSONAS?

If you are creating content, you need to create personas to reinforce that you are talking to people with real concerns. It's so easy to fall into the trap of talking about your products and services rather than focusing on the needs of your customers. Remember the story of Brian, from Chapter 1? He was the salesman who focused on the customers, until in training he learned about products. Then he focused on the products and stopped focusing on people's needs. He was not able to sell effectively until he learned to combine his approach: First, focus on your customer's needs, then find the product or service that is best for her.

There are three important reasons to create, use, and regularly update your organization's personas.

Personas:

1. *Identify and target your audience*: Personas help you to identify your audience so you can create compelling content that keeps them coming back for more.

   Personas breathe real life into your audience so you don't fall into the trap of depersonalizing your customers by thinking of them as users rather than considering them real flesh-and-blood people. Personas help all content creators focus on the customers, putting their needs, worries, and responsibilities foremost, rather than our own.

2. *Put the team on the same page*: Personas help create alignment among your content creation team. If everyone knows that your audience consists of Avery, Peyton, and Bristol (more modern-day names for Tom, Dick, and Harry), then they will be able to better plan for content and to edit each other's work.

3. *Keep you out of the danger zone*: Without personas, companies often tend to forget who is consuming the content on the other end. This leads to what I call the "Danger Zone", which causes customers to zone out because the content is either way too vanilla or lacks any competitive differentiation on the web.

HOW TO CREATE PERSONAS

There are many useful resources you can reference when creating your personas. Jared Spool has several articles at User Interface Engineering (www.uie.com). Ginny Redish has excellent information in her book, *Letting Go of the Words, Second Edition: Writing Web Content that Works*. Her directions and highlights include:

1. *Gather information about your site visitors*: Include customer service inquiries, web feedback, reviews, recommendations, social media, web analytics, blog comments, online questionnaires, and usability testing. You can also consider offline research activities to find out more about your audience by conducting interviews, focus groups, and other types of market research.

2. *List groups of site visitors*: Ask how your audience self-identifies, how you identify them, and what they need to know to help you create better content for them.

3. *List major characteristics for each group*: Think about the vocabulary they use, their emotions when interfacing with your content, their values, and the technologies they might be using (Redish, 2012).

PERSONAS WORKSHOP

My favorite way to create personas is to hold a workshop with your digital and/or client team. This, of course, comes after you've spent time with your stakeholders so you can get their view of the target audiences. Or, (even better) invite the primary stakeholders to the workshop.

Creating personas using workshops is helpful for a few reasons:

1. *Contribution*: Everyone gets to contribute, which goes far in ensuring that you're not missing a major audience segment or fact that makes a difference in the final personas.

> Personas breathe real life into your audience so you don't fall into the trap of depersonalizing your customers by thinking of them as users rather than considering them real flesh-and-blood people.

2. *Connection*: By using a workshop format, people connect to the development of the personas; it feels like a team effort. Therefore, your team is far more likely to use the end product personas. In addition, people from different departments hear each other's viewpoints and connect to each other, thus creating a vibrant team environment and team ownership of the personas.

3. *Challenge*: By challenging each other's assumptions, you ensure the personas are solid and will help drive the entire strategy effort by clearly defining your audience

Questions That Will Get You Started

Think about persona creation as that game you played as a child, called *Twenty Questions*. A review of the rules: one player thinks of a person, then the second player tries to guess who it is and each person gets a turn to try to guess before the 20 questions run out.

During persona development, unlike the game, you are not limited—you can ask as many questions as you want. And of course, your sets of questions will change depending on the type of product or service you sell. If you sell auto parts, you are not going to ask how your personas look up healthcare information. If you provide air duct cleaning, you may want to consider how people access information about asthma, air quality, and how it affects their overall health. It's all about putting yourself in the minds of your audiences and thinking as they do. Here is a sample of some questions you should be asking:

- How old are our customers?
- Where do they live?
- Where did they grow up?
- What is their level of education?
- How much money do they earn?
- What types of professions do they have?
- With whom do they spend their time?
- Do they have significant others or families?
- Where do they shop?
- What types of stores do they frequent?
- What do they eat?
- Who prepares their food?
- What types of cars do they drive? Do they use public transportation?
- What types of technology do they use?
- Do they access content from a desktop computer or a mobile device?
- Do they have a smartphone or a tablet?

Spend time answering these questions with your team. You can create persona projects in a day. But you'll then need other types of research to back up your assumptions. So make sure you triangulate your research; meaning, find other sources of data to back up your creations. We talked about different types of research in Rule #1. These included customer research, interactive data, ethnographic studies, focus groups, surveys, and consumer trend research.

My suggestion is to do the workshop for half of a workday. Bring everyone in the conference room with pictures from magazines. Let people cut and paste pictures that represent who they think the personas are to their heart's content. Then they can present their composites to the entire team.

I know you may be skeptical, but trust me—teams really enjoy this activity: It spurs their creativity. By sharing with each other, they are able to find gaps in their knowledge about the target audiences and if any messages are scrambled. Speaking of eggs, don't forget to serve breakfast, lunch, or good snacks. Meetings over food take on a different tone, making everyone feel comfortable enough to confirm or critique others' persona presentations.

BACKING PERSONAS UP WITH DATA

No matter how you create your personas, you must ensure you reinforce them with data. As Paul Bryan, a user experience professional, points out, "When a team formulates personas on the basis of real customer data rather than just making them up, personas accurately represent the needs, wants and cross-channel interactive behavior of large segments of customers." He recommends the following hybrid approach to persona development:

1. *Use data*: Use analytics and all available customer data to generate a set of characteristics and behaviors.

2. *Do a deep-dive on developing personas*: Interviewing customers in their homes, conducting video-diary exercises and shop-a-longs.

3. *Connect the dots*: Wire those archetypes to analytics, figuring out the distinguishing behaviors that match the specific attributes (Bryan, 2013).

By using this process, you ensure that you are using all different types of customer data to verify that your personas are appropriate for your brand.

What Should Our Personas Look Like?

In the beginning, while you are engaging in the workshop, you can use large pieces of poster board to create your personas with your team. Once you are finished, you will put them in charts within your style guide or brand guidelines. For now, you just want to create a rough outline of the personas.

Figure 6.1 Persona example—Lisa.

It's important that your team, to feel personally connected to the personas, relate to them as real people. To that end, give them names and find an "image" of him or her; someone that your team can truly connect with. It's not too far-fetched to post these "customer images" on the wall of your main conference room and refer to them by name. I typically recommend no more than five personas per organization, but for those that have different products or service lines, it may make sense to create umbrella personas. The detailed personas may only exist for segmented parts of the organization.

Let me introduce Lisa (Figure 6.1) and Marcus, two rough personas that I use here as examples.

Now remember what we said earlier—try to ignore the usual characteristics of audience that we all tend to focus on—gender and age. So, with that in mind, let's say that Lisa is studying and likes to party but that doesn't mean that she is in her twenties and at a fancy, expensive college. Marcus (in Figure 6.2) just got married but that doesn't mean he is under age thirty.

If we are to be successful in developing content to reach as many people as possible, we need to free our minds of the usual characteristic-based constrictions.

So, what do we know about Lisa? She:

- Studies at college
- Likes to party, but also takes school seriously

Marcus

Figure 6.2 Persona example—Marcus.

- Interacts with her friends via her iPhone, using various forms of social media and chat

We can add other things about Lisa to the mix, depending on who we are as a company. If you sell shoes, then Lisa may be a target customer. Does she like shoes? When does she shop for them? Online or with her friends in retail stores? How many pairs of shoes does Lisa have? How many would she like to have? Does she pay for shoes herself or do her parents still let her use their credit cards? Does Lisa have a job to pay for her shoes? The questions are endless and by answering them you nail down the details you need to know about Lisa so you can better shape your content for her.

What do we know about Marcus? He:

- Lives in NYC and does not own a car. Therefore, he uses the subway to get around
- Works as a stockbroker on Wall Street
- Is a runner
- Got married in the past year

What product do you want to sell to Marcus? Car oil? He doesn't own a car, so he's not a good example of a persona that suits your company. Life insurance?

Well, now you can add in relevant details that help shape your content around life insurance.

How much money does Marcus make? Does he have life insurance through his job? Does his wife carry life insurance? Marcus is young—what would make him think about life insurance? Are there financial benefits for him in the different types of life insurance he might choose to buy? As a stockbroker, Marcus is probably savvier than most customers about finances—or is he? Does he pay attention to his personal finances? These are all important questions to answer about Marcus.

Developing customer personas like this help you to identify with your audience. During a meeting, you may have talked about the wealthy professional in his early thirties who is part of your target audience. Now that Marcus has a name and a face, your team will undoubtedly do a better job of creating directed content for him.

A word of caution: I have seen all types of personas—incredibly detailed down to what a person eats for breakfast, lunch, and dinner. I have also seen very loose personas that don't answer all the questions you need to know about your target audience. My advice? Make them as detailed as they need to be, but targeted toward the product or service you are selling. For example, if you're a government agency who regulates financial securities, you don't need to know what your personas are eating at each meal. If you're a government agency who is trying to get information to people about nutrition—then yes!—you need those descriptions.

Some content experts argue that your personas should be as specific as possible and others say that you don't need to obsess over your personas—some bullet points can suffice (Halvorson & Rach, 2012). I think the types of personas you choose to create, and how detailed they are, depend on your organization, business objectives, and most importantly, what you are trying to sell or achieve.

When personas get too concrete, they lose their power. Your team needs a starting point that feels very solid to them, but they don't need unnecessary details clouding their perception of the person. Remember, personas are *representative* of a member of your target audience. Keep the details centered on your organization's business objectives. You're not Dr. Frankenstein; meaning, you're not trying to create a real person out of cardboard, magazines, and glue.

Each organization needs to pick the right number of personas to use in a way that shapes an artful conversation. Don't pick too many—more than five and it will get too confusing. The goal of personas is to become familiar with them so that they feel like real people that are, by extension, a part of your team. When you talk about them, they feel real and it makes talking to them—and therefore crafting content for them—easier.

Just like brands evolve and change, so too, personas will evolve and change. Ensure you're looking at your customer personas at least once a year to keep them fresh, relevant, and aligned with business objectives. What's most important to identify about a persona is their mindset, or where they are in the decision-making process. This brings us to the different types of journey maps you can create and which ones are best suited to your organization's content.

Knowing Your Audience

It's not too difficult to understand that Neiman Marcus and Wal-Mart are targeting two very different audiences and that the personas to which they direct their content vary greatly. Take these two Valentine's Day web ads—Neiman Marcus doesn't even mention Valentine's Day in theirs, just shows photos of a few items framed in pink and leaves the audience to figure it out. Wal-Mart, on the other hand, is catering to a different group. By using a wordier approach, with many more choices to buy for your sweetheart, they are fulfilling their brand promise of the widest variety of products at the lowest price (Figures 6.3 and 6.4).

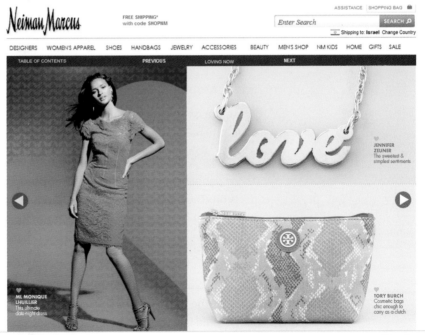

Figure 6.3 Neiman Marcus ad.

(Continued)

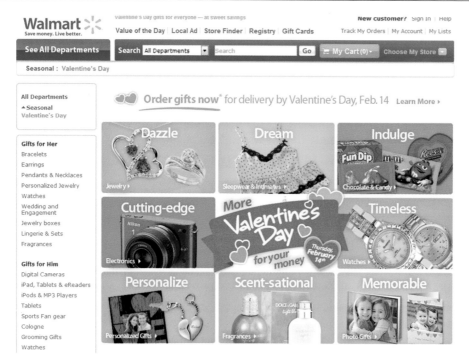

Figure 6.4 Wal-Mart ad.

THREE CATEGORIES OF JOURNEY MAPS

Once you create up to five major personas, you may want to create journey maps detailing how they access content and change their content consumption process as they gather information. There are three categories of maps and scenarios to guide you:

- *Seeker Maps*

  These are customers looking for information—a phone number, a coupon code, the name of a contact person.

- *Decision Journey Maps*

  These people want to add to their knowledge base so they can make a decision. They might want to buy a product, choose a health professional, pick a hotel for a vacation, or buy a household appliance. They need information so they can complete a very specific task.

- *Interactive Scenario Maps*

  These tells you what your customers are doing while they access your content. Consider the following: You use a video to demonstrate to customers why they should buy your product. But in a mobile situation, it may take too long for your video to download. So it's important to know what your customers are doing when they interact with your content so you can help support them as they try to get a piece of information or complete a task.

A useful way to think about how to use these different types of maps would be:

If You Think People Are Interacting with Your Content Because:	You Would Want This Type of Map:
They need information →	Seeker
They want to buy something or make a decision →	Decision Journey
They are in a situation where all of your content is not accessible to them at that moment →	Interactive Scenario

We'll talk more about some of these types of maps in Chapter 11.

SEEKER MAPS

When you create a seeker map, you sketch a profile of the path an audience member will take while they look for a piece of information embedded in one of your types of content. It could be something like a phone number, or what types of fruits are illegal to bring back into the United States after an overseas journey. Seeker maps might also detail a person looking for news or a piece of trivia. They may also be in search of health information to use later when they come to the decision-making process of their journey.

Seekers are gatherers of information—either a piece or pieces of information— to satisfy a need. Creating maps for seekers has a lot to do with the type of content you produce and why you produce it. For example, if you run a huge news site like CNN, you probably have broad maps, because CNN covers many types of news. If you're a celebrity gossip site like *US Weekly*, you may have more specific maps, because you know the members of your audience are people who like celebrity gossip. Your maps might get specific, based on TV shows, movie stars, and fashion.

DECISION JOURNEY MAPS

Decision journey maps describe people who are in search of information to help them make a buying decision. They are perfect for the customer loop we described in Chapter 2.

Buying decisions usually require gathering information, which is why your map should begin at the top of your customer loop as a broader sketch; the few bullet points we referenced before—who are they, where do they spend their time, and so on. As they make their way through the customer loop, clarify what happens as they sharpen their decision based on information. That way you can develop, build, and create content that is relevant for them depending on what content they may seek at that step.

Figure 6.5 AJ Madison refrigerator sorter.

For example, the website AJ Madison (www.ajmadison.com) sells kitchen appliances. If you use a search engine for a particular model or appliance, you can usually end up on their screen that shows that appliance. But if you start on their home page and select one of their top menu items you will find an appliance sorter which allows you to refine by price, color, brand, and size (Figure 6.5).

When you hit the content page, you can read about the content, and can even dig deeper, finding a photo, pricing, description, and appliance specs to help in kitchen design.

Layering this content gives your audiences the different pieces of information they need to make the purchase decision. Providing different formats of content at each step helps them to make those decisions.

Therefore, seeker personas may start at the top of your customer loop but as they move their way down the stages of the loop their questions change. This means you have to create content for them wherever they are in their decision-making process.

Sales Lead Stage	Action	Persona Stage
I	Gathering information	Seeker
II	Narrowing the decision	Comparing products
III	Reading reviews	Ready to purchase
IV	Buyer	Customer

A very rough sketch of a decision journey map for AJ Madison might look like this (Figures 6.6–6.8).

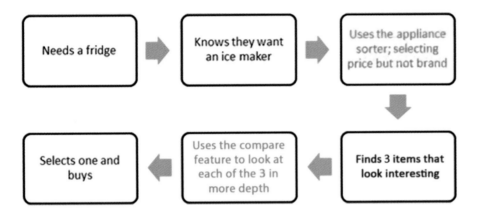

Figure 6.6 Decision journey map: The text in blue signifies the point at which the customer uses an interactive feature to narrow her decision.

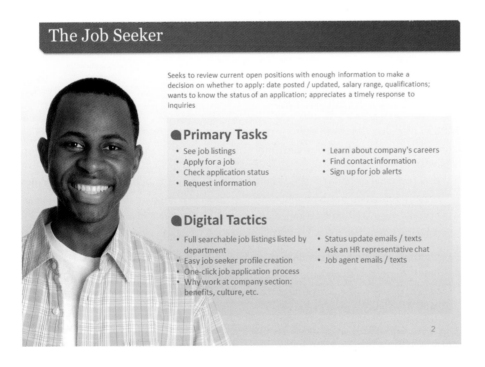

Figure 6.7 Job seeker persona. Here's an example of a person who is described by their decision journey (Credit: EPAM | Empathy Lab). In Figure 6.8, you can see the journey mapped.

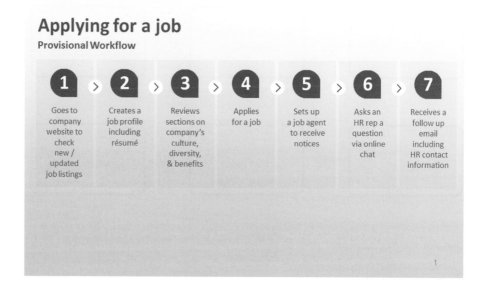

The Job Seeker

Applying for a job
Provisional Workflow

1	2	3	4	5	6	7
Goes to company website to check new / updated job listings	Creates a job profile including résumé	Reviews sections on company's culture, diversity, & benefits	Applies for a job	Sets up a job agent to receive notices	Asks an HR rep a question via online chat	Receives a follow up email including HR contact information

Figure 6.8 The job seeker's decision journey. In this map, Empathy Labs mapped the provisional workflow for applying for a job. This gives them important information about the interactive touchpoints for the persona. (Credit: EPAM | Empathy Lab).

INTERACTIVE SCENARIOS

Another map you can use in persona development is an interactive scenario. Interactive scenarios describe *what your customers are doing when they access your content.*

> User [persona] scenarios anticipate the needs of a user in a mobile situation, when his or her information needs might be different than in a standard desktop situation (and by that I mean a situation where a user has a full interface and is not pressed for time). A typical interactive scenario would look like this:
>
> *Customer A is at one of our physical stores. He wants to know how much the camera that he is holding in his hand would cost online. Can he save money by buying the camera or any of the accessories online? Is it possible to use the online price in the store to negotiate for a better deal?*
>
> (Leibtag, 2011)

Interactive scenarios are critical because today at least a third of the world's population is consuming content on a mobile device. This means that not only is your audience important, but the way in which they access your content is also critical (UX professionals call this context). You want to make sure you are delivering content they can access, or that will influence them, no matter the device or format.

Lisa's Scenarios

Figure 6.9 Lisa's customer scenario.

Here is an example of Lisa and Marcus' interactive scenarios (Figures 6.9–6.10):

- Lisa works as an intern, which means she has access to her iPhone the entire day.

- She uses the iPhone to check on flights back home for spring break.

- She also uses it to shop for her favorite shoes.

- Lisa travels around her college campus on foot and uses the ATM located near her dorm to get cash (Figure 6.10).

- Marcus accesses content to read *The Wall Street Journal* and view other financial news-related sites.

- He and his wife eat out often, so he may use a restaurant app to make reservations.

- As an outdoor runner, Marcus likes to use his phone to check the weather.

- He wants to buy his wife a diamond pendant for their first-year anniversary, but he doesn't want her to see it on their home computer. So he buys it from his phone.

Knowing about your target audiences' daily behaviors helps you put their content consumption into context. This will help you as you continue to build and grow your content programs.

Marcus' Scenarios

Figure 6.10 Marcus' interactive scenario.

Remember: this doesn't change what we said in Chapter 4. You need to be ready for multichannel publishing and have your content available on any device. But knowing if your customers are likely to purchase your products from a mobile device, or if there is something about the way you're presenting the information that makes them abandon your mobile site, is powerful information you must have.

In the end, your audience engagement team may end up creating a variety of different personas that mix all of these elements together. For example, most of my persona workshops end up with a persona characteristic that describes how people access content—either through a tablet, PC, smartphone, or combination.

Another example of how you can mix personas and maps is talking about a customer who requests a phone number or directions using a mobile device. Ensuring that the content is mobile-ready and that all they have to do is click on the link to the phone number to have their smartphone make the call, is an important hallmark of organizations that make the customer the focus of their digital efforts.

THE CHALLENGES OF USING PERSONAS IN LARGE ORGANIZATIONS

When I introduce the idea of personas in large organizations, many digital strategy teams begin to feel overwhelmed. "We have so many different types of customers," they say, or "How detailed should we get?" If you are thinking about hanging five poster boards in the conference room with different names and pictures to describe your different customers, and think this will feel too hokey for your team, then do not do it. I want you to find success with personas, scenarios and maps, not have it muck up your process.

So think about doing what Ginny Redish advises—creating what she calls mini-personas. "You may also want to have scenarios for a few secondary personas. For example, if your main personas are frequent shoppers and casual shoppers but you also have investors and reporters coming to the site, you may want to do 'mini-personas' for them along with their scenarios" (Redish, 2012). We talked about that earlier: In large organizations, it may be helpful to have enterprise customer personas and have specific personas for different departments or product lines.

The most important thing you can do when you create personas, scenarios, and maps in a large organization is publicize them and let others know to use them. Even if they are mini-personas or a few bullets, they will not make a bit of difference if the teams creating content do not know whom they are. For this you need training, consistency in editing content, and a centralized style guide, which we'll talk about in Rule #5.

ALIGN CONTENT DEVELOPMENT WITH THE LARGEST PERSONA GROUP

Another important issue to discuss in persona development is what percentage of business a particular persona brings to your organization. In the case of a university, most of their content is geared toward attracting prospective students. However, alumni give money to the school and keep school spirit and strong reputations alive. Universities always want to receive research funding from governments or other institutions, so it's important for the university to publicize its successful research outputs.

In this case, the university needs to look at what the business objectives are for the organization in the next few years. They probably want some combination of growing the student population, growing alumni engagement and support, and increasing chances for government or other funding. Senior management has to decide how to rank those priorities. Based on that, you know how to focus your content development. Let's imagine that the university administration decides on these priorities by percentage (Figure 6.11).

University Business Priorities

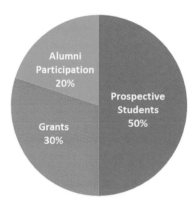

Figure 6.11 University business priorities.

The university's content team needs to spend 50% of their content development time on creating and managing content for prospective students, 30% on grants, and 20% on alumni participation. There will, of course, be other personas to develop and manage content for as well, such as faculty and current students. So, the team directs 80% of their time toward the three main personas. Then, they divide the remaining 20% equally between faculty and current students.

In this way, content development efforts are structured toward business objectives, making it easier for teams to know where they should be spending their time. By knowing which of the personas bring the most business, teams can focus their efforts effectively.

SUMMARY

You cannot create valuable content until you know your customers. And, you cannot know your customers without doing some hard work and conducting real research. Remember, your audience interacts with your brand because they are hopeful that you will provide knowledge, news, or data they can use. They interact with your digital properties—your website, blog, and social media channels—because they are hungry for information. Sometimes your audience will convert to customers; sometimes they won't. But you have a better chance of making that conversion happen if you know who they are and what really matters to them.

Your customers' identities are your starting point and serve as the building blocks of your digital strategy. Now you know how to create personas, scenarios, and customer maps to define them. Once you've done that, you need to be able to tie your content back to your company's business objectives, so your C-suite can appreciate why it is so important.

Don't underestimate how powerful personas are for aligning your digital strategy teams. When done properly, your teams will begin to refer to "Avery and Peyton," making it seem as though they are in the room when you are talking about creating content. And when Avery and Peyton are in the room when content is created, you're invariably going to have better conversations with them.

In creating personas, you now know who your audience is. Now you need to learn how to define who you are. Let's find out how to do that in Chapter 7.

REFERENCES

Anderson, M. (2013). *J.C. Penney apology: We erred … come back*. Retrieved from http://www.csmonitor.com/Business/Latest-News-Wires/2013/0501/J.C.-Penney-apology-We-erred.-Come-back-video.

Bryan, P. (2013). *Are personas still relevant to UX strategy?* Retrieved from http://www.uxmatters.com/mt/archives/2013/01/are-personas-still-relevant-to-ux-strategy.php.

Halvorson, K., & Rach, M. (2012). *Content strategy for the Web* (2nd ed.). Berkeley, CA: New Riders, p. 105.

Handley, A., & Chapman, C. C. (2011). *Content rules: How to create killer blogs, podcasts, videos, ebooks, webinars (and more) that engage customers and ignite your business*. Hoboken, NJ: Wiley.

Hsu, T. (2013) *J.C. Penney ad apologizes for missteps*. Retrieved from http://articles.chicagotribune.com/2013-05-02/business/chi-jc-penney-ad-apology-20130502_1_youtube-social-media-sites-goldman-sachs.

Leibtag, A. (2011). *Mobile content strategy: Creating user scenarios*. Retrieved from http://www.cmswire.com/cms/web-engagement/mobile-content-strategy-creating-user-scenarios-010673.php.

O'Connor, K. (2011). Personas: The Foundation of a Great User Experience. *UX Magazine*. Retrieved from http://uxmag.com/articles/personas-the-foundation-of-a-great-user-experience.

Redish, J. (2012). *Letting go of the words writing web content that works*. Waltham, MA: Morgan Kaufmann.

FRAME YOUR CONTENT

CHAPTER 7

At every Ritz Carlton in the world, management refers to their staff as "ladies and gentlemen." In every morning meeting, every training session, every conversation, employees at all levels—from executives to managers to floor staff—treat each other genially and with respect.

Why do they go through all this formality every day? Because the Ritz Carlton stands for unique, consistent, luxurious service. By talking to staff with courtesy and respect, management communicates an expectation of how others should be treated—no matter what. In its daily interactions, the Ritz Carlton communicates brand values to their employees, and this kind of training pays off—the hotel chain received top honors in all categories in the 2011 Luxury Hotel Guest Satisfaction Survey carried out by JD Powers and Associates (Jakobson, 2011). It's no wonder Steve Jobs turned to the Ritz Carlton for a model for how to build his Apple retail stores. The management at the Ritz Carlton knows how to *frame* experiences and conversations.

In this chapter, you're going to learn how to frame your content, how to create tools to help build your content so your audience will return to it time and again. I use the term *framing* because I think the metaphor is apt for what we're going to learn how to do in this chapter: decide what we are constructing, what it looks like, and how to keep it within building code.

WHY FRAME?

Framing is something that all contractors and builders do before they build a house because it gives the building structural integrity. First, builders use blueprints so that they have one guideline of how to build a house.

They already know for whom they are building it: a family of four with a dog and a need for a mudroom. Concealed within these blueprints are a million things that the family will take for granted, even though those things will greatly affect their comfort and serenity. Electrical wiring, plumbing, window placement, how the doors swing, and so on, are all captured and documented within these blueprints. These blueprints are *exactly* the same no matter which professional is working on the house: electrician, plumber, window installer. If the professionals were working from different blueprints, then you would have a house no one would want to live in.

WHAT IS "FRAMING YOUR CONTENT"?

Framing your content means defining and creating three major characteristics that will help define your brand so you can communicate effectively with your audiences:

- Identity pillars
- Messaging architecture
- Voice and tone

Like the builders, you already know who will live in your house because you followed Rule #1 and you just finished Chapter 6. You have the philosophy and the tools to apply a clear identity to your customers. Now that you know who you are talking to, you need to define who *you* are so you can create great conversations.

Framing your content means that you will decide what upholds your brand—the pillars that define who you are. Then you will decide on messaging and hierarchy of that messaging: what are you trying to say and in what order? Finally, we will learn about voice and tone—how we say it is as important as what we say.

IDENTITY PILLARS

As we learned in Chapter 1, if you don't understand what your brand represents for your audience, your content efforts won't be successful. Identity pillars aren't just about what people think of when they think of you (brand attributes), it's also about *what you want your brand to represent to them*.

Identity pillars are the core principles of your brand.

To create identity pillars that will help you shape your content efforts, we must first define brand attributes. Then we can tie those into the product or service you are trying to sell.

BRAND ATTRIBUTES

Brand attributes are what defines your brand. In other words, *who* is your brand? I use "who" because I believe that you should think of a brand as a personality. What are the characteristics people think of when they think of your brand? Are you fun, playful, affordable, dangerous, caring, technologically advanced, classy, elegant, chic, exciting, boring, reliable, controversial, or dull? Do people laugh or cry when they see your logo? Do they sometimes laugh and sometimes cry, depending on the type of business they do with you? (I'm thinking here of the government agency that regulates taxation—people laugh when they get a refund, and cry when they get any other kind of letter.)

Who is your brand? What does that brand mean to the world? What do you *want* the brand to mean to the world? You need to know it and define it. Because just like those blueprints, if you don't have a way to marry your content to your identity, your content won't hold together.

HOW DO WE DEFINE OUR BRAND?

As we said in Chapter 1, branding should really come from the highest executive leadership in the organization. However, you may not be working in a company where things work quite that way. For example, you may be the senior leadership, or you may be tasked with creating content, but may not be 100% sure of what your brand should be. Talk to people within your organization to define your brand. You may be able to do this on your own, or you may need to hire an excellent branding firm. In either case, you can't move ahead with your content if your identity pillars are shaky.

If you must move ahead on your own, then go ahead and carry out the exercises below, have your senior management sign off, and then go forth and create your content. I have been on many content projects where clients used just this approach and it worked—very successfully, in fact.

As Margot Bloomstein, a content strategist, explains, the goal of this exercise is to "translate high-level business and brand guidelines into actionable messaging priorities" (Bloomstein, 2012). No matter what size organization you are responsible for—or whether you have branding specialists on speed-dial—the goals of creating identity pillars are still the same. You need to know what the business objectives are, what the brand is, and combine those two pieces of information into an executable communication strategy.

BRAND ATTRIBUTES VERSUS IDENTITY PILLARS

Remember, *brand attributes are the characteristics* that describe your brand. Brand attributes are what people think about the brand, and, possibly, what the brand thinks about itself. Identity pillars are a way to establish how you want to communicate with both your internal team and your external customers. Identity pillars:

- Provide the vehicle to move the perception of the brand forward
- Define communication goals (in the context of content) within the company

In other words, identity pillars give you a roadmap for how to improve the perception of your brand through content, and communicate internally within

You can't move ahead with your content if your identity pillars are shaky.

Brand attributes are the characteristics that describe your brand. *Identity pillars* are a tool used to describe the core principles of your brand.

Figure 7.1 Knowing where you want to go will help you move forward with content.

your organization about content priorities and objectives. They show you how to move forward from where you are to where you want to be (Figure 7.1).

CREATING IDENTITY PILLARS

As with everything in content, we need to understand where we are, where we want to be, and how we are going to get there. Establishing identity pillars requires a four-step process:

1. Analyze your current business objectives
2. Understand what your *current* brand attributes are
3. Express how you are trying to move the brand
4. Create identity pillars that articulate the promises of your brand

Let's walk through two examples—one a service and one a product—so you can get more comfortable with this process.

EXAMPLE #1: HOSPITAL CURE

Let's talk about "Hospital Cure," a fictitious hospital that has a reputation for working with severely ill cancer patients, among other medical specialties. At Hospital Cure, we would create identity pillars by examining what brand perception currently is, and where hospital leadership would like to move it. People around the country may know Hospital Cure for its excellent doctors, as well as for curing challenging cases of cancer. They may also know it as that place people go when there's no hope left.

The senior leadership of Hospital Cure, while analyzing healthcare trends, recognizes that, aside from treating cancer patients, they need to attract patients who have more common ailments, such as gallstones, kidney stones, tonsillitis, and appendicitis—general everyday conditions that are not usually life-threatening.

Let's look at how we would map this out for Hospital Cure. First, let's look at their business objectives:

- Grow overall patient volumes
- Specifically, bring more people into the hospital for routine medical procedures and treatments

- Increase people who use the primary care physician practice associated with Hospital Cure

- Increase the number of people who enroll for clinical trials, to increase government funding to study cancer diagnosis and treatment

Current Brand Attributes (What people think of us now)	What We Want Brand Attributes to Become (What we want people to think of us)	Identity Pillars (How we will communicate our brand promise—both internally and externally)
Advanced medicine	Advanced and "regular" care	Complex and routine medical care
Excellent physicians	Excellent physicians and nurses	Fantastic doctors and staff
The last resort	We treat everything	We are here for all your health needs
Big and confusing	Caring and compassionate, but with care like no other	Friendly experts

How can the senior leadership expect to increase the number of people who come for routine services and still increase clinical trial enrollment for hard-to-treat types of cancers? Does that seem incongruous to you?

No, because you can do both. Look carefully at the wording of the identity pillars. We know people already think of Hospital Cure as a large cancer research organization. We don't want them to lose that brand attribute, but we still need to grow routine care patients. Therefore, we use terms that encompass an entire range of healing, so people will shift their understanding of the brand over time.

EXAMPLE #2: AMERICAN FAUCET MAKER

An American faucet maker—we'll call them Fawcet—is struggling with increasing competition from European competitors who are designing sleeker, more modern faucets that are so in fashion now in American kitchens. Fawcet has followed Rule #1 and knows exactly what their customers think: They make a nice product; but Americans think European products look better in their kitchens. Their research also revealed that people don't think their American-made faucets have the same quality as their European counterparts.

What are the business objectives here?

- *Show* people that Fawcet's faucets are just as beautiful as European designs

- *Remind* people that Fawcet is a strong American brand and makes excellent products

- *Demonstrate* that Fawcet will last a long time

- *Increase* awareness of Fawcet in Europe to compete there

Current Brand Attributes (What people think of us now)	What We Want Brand Attributes to Become (What we want people to think of us)	Identity Pillars (How we will communicate our brand promise—both internally and externally)
Nice, but boring	A style to fit any taste (after all there are people who don't like the modern look)	With so many choices, we'll find the right Fawcet for you
Not as attractive as European competitors	Beautiful to look at	Look at how beautiful our Fawcets are
Will break	Well-made and lasts forever	Competes in terms of longevity with any other type of faucet

Now that we've gone through two examples of creating identity pillars, let's talk about a messaging architecture.

MESSAGING ARCHITECTURE

Margot Bloomstein defines it this way: "A message architecture is a hierarchy of communication goals; as a hierarchy they're attributes that appear in order of priority, typically in an outline." She explains you must, "start by engaging the client around their communication goals and priorities—you can't have one without the other if you want to establish a clear value proposition for the brand. Why does prioritization matter? It's rare for initiatives to have a single purpose or stakeholder; that's why 'this too!' is the battle cry of so many departments jostling to have their content dominate the homepage, breaking templates with countless content modules" (Bloomstein, 2012).

Identity pillars are the beginning of messaging architectures—they give you your high-level statements so you know who you are as a brand—your personality. Messaging architectures go two steps further:

1. They give priority to your business objectives
2. They give you firm documentation for explaining why certain content—and messages—need to come first

CREATING A MESSAGING ARCHITECTURE

Margot describes an in-person process in her book, *Content Strategy at Work,* called a "card sort," to define your messaging architecture. Using about 150 cards with adjectives printed on them, all the stakeholders in the room sort the cards according to the following:

- Who we are
- Who we'd like to be
- Who we're not

This is very similar to what we described in the identity pillars exercise. By describing who we're not, as well as adding in a step to filter adjectives and then prioritize and choose, an organization develops a very clear picture of their messaging and priorities.

I recommend using identity pillars first, because priorities of messaging should fall back to the business objectives of the organization. While defining the brand internally is very important, the real goal of content is to meet your audience's needs and make money for your brand. Executives who write strong, solid business plans have this knowledge. That is who will be able to tell you what the business objectives of the organization are.

I recommend using the card sort if you need to understand your brand's values with all stakeholders present. This gives everyone an opportunity to chime in on what he or she thinks the brand represents. However, at the end of the day, what sets priority should be the business strategy. So let's see how to put identity pillars together with the priority of a messaging architecture and the clear guidelines of what comes first.

ESTABLISHING PILLAR PRIORITY

To establish pillar priority you need to ask your executives to order their business objectives, including percentages of how important these business objectives are. This process is similar to the prioritization of personas that we discussed in Chapter 6—it's all linked back to business objectives. This activity will also help strengthen your case when you talk about divvying up your content resources.

Let's go back to Hospital Cure, our earlier fictional example. Their business objectives were:

- *Grow* overall patient volumes
- Specifically, *bring more people into the hospital* for routine medical procedures and treatments
- *Increase* the use of the primary care physician practice associated with Hospital Cure
- *Increase* the number of people who enroll for clinical trials, to increase funding from the government to study cancer

> Use identity pillars first, because priorities of messaging should fall back to the business objectives of the organization.

Branding Review

Branding attributes are the way you define your brand—its personality.

Identity pillars are communication statements that express how you want to move your brand forward for both your internal communications team and external customers.

Messaging architecture is how you set the priority of those messages.

When the executives order those business objectives and give percentages of priority, you might receive this:

Priority	Objective	Percentage	Associated Branding Pillar
1	Bring more people into the hospital for routine medical procedures and treatments	50%	Complex and routine medical care
2	Increase the use of the primary care physician practice associated with Hospital Cure	25%	Fantastic doctors and staff
3	Grow overall patient volumes	15%	We are here for all your health needs
4	Increase the number of people who enroll for clinical trials, so we can increase our funding from the government to study cancer	10%	Friendly experts

Now that you have the priorities of the identity pillars, you can begin to create your messaging architecture:

1. Complex and routine medical care

   • Start with the best, no matter what your condition

   • If we can handle the big stuff, we can handle other things too

   • Our expertise means that you are getting the very best no matter what your level of care

2. Fantastic doctors and staff

   • We have amazing primary care doctors who have daily communication with specialists, in case you should need one

   • Our staff of nurse practitioners, nurses, and therapists will provide you with excellent care

   • Employed by the best, we deliver the best

3. We are here for all your health needs

   • Superior medical care across our institution

   • One of the top five institutions in the region, as noted by a popular consumer ranking system for hospitals

4. Friendly experts

   • Our specialists are experts, which means they deal with serious conditions on a daily basis, but they still will treat you with warmth and compassion

   • As experts, we engage in research that benefits not only our patients, but the medical world at large

   • We use our expertise to broaden our understanding of disease processes through research

Hospital Cure chose precise wording to articulate the messaging supported by the identity pillars. Messaging is so delicate and so important because it involves three unique exchanges at the same time:

- Who we are

- What we stand for

- How we articulate those two things

Let's explore that a bit more.

The Interplay of Messaging and Branding

Messaging is how you communicate the particulars of your brand promise. Messaging is not taglines: Taglines are one method that we may use to communicate brand promises. They are not messaging in its entirety. As we saw from the exercise above, most of those messages could not be turned into taglines.

Take Nike. The company's tagline is *Just Do It*. The tagline communicates an attitude towards exercise and physical activity that encompasses a "take no prisoners" attitude. "Just Do It" lets you know that people who choose to wear Nike are serious about physical fitness—it is a major priority for them. *Just Do It* captured the imagination of the world, the way awesome taglines often do.

Another simple tagline that encapsulates a brand is Apple's *Think Different.* The brand promises that Apple envisions technology and communication differently to affect change. *Think Different* effectively focuses consumer attention on the unique attributes of an Apple product—no matter what the product might be—the iPhone, iPad, or MAC.

What about Coca-Cola? This company has changed its messaging and taglines countless times over many decades. In the 1970s, it was "Have a Coke and a smile." In the 1980s, it was "Coke is it." In the 1990s it was, "Always Coca-Cola." In the 2000s, "All the world loves a Coke," was targeted at a global audience. Close your eyes for a minute and imagine the iconic Coca-Cola script and red background. What comes to mind? Look back at all those taglines. What do they have in common?

They communicate that:

1. Coke makes you happy
2. Coke is better than any other soft drink out there

That's messaging. Coke knows who they are as a brand, and they articulate that meaning through their taglines, which are a synthesis of their brand attributes and the expression of those attributes over time. Their voice—or their brand personality—comes through in every commercial, every piece of content, every encounter you have with their brand—we make you happy and we are happy doing it.

Coke understands their voice and they use it consistently. (Have you ever watched a Coke commercial and walked away thinking, "Wow, that was a bummer?") As a brand, you also have a voice you use when you converse with your audience. Let's talk more about voice and tone now—the third step in framing your content.

VOICE AND TONE

A voice is an expression of your brand's personality. Tone is the reflection of the feelings we have when we communicate. Tone comes from the stresses we put on words—otherwise known as intonation. Consider the following sentence:

"Come here right now."

Now imagine that sentence uttered by your parent, boss, friend, or lover. The stress on each particular word in the sentence, as well as the hardness or softness of that person's voice will tell you how they are feeling when they say that sentence.

No one ever says, "Don't use that voice with me, Missy," but they do say, "Don't use that tone." Tone changes—voice should not. That is why emoticons are so popular: Because written digital text can be so flat and devoid of tone, we've resorted to using graphic smiley faces to communicate what we truly mean.

It is doubtful, however, that your brand can use emoticons, as it would probably be considered unprofessional in certain contexts. The articulation of your brand comes down to your voice and tone. How do you define and use your voice and tone within your organization?

DEFINING YOUR VOICE

First, we want to pick a human voice. We're not robots speaking to people with dictionaries. When you create content that speaks human to people, you ignite real conversations, not boring exchanges of information that go nowhere for either party. "The human voice is unmistakably genuine. It can't be faked" (Hay, 2013). People know when there is another person at the other end of the communication. They are not fooled by corporate speak and business lingo. They want transparency, reality, and solid interaction. As Steph Hay, a content strategist, points out, "being real builds trust" (Hay, 2013).

So decide now—your voice will be human. There are many types of human voices. So which one is yours?

Picking your voice comes from your identity pillars, from within your industry, as well as how you want to position yourself against your competitors. Kate Kiefer Lee, a voice and tone expert, provides four excellent questions to ask when trying to define your company's voice (Kiefer Lee, 2012):

- What does your company do?
- Why do people visit your website? (Why do they interact with your content?)

- If your brand were a person, how would you describe him or her?

- How do you want people to feel when they visit your site?

Once you answer these questions, look back at the card sorting exercise you did, or the bullet points of adjectives you used to describe your brand. Be careful to also look at how you didn't want your brand described. That will give you some ideas of how to define your brand's voice:

- Educational but not preachy

- Expert but not cold

- Reliable but not boring

- Fashionable but not flaky

- Fun but not over the top

- Relatable but not inappropriate

- Serious but not stodgy

When you have those broad definitions, you can start to determine your brand's voice—the expression of your brand's personality. Once you know the brand voice, "Create voice guidelines that fit into your company's culture. Keep in mind that just like a human's voice, your brand's voice will adapt and mature over time. Creating flexible voice guidelines makes it easy to revise and tweak them when the time is right" (Kiefer Lee, 2012).

DEFINING YOUR TONE

Tone is how you sound in different situations. Your brand can be fun, but if a customer is annoyed, a cheeky email that may come across as cute in one situation may be a major turnoff in another. Tone is so important for brands that you need to think through this part critically.

Your tone should be adjusted based on the conversation and where your customer is in the customer loop. That's why you should plot tone to the customer loop, content formats, your different personas, distribution channels, and identity pillars.

This obviously takes a lot of time and thought, but like all our processes, it's an iterative one. My one guiding rule is—when in doubt, leave it out. So even if your brand is fun, but you're communicating about an order gone wrong, try to keep it approachable and empathetic. In other words, don't say, "Hey, we're sorry, but we like totally lost your order and are still looking through our shipping system for it." Instead, you should say, "We apologize, but it seems we lost your order. We would like to give you two options: Place the order again and we'll pay the shipping charge OR cancel the order now." Meaning, if your tone doesn't change to accommodate your audience's need at the time they engage with your content, then you come across as unfeeling—something you NEVER want.

As an example, let's consider Zappos.com, the online retailer. Zappos has developed a fun, lighthearted approach for its content. When you order a product, you receive an email congratulating you on your good taste. When you want to return something, their service is impeccable, which is one of their identity pillars—they *stand* for excellent customer service. Their return policy's voice is still light, yet the tone is a tad more serious than the rest of the site:

> Unlike many other web sites that have special rules and lots of fine print, Zappos.com offers free shipping on all domestic orders placed on our website, with no minimum order sizes or special exceptions.
>
> Just because shipping is free doesn't mean it should take a long time. Zappos.com understands that getting your items quickly is important to you, so we make every effort to process your order quickly. When you order from our website, you can expect to receive your order within 4-5 business days.
>
> (Zappos.com, 2013)

While Zappos wants to be casual, they also understand that sometimes they need to be direct and formal. That's a great example of adjusting tone—*you shift how you sound based on the situation.*

GOGO—GETTING VOICE AND TONE RIGHT

Gogo In-flight Internet is a company that has nailed voice and tone. Their voice is fun and conversational; after all, they sell Internet access on airplanes, so they know they are dealing with a certain persona. It doesn't matter if the customer is a business traveler, someone looking to stream a movie, or someone who's checking on an auction on Ebay—their customers want strong, reliable Internet access 10,000 feet up in the air.

See how they describe their service:

Is Gogo fast? Is the sky blue? The Gogo experience is best compared to mobile broadband service on the ground—except with a whole lot more altitude. All you need is a Wi-Fi enabled device, a Gogo account, and a burning desire to access exclusive in-air experiences available only on Gogo.

Phrases like "is the sky blue" and "a burning desire" inject typical prose with some brand personality. They're telling their customer audience: We're passionate about delivering a fantastic in-air Internet experience and we're cool enough to be friends with you.

Look at how they express their brand's history (Figure 7.2).

On Gogo's Facebook page, they feature the following mix of content:

- Contests to win Bluetooth speakers
- The Gogo bear who asks you about your weekend flying plans
- Updates about weather that may affect flights

Figure 7.2 Gogo's history page conveys its brand by its cool, fun, yet informative tone.

But, when they are answering a potential complaint, look at how they manage their tone:

Thanks for taking time to submit your feedback. We appreciate your help and look into each report we receive. While we cannot guarantee a response, we can assure you that the report will be read and investigated.

While they're still kind and friendly, they know people may be angry when contacting them. They keep their tone even, letting customers know they may not receive a response right away (or ever). That is honesty—they are setting an expectation, so that customers who are not contacted cannot say they were not warned.

THE PAYOFF OF FRAMING

I know framing seems like an intense amount of work. However, nothing will help you build a reliable set of content assets more than framing your content. After all, the key to wearing the digital crown is engagement and all of the tools we described—identity pillars, messaging architecture, and voice and tone—will guide you in creating engaging, robust, personable content.

We will talk more about how to use your identity pillars, messaging architecture, and voice and tone guidelines to help frame **design** in Chapter 11.

For now, let's focus on some final items about content framing.

HOW DO WE EXPRESS THESE GUIDELINES?

We want to be very clear within our style guide and other training manuals about voice and tone. Here is a brief I once received about voice and tone:

"Overall, the tone needs to be confident, convincing and inspiring. Additionally, it should convey a tone of comfort and compassion (and discretion)."

How exactly was I, the writer, supposed to interpret that? There were no examples to go along with the direction. How is one inspiring and comforting and compassionate and discrete? What does *overall* mean? Does that mean that sometimes I can break from tone?

Again, it's best to give examples of what you *are* and also provide your content creators with a list of adjectives that describe what you *are not*. No one in the organization is going to absorb this material by osmosis. Therefore, you must train your content creators, customer service reps, and others to follow voice and tone guidelines.

Where Should These Guidelines Live?

Most content professionals will advocate for a shared, centralized style guide where all of this information lives, accessible by anyone who touches content within your organization. We'll talk more about shared style guides in Rule #5.

Who Owns the Content Framing?

Hopefully, you have Captain Content within your organization who owns the content framing. You may have a content strategist on staff, or it may even be the responsibility of the Director of Communications and/or Marketing. In either case, make sure someone owns it, because if no one does, it will quickly become out of date and unreliable.

How Often Should We Review Our Content Frames?

Reviewing framing should happen once a year or more frequently if business objectives shift. When your team uses these tools on an everyday basis, it will be easy to know when they need to be updated or changed.

SUMMARY

Framing your content means defining and creating three major characteristics that will help define your brand so you can communicate effectively with your audiences: Identity Pillars, Messaging Architecture, and Voice and Tone. Without clear documentation about who you are, the priorities of your messaging and how you represent your brand to the outside world (a solid frame), your content will begin to crumble. Creating a framework provides structure that will meet your business goals, ensure consistency of messaging, and get the right voice and tone for each and every piece of content.

Now we're going to talk about more tools you can use for your content, but these tools focus on how to establish a concrete content publishing *process*—a content strategy.

REFERENCES

Bloomstein, M. (2012). *Content strategy at work real-world stories to strengthen every interactive project*. Waltham, MA: Morgan Kaufmann, p. 25.

Hay, S. (2013). *Being real builds trust*. http://www.uie.com/articles/being_real.

Jakobson, L. (2011). *The Ritz-Carlton tops luxury hotel guest satisfaction survey*. http://www.incentivemag.com/article.aspx?id=7399.

Kiefer Lee, K. (2012). *Tone and voice: Showing your users that you care*. http://uxmag.com/articles/tone-and-voice-showing-your-users-that-you-care.

Zappos.com. (2013). Retrieved from http://www.zappos.com/shipping-and-returns. Accessed 30.01.13.

CHAPTER 8

We are going to continue to explore the details of how to set up a publishing system for content in your organization. As we have learned, there are two major challenges around content. One is getting the right information to the right people to create the right kinds of content. The second challenge involves publishing the content itself and keeping it fresh and consistent. We can solve both challenges by implementing a content strategy.

THINKING LIKE A PUBLISHER

If you are in business today and you own digital property, such as a website, blog, or social media channel, you are a publisher. Even if you don't publish anything on actual paper that's distributed to people, you're a publisher. You are responsible for keeping that digital property up to date with relevant information about your business.

Being a publisher requires thinking differently about information. Publishers know they need to inform, surprise, inspire, and educate people so they return to their publications. You may feel that you don't even know where to start with thinking about your organization as a publishing entity.

Content strategy solves that challenge. To understand how to think, communicate, and produce content like a publisher, you need to understand content strategy. It is the how, when, what, and who of the content equation. A strategy is a set of tactics you use to achieve a goal, or as Diana Railton, a content strategist, says, "A carefully worked plan of action to meet one or more goals" (Railton, personal communication). Your goal is to manage your content so that it speaks to your audiences and helps you reach your achievement threshold.

Content strategy is a system designed to help your organization manage its content assets. How do you create, update, and manage all of it—the product descriptions, forms, bios, whitepapers, videos, podcasts, position descriptions, and so on?

A content strategy lifecycle provides guidance about how to publish content according to a system. We move through each step to manage the lifecycle of our content, similar to following the steps of a recipe. Content strategy provides guidelines for actual management of content within an organization—how information becomes content and is distributed to your target audiences.

Many creative people balk at systems and are even offended by the suggestion that they need them. They feel they have more freedom without the structure of a system or strategy. They couldn't be more wrong.

Systems allow for freedom, they don't stifle it. By building in workflows and reviews, you create a structure of consistency around your conversations with your audience. This structure benefits both your internal process and your business objectives. It also lessens the tensions inherent in any development process. When everyone agrees to a process, knows their stage, their role, and the roles of others within it, they are less nervous about their own work and they appreciate the teamwork. Content is a big job regardless of the size of your organization.

Now that you know to whom you're talking, as we learned in Chapter 6, and who *you* are, as we learned in Chapter 7, we're going to focus on aligning your internal teams so they publish content using a repeatable lifecycle (always keeping in mind Rule #3: Keep it Iterative). You're already walking into the planning phase armed with three major tools you need for content strategy: customer identity profiles, identity pillars, and messaging architecture.

> Create a structure of consistency around your conversations. You and your audience will benefit.

READY TO EXECUTE

At every step in the content strategy process we need to look at those personas we tacked on to our conference room wall and remember that we are creating content to reach them. Here is a good way to keep that in mind: using the content strategy graphic (Figure 8.1) as a guide, use this chart that lists one or two critical questions to answer at each stage.

Phase	Questions
Plan	What does my audience need to know? What goals are we trying to meet?
Create	What are the best content formats to get those messages across to them?
Publish	What technology platforms make the most sense? What online publishing tools do we use?
Distribute	Which social media tools do we use?
Analyze	How did we do? Can we do better?
Govern (Central to the entire process)	How are we caring for our brand across the web and within the ecosystem of content in our organizations? Are we consistent? Are we up to date?

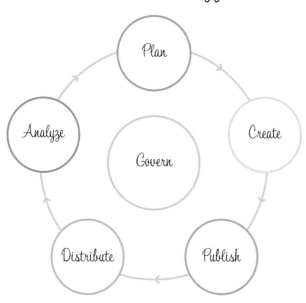

Figure 8.1 The lifecycle of content strategy. Ahava Leibtag. All Rights Reserved.

All of those questions focus on your audiences, their needs, and their responses to your information expressed as content.

FOCUS ON THE TOOLS IN THE BOX

For this chapter, I've chosen to focus on the tools a content strategist uses within each phase of the lifecycle. The reason for this is twofold:

1. *Trust the process*: Content strategy is a never-ending, constantly evolving practice. But just as a surgeon has some basic techniques he uses every day in the operating room and a dancer learns the basic steps and then adds variety to spice up routines, so, too, content professionals must trust the basic process of content strategy. Trusting the process means learning what the tools are, what they do, and how to use them effectively on a daily basis. Great content professionals also know how to adapt these tools for each project.

2. *Focus on the tools, not the deliverables*: So much of today's business world is focused on deliverables (work you can hand off to a client or use internally as a guide), particularly if you're a consultant. Content strategy is indeed a consultative practice, and the tools we're going

to talk about in this chapter *can* double as deliverables. But don't fall into the trap of thinking that because you've finished the deliverable, the work is done. The process of content strategy is designed as a cycle that you keep improving. So rather than thinking of them as end deliverables, think of them as tools in your toolkit.

So let's talk tools. You'll use tools in each of the stages: Plan, Create, Publish, Distribute, and Analyze. Then, in Rule #5, we'll talk in depth about why governance is the center of any content strategy lifecycle. In that rule, we'll also talk about the tools you can use to keep your brand consistent, regardless of the channel on which your audience finds your content.

FRAMEWORK: PEOPLE, PROCESS, TECHNOLOGY

Content strategy helps you manage the intersection of people, process, and technology when it comes to publishing content within your organization (Figure 8.2). All of the tools we'll discuss exist within this overlapping framework. Managing these tools efficiently means processing all of the information you have about your own company's talent, business cycles, and what types of technologies will help you create, publish, manage, and update content.

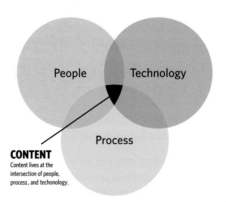

Figure 8.2 Content is at the intersection of people, process, and technology.

Note: This is by no means an exhaustive list—there are entire books that focus on content strategy. Rather, this is a list of the basic tools every organization must master to keep on top of their content. Here is how Shelley Bowen, a content strategist, shows the potential deliverables and tools for a content strategy (Bowen) (Figure 8.3).

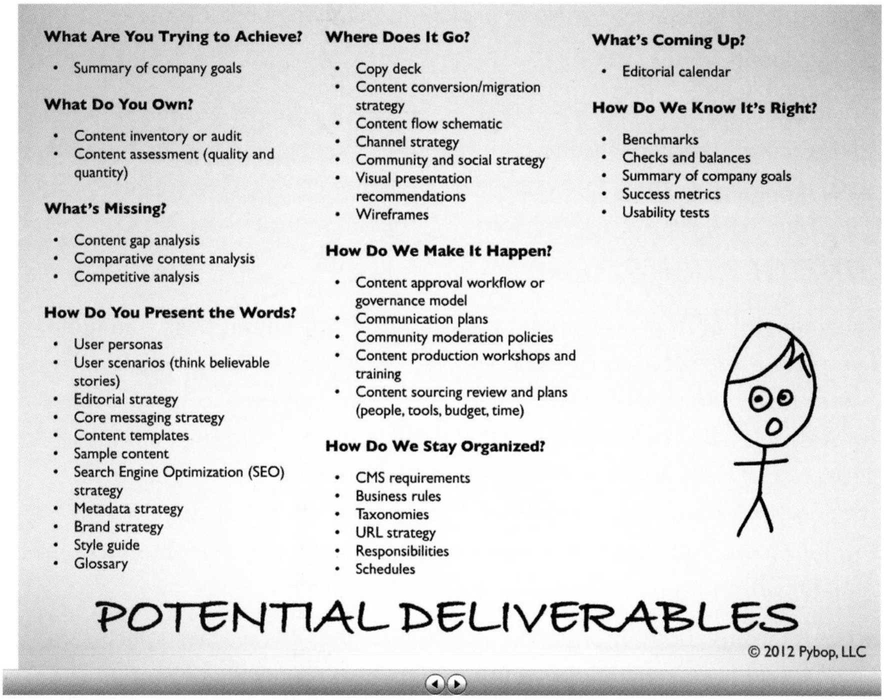

What Are You Trying to Achieve?

- Summary of company goals

What Do You Own?

- Content inventory or audit
- Content assessment (quality and quantity)

What's Missing?

- Content gap analysis
- Comparative content analysis
- Competitive analysis

How Do You Present the Words?

- User personas
- User scenarios (think believable stories)
- Editorial strategy
- Core messaging strategy
- Content templates
- Sample content
- Search Engine Optimization (SEO) strategy
- Metadata strategy
- Brand strategy
- Style guide
- Glossary

Where Does It Go?

- Copy deck
- Content conversion/migration strategy
- Content flow schematic
- Channel strategy
- Community and social strategy
- Visual presentation recommendations
- Wireframes

How Do We Make It Happen?

- Content approval workflow or governance model
- Communication plans
- Community moderation policies
- Content production workshops and training
- Content sourcing review and plans (people, tools, budget, time)

How Do We Stay Organized?

- CMS requirements
- Business rules
- Taxonomies
- URL strategy
- Responsibilities
- Schedules

What's Coming Up?

- Editorial calendar

How Do We Know It's Right?

- Benchmarks
- Checks and balances
- Summary of company goals
- Success metrics
- Usability tests

POTENTIAL DELIVERABLES

© 2012 Pybop, LLC

Figure 8.3 "Potential Content Strategy Deliverables" by Shelley Bowen, 2012 ©Pybob, LLC.

CONTENT STRATEGY: TOOLS YOU CAN USE

Take a look—here is a brief overview of the types of tools you need to use at each phase of the process.

Phase	Tools
Plan	Personas, messaging architectures, identity pillars, content audits, centralized style guides, content usability testing, competitive analysis
Create	Editorial guidelines, goal matrix, style guides
Publish	Editorial calendars, workflows, publishing guidelines, CMS documentation, archiving guidelines
Distribute	Channel mapping, social media guidelines, recommended character guidelines, best practices for content types posted on different social media channels
Analyze	Analytics reports, engagement metrics, site search analytics (SSA)

Now let's dig deeper.

PLAN

When you plan your content, the magic begins. This is exciting, because it's the starting point of a step-by-step process that moves you forward so that you can achieve your goals.

There are four tools we're going to explore in the plan phase:

- Content Audits
- Centralized Style Guides
- Content Usability Testing
- Competitive Analysis

CONTENT AUDITS

Marcy Jacobs, a UX professional in Washington, DC, says it best: "Imagine if you had every piece of clothing you've ever worn in your entire life in one closet, the size of a small room. Every shoe, every accessory, even clothes you've borrowed from others. How would you organize all those pieces of clothing? By size? By age? By event? This isn't a museum of the clothing you've worn your entire life. So can you get rid of some of this clothing? You're probably not wearing size 3T anymore" (Jacobs, personal communication).

Jacobs is talking about information architecture (IA)—the way we structure the back-end file system of our websites so that we organize our content in an intuitive way for our audiences (Figure 8.4). But her point is that before we do anything on our digital properties, we need to know what we already have. You may not want to keep your first pair of shoes, but you may find a nice tie from 2006 you completely forgot you had that is still in style.

Here is another way of putting it—Lou Rosenfeld is a recognized authority on information architecture and defines it as:

1. The combination of organization, labeling, and navigation schemes within an information system.

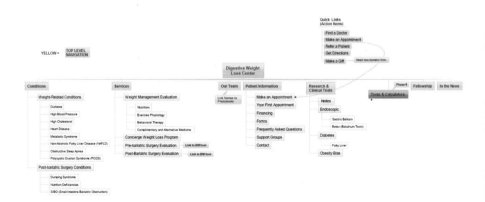

Figure 8.4 An example of an information architecture, a visual depiction of the back end file organization of a website.

2. The structural design of an information space to facilitate task completion and intuitive access to content.

3. The art and science of structuring and classifying websites and intranets to help people find and manage information (Morville, 2012).

So, before you organize all the shared content assets of your organization, you need to inventory them.

Why Do a Content Audit?

I'm not going to sugar-coat this. Content audits can be mind-numbingly boring and time consuming. They require an incredible amount of patience and curiosity. Someone has to look at the content with a fresh eye and suspend judgment because any findings from the auditing stage will be the foundation of all conversations regarding the future of the content.

However, content audits are essential—not just important or nice to do. I can't emphasize this enough. You just cannot know what you have unless you go through it piece by piece, format by format. You may be able to automate some of this process (there are tools out there), but at the end you need to know:

*   How much content you have
*   Where the content lives
*   If the content is relevant

Chris Detzi, an information architect, describes four reasons to perform a content audit (Detzi, 2012):

1. *Reveal* the true scale of the website's content

2. *Clarify* and refine the project scope

3. *Facilitate* strategic discussions about design objectives and direction

4. *Establish* a common language for the team to use throughout the project

What Type of Audit Should You Do?

If you are truly auditing all the content assets of an organization, you need to look at all of their digital properties—not just their website. There are five types of audits:

1. *Quantitative audit*: This results in a basic list of the content on your site, including URLs, page titles, and downloadable documents. This is really an inventory of the content on your digital properties.

2. *Qualitative audit*: A more in-depth accounting of the content, including an analysis of the writing, multimedia, accuracy of the content, value for the organization, etc.

3. *Mapping audit*: Mapping allows you to see the content you have, visually, in the form of a site tree. It looks very much like an information architecture, but allows you to see the relationship that different pieces of

content have to each other. It also gives you a sense of how deep the site is and therefore how layered the content is (Leibtag, 2010).

4. *Rolling audit*: These audits never end—meaning you're always auditing some digital property to know what you have and what is being added. The best way to perform rolling audits is to pick a part of the site and then audit it until you have finished. Then move on to another digital property or part of the site. When you get back to the beginning, you start again. (Have you noticed yet the inherent circular theme within content strategy?) "The benefit of a rolling audit is that more content gets looked at, in a more careful manner, more often" (Halvorson & Rach, 2012).

5. *Thin slice audit*: Matthew Grocki, a content strategist, recommends doing this type of audit to break a large site down by sections. By auditing some of the pages, you get a "thin slice" view of the content in that section.

With a quantitative audit, you can see how much content there is on the organization's digital properties. When you do a qualitative audit, you can get a sense of the quality of the content. With a map, you can see the relationship the different pages have to each other. The content mapping audit process works well when you need to make a case for creating new content or for changing certain parts of the IA.

Picking the right type of audit to perform is not something you should agonize over. There's no time for paralysis through analysis. Time and budget often dictate which one you should perform, but you must know as much as you can about the content so that you can know how to change it or make it better.

Another Way: Multidimensional Content Audits

You may want to think about combining types of audits to reveal information that, combined, gives your stakeholders a true taste of the current state of your content.

Instead of spreadsheets that list your content, this type of audit is a multidimensional group of documents that help tell a story—not just about what you have, but its performance in the outside world. Consider the following types of multidimensional content audits:

Multidimensional content audits help to tell a story about how content is living in the outside world.

- *Combine your analytics and content audits* in a spreadsheet so you can sort according to information architecture (IA) order or by page views.

- *Pull interesting notes* from your analytics and display those in graphical format: peak user times, top pages by entrance and exit, whole sections that are ignored.

- *Have your developers count the number* of design templates or databases you are using.

- *Request information from the call center* about the top 10 issues or concerns they deal with on a daily basis and look at the analytics for that content.

- *Compare your mobile analytics with your desktop analytics* to see if there are major differences in the way people consume your content using different platforms.
- *Count the top types of content that are used.* For example, does video score high? Audio? Downloadable PDFs?

The goal of collecting this data is to inform your decisions. Having multidimensional content audits will help you move forward in your content strategy efforts. Why? Because you need to be able to tell a story.

Showing clients, or your C-suite, a content inventory spreadsheet is never enough—they need a visual representation to better understand how much content they have and how the content is performing. You can see an example of an audit I performed for an international information technology supplier in Figure 8.5. I wanted to graphically represent how each page performed by merging Google Analytics information into the audit. Building a story for the client of how content performed was important for explaining why they needed different types of content formats (more videos, fewer whitepapers).

Key:
Peach = Advanced Services (1)
Green = Other Services (2)
Blue = Technical Services (3)
Major Services
Sub Service
Top 25 pages

#	Page ID	Page Rank		URL	Content types	Notes	Business Model	User Goals
1	0.0	4	Home					
2	1.0	7	**Advanced Services**	URL HERE	PDF	flash piece and 3 callouts at bottom: cloud, unified communication services		
				URL HERE				
3	1.2.1		**Application Management**	URL HERE	data sheet, at a glance			
4	1.2.2		Services Literature	URL HERE	3 PDFs--repeats of before			
				URL HERE				
5	1.3.1		**Carrier Ethernet Services**	URL HERE	PDF at top, 2 videos	a lot of paragraphs with no CTA then at bottom operate		
6	1.3.2		Services Literature	URL HERE				
				URL HERE				
7	1.4.1		**Customer Care Services**	URL HERE	8 PDFs			
8	1.4.2		Services Literature	URL HERE	same material repeated			
				URL HERE				
9	1.5.1		**Data Center Services**	URL HERE				
10	1.5.2		IT Infrastructure and Deployment Services	URL HERE	13 links to subservices and crosservices			
11	1.5.3		Business Continuity Planning	URL HERE	Data Sheet repeated on			
12	1.5.4		Services Literature	URL HERE	Data Sheet			
13	1.5.5		Data Center Migration Services	URL HERE	PDF			
14	1.5.6		Services Literature	URL HERE	same PDF as above			
				URL HERE				
15	1.6.1		**Data Center Testing Service**	URL HERE		link to data zone and other data management service		
16	1.6.2		Services Literature	URL HERE		there is no link to this page from the "parent" page		
				URL HERE				
17	1.7.1		**Data Center Switching Services**	URL HERE	1 PDF	4 links, 1 not highlighted to other related services		
18	1.7.2		Services Literature	URL HERE	5 PDFs			
				URL HERE				

Figure 8.5 Multidimensional content audit representing how each page performed. Ahava Leibtag.

Do I Really Need to Audit the Entire Site?

If you need to save time, or you are running a content strategy pilot project, you can use the 80/20 rule when it comes to content; that is, 80% of your traffic comes from 20% of your pages. Examining those top pages will reveal some important facts:

- What are your hardest working pages and how can you improve them?
- Are there any noticeable traffic patterns that reveal weaker pages?
- Are the owners of these pages keeping the content up-to-date and relevant?

You can also use a representative sample of your content to get a better understanding of it without auditing everything. What size sample is appropriate? There are some suggested sample sizes depending on how large your site is and how many pages or chunks of content you have, but I would recommend considering the following before deciding how much of the content to audit:

- How much time you have
- Your budget
- If you can automate any of the process and still get the information you need
- The level of detail you want
- How much you think your client already knows about the audience

Use the Content Audit Wisely

The content audit is the basis of your roadmap. It tells you what you have, not what you should do. But, once you've spent the human and other resources creating it, it pays to think carefully about how you use it. Detzi describes how content audits can help facilitate discussions about the plans for content:

- "Is all of this content still relevant? What business, customer, or employee need does it support?
- What new content must be created in the coming months? What's driving those needs?
- What drove decisions about file types and/or variations in format that exist? Do these decisions still hold?" (Detzi)

Your content audit will be used to focus on priorities. This will shape the conversations about how to create and manage content in the best way to develop solid, lasting relationships with your target audiences.

Go into the audit process knowing why you are doing it and what you hope to get out of it. This will help shape the way you ultimately deliver the information to your team. When presenting the results of audits, it helps to make the reports as visual as possible, accompanied by text.

More important, though, are the *conversations* you have with the others on your team, with the stakeholders, or with the C-suite, about the findings. Sometimes, stakeholders really have no idea what content exists or what may not be performing well. A content audit is the perfect time to pull the veil away and expose the reality of the current situation: The content may be messy, out of date, inconsistent, or the worst—just plain confusing.

CENTRALIZED STYLE GUIDE

Many content strategists would argue that a centralized style guide—a guide that encompasses your personas, messaging, editorial guidelines, and styles for both design and content is a tool that we should talk about when discussing governance. I would argue that because governance is central to the content strategy process, a style guide needs to also be a part of the *planning* process, because it sets the stage for what you're really trying to say, who you are trying to say it to, how to listen, and how to respond.

We will learn how to build a great style guide in Rule #5, but do include it in your planning process. Your content will be stronger for it.

CONTENT TESTING

Would you ever launch a product without detailed product testing? And yet every day, millions of pieces of content are published online without ever being tested by audiences. Why do we do this?

Well, one reason is that it is so easy to publish content now. The second reason is that for a decade, the web world was so focused on design, that content was often ignored. Now that we've realized content is king, we need to get back to testing our content.

I've tested content many times and I'm always astounded by what I learn. You will be too. Content testing should include:

- *Goals*: What are we trying to uncover by testing the content?
- *Participants*: Find members who represent your target audiences.
- *Scripts*: Distribute the scripts throughout your team, and ask for feedback, so you know you are asking the right questions.
- *Usability software*: There are many versions you can purchase. Now with web cams in almost every computer, you can easily film your participants using and interacting with the content.
- *Reporting mechanism*: Your findings should be distributed within your group. Most importantly, use the findings to shape your planning process with content.

Content Testing Case Study

Working with an international powerhouse medical institution like Johns Hopkins Medicine can be daunting: Trying to get the medical minds to agree on the content of the medical system's website is incredibly challenging.

When tasked with testing whether the website was effective, our team (Aaron Watkins, Director of E-Strategy at Johns Hopkins Medicine, and Ahava Leibtag) decided to focus on testing the content, instead of testing the site itself. Testing actual content would enable us to convince the stakeholders that less content might actually be more—a tough sell for academic medical professionals whose careers depend on publish, publish, publish.

So while a usability test may have focused on completing tasks while interacting with the interface, for content testing we wanted answers to the following:

- Can users find the content they need?

- Can they read the content? (Was the font size large enough?)

- Can they understand the content?

- Will they act on the content?

- Will they share the content?

These questions seem simple, but required a sophisticated framework for testing individual users. How do we answer the above questions in a reliable and methodical way? How do we avoid asking customers if they like content but instead focus on the following questions:

1. How relevant do you find the content?

2. Will you act on the information from the content?

3. Did you find this content useful to you?

Our team tested at several locations and watched in person or via webcam as people went through the website and attempted to answer a set of questions. Some of our findings were incredibly revealing, including that people *who did not watch* an online video got the answers right more often than those who did watch it.

Some lessons learned from the experience include:

- *Use an iterative approach*: Test, fix, and test again until you are sure your content satisfies the majority of your audience(s)

- *Pick the right content to test*: Pick areas of the site to test that are business critical and user experience critical

- *Know who you are testing*: Clearly define your customer groups

- *Use moderated usability testing*: Have a person directing the test instead of using automated software to test content

- *Test the content, not the person*: Make it clear you are testing the content, not the customer

- *Use the testing opportunity wisely*: Find out everything you can about how your customers understand and integrate the content into their thinking (Leibtag and Watkins, 2011)

COMPETITIVE ANALYSIS

A competitive analysis is important when you are planning your content because it will help you discover what types of content your competitors produce, as well as their levels of engagement with their audiences. On a high-level, it gives you the lay of the land as well as the market context.

Some questions you may want to ask about the competitors' sites:

- How up-to-date is their content?
- Do they interact on social media channels?
- Do they have a mobile website or any mobile apps?
- Are they doing things we should be doing?

Jason Withrow, a user experience expert, recommends breaking up the competitive analysis by content and functionality: "Broadly speaking, content refers to informational pages while functionality is what users can do while they are at the website" (Withrow, 2006). In other words, Withrow is defining content as information, while functionality refers to interactive forms that customers use to complete or further a task, such as making an airline reservation or buying a product.

Use a high-level inventory to demonstrate what information and functionality your competitors have. This will help open up new conversations surrounding your competitors' offerings, as well as what you can and want to offer in the way of content and functionality.

Beware, however, of the "Ooh, they're doing it, we have to do it too!" syndrome. I've been on projects where we were moving in one direction and because a competitor launched something new we suddenly changed course.

This is not a good idea—ever. Here's why:

Once you have done the heavy lifting we've described in the past two chapters, you should not change course just because of a competitor. Who says they're doing it right? You do not have access to their data—therefore, you cannot make decisions based on their content moves. Their strategy is based on a problem they are trying to solve for—let's say it's X. Your strategy is based on trying to solve for Y. Knowing what content and functionality your competitors offer does help keep you on top of any content innovations within your industry. If it makes sense to create something similar because it helps you solve for Y, then by all means, approach it strategically. But, remember, you are not a butterfly. You don't have to change the color of your wings to mimic the competition. To keep up to date in your industry, perform at least one competitive analysis each year (Figure 8.6).

II. ▨ Competitors at a Glance

Competitor	Clicks from home page	Multimedia	Content	Physician entries	Patient testimonials	Contact info and directions
▨	1	Some, but buried. There is a lack of photos.	A lot of good content. The organization is around diseases and treatments—currently the best practice.	Yes, bios are available, although an extra click away.	Some, in videos, but not highly visible.	On some pages and in some centers.
	1	Yes, pictures are used on almost every page. But no videos.	Content is robust and relational; meaning that on a condition page you can find the name of a treating physician and related treatment information.	Find a cardiologist is similar to ▨ form. There are pictures and bios but they are not arranged in a list—rather they are connected to the condition.	Yes, there are quite a few, and that menu option is high-level.	The main number is listed at the bottom and numbers are listed along with physicians' bios, but there is no main heart number.
	1	1 video and 1 podcast. Photo galleries in some sections.	A lot of robust, well-written content.	Not posted in a visible place—can use their standard database.	Yes, a central part of the campaign.	Obvious.
	4	Yes.	Robust content, detailing almost all aspects of their services.	No bio or picture. Just contact information.	Yes.	Yes, contact information listed on the right hand.
	2	Yes, and all posted in one place.	A lot of content—some of it is very patient focused, some not.	Physician Leadership bios and pictures posted.	None.	Yes, on top of every page.
	2	Tons of pictures, multimedia, and calculators.	Content is organized according to patients' thought processes.	Annoying databases, but they are there.	6 in different treatment areas.	Tons of calls to action all over the pages.

Figure 8.6 An example of a competitive landscape analysis. In this case, there was a comparison of content, as well as other issues important to competition.

CREATE

Creating content is fun—often it's the part of the process that teams enjoy the most. However, creating content requires patience and the ability to break down the silos that hold the information you need to create great content.

The following tools will help you:

- Goal Matrix
- Editorial Guidelines and Style Guide

GOAL MATRIX

Often the best place to start when creating content is with the *format* of the content: written, visual, multimedia, interactive, or some other type. (For a reminder of different content formats, revisit Chapter 3.) Once you know what content formats you need to create, you can select the right person or groups of people on your team who are experts in creating those.

If you are producing different content formats, have a short but sweet list to let everyone involved in production know the goals of this piece of content and what part it plays in the big content picture.

Content Goals Matrix	
For which persona or audience?	*Primary Persona*: Sporadic Shopper *Specifically*: Customers who haven't visited the site in two months
Content Format?	Written/Email blast
Goal?	Inform these customers they are eligible for a 20% savings coupon
Author?	Name of person
Call to Action?	Visit the site and use the coupon

Using a simple form like this for every content format will help the entire team refine clear goals for each piece of content. It will also train them to start thinking about creating content for *people*, rather than to just create and publish.

EDITORIAL GUIDELINES AND STYLE GUIDE

Your editorial guidelines should be a part of your style guide. Depending on how distributed your content workforce is (meaning do they sit outside central web, marketing, and digital communications functions?) it is going to be hard to align everyone with a huge style guide that encompasses branding, design, voice, and tone.

You may have hundreds of writers, or even assembly line content posters (the people who change phone numbers, publish parking information, and change bios) throughout your global organization. So make sure you select the elements that really matter and create checkpoints to ensure your content workforce is following those. I cannot emphasize how important training is to your governance endeavors: Training those and other CMS authors will keep your content consistent.

PUBLISH

Publishing content means getting it out into the world. There are many tools you can use during the publish phase:

- Editorial Calendars
- Workflows or Publishing Guidelines
- CMS Documentation
- Archiving Guidelines

EDITORIAL CALENDARS

Editorial calendars are incredibly important for the planning process. However, they really belong here, in the publish phase, because they dictate when you will publish content.

You can use many different types of editorial calendars; there are some great software programs out there. Or you can just use a shared Google doc. However you decide to update your editorial calendar, make sure only certain people can edit it, but that many people can view it. This will encourage a cultural mindset to work from an editorial calendar. You editorial calendar should include:

- Post date
- Author, Editor, and Publisher
- Tentative title
- Keywords
- Categories or Type of Content
- Tags
- Call to action
- Status (Linn, 2010)

WORKFLOWS OR PUBLISHING GUIDELINES

Workflow includes how content is planned, created, published, and distributed. That means you need the right talent in the right roles. The best way to handle workflow is to sketch out how the workflow currently operates. For example, try filling in the following chart:

Role	Definition	Who?
Requestors	The person that requests that this piece of content be created	
Providers	The sources of the factual information behind the building of the content	
Creators	The creators of the content. Can be authors, videographers, graphic designers, etc.	
Editors	The people who make sure that the content is factually correct and follows brand and editorial guidelines	
Approvers	The people who approve the content—could be legal or subject matter experts	
Publishers	The people responsible for publishing the content	
Audience Engagement (Social Media) Managers	The people who manage the distribution of content on different channels and engage with the audience regarding the content	
Analyzers	The people who review data regarding the content to inform the team at a later date. Remember to pick metrics that measure the right data so you can use that to make better decisions about your entire content process	

Once you know what the current workflow looks like, you need to ask:

- Do we have the right talent within the organization or do we need to hire new talent?

- Are the content professionals on staff equipped with the right skills or do they need further training?

- Would outside consultants, writers, editors, or videographers make sense for specific projects?

Examining these issues is critical to understanding how to establish a successful content strategy.

You may already have the right staff, but the wrong talent in the wrong roles. For example, a writer may have been pushed into a project manager position because she showed an aptitude for keeping people on schedule. However, she really wants to write, so she pays too much attention to the creation phase of the content, instead of focusing on the management of the project. There are hundreds of other examples of these types of workflow issues. We will discuss workflow more in Rule #6.

Workflow takes a long time to examine, analyze, switch, and get right. That's okay. Finding the right people for each role is critical: It will take patience and effort. But once you have a well-functioning, well-oiled machine, you'll see how it really makes execution seem effortless.

CMS DOCUMENTATION

We talked about CMS authoring in Chapter 4. Giving instructions to your CMS authors and the people responsible for posting the content is a little bit like paint by the numbers. You may not feel like this is your most "creative" activity, but then again it isn't supposed to be. Remember, our goal is a unified brand personality regardless of which channel our audience finds us on. By giving clear and explicit instructions about display, editorial guidelines, and SEO within the CMS, you will accomplish that goal. Again, this is a place where training is vital so people can master the necessary skills.

ARCHIVING GUIDELINES

When you publish a piece of content, program your CMS to take it down or move it into archives at a certain date. Or, create once a year reviews for content owners so they know that by a certain date they need to review the content and make changes or it will be archived. When they are faced with the possibility of their content disappearing, most content creators pay attention.

DISTRIBUTE

We talked a lot about distribution in Chapter 5. There are important distribution tools you can use, including:

- Channel Mapping
- Policies and Guidelines

CHANNEL MAPPING

"When you take a close look at all of the channel connections and user relationships, you are able to better focus future content efforts—avoiding duplication and improving the overall user experience" (Halvorson & Rach, 2012). Meaning, don't say the same thing on every channel. Instead, understand who is hanging out around that particular watering hole and tailor the content for them.

Your message should never CHANGE for a channel. Rather, it should adapt for it, and you should let your personas serve as a guide. If you've determined that your personas spend more time on Facebook than Twitter, then you should modify your messages for Facebook. Take advantage of the potential that each channel gives you.

POLICIES AND GUIDELINES FOR DISTRIBUTION (SOCIAL MEDIA)

You only have to read a couple of horror stories about social media and audience engagement gone wrong to be convinced that you must have social media policies and guidelines for both your internal teams and your audience. Let's call them audience engagement policies and guidelines from here on in.

If your teams aren't trained in how to create these very important documents, and if you don't have attorneys reviewing your plans and perhaps even involved when it is happening, you are going to look terrible—in a very public space. So ensure there are clear audience engagement policies and guidelines in place and that they are posted. Ensure it is clear how you will handle negative or potentially problematic conversations.

ANALYZE

You need to understand how your content is performing *now* before you can make decisions about how to proceed in the next iteration. During the analyze phase, you and your teams will examine how audiences search for, react to, and share your content.

So … love your data because you are going to be spending lots and lots of time with it. But that's a good thing. You will finally be able to see the true fruits of your labor as well as where you may need to make some changes to improve even further. Some of the tools you can use during the analyze phase include:

- Analytics Data
- Engagement Metrics
- Site Search Analytics (SSA)

ANALYTICS DATA

Ah, Mrs. Stone, my math teacher from high school. I once told her that I would never need to understand the math she was teaching that day because I was going to be a writer. Luckily, I caught up with her later in life and apologized.

Do not underestimate the power of data—numbers tell a story. So don't zone out on your data—trust me, there's a Mrs. Stone somewhere in your life, too. Examining your analytics will let you see how people are engaging with your content. Analytics should tell you the devices people use to engage with your content, what they spend time looking at, and whether, sales-cycle wise, they buy your products or download content.

Analytics should inform and refine your teams' thought processes around digital content (Leibtag, 2011). To get there, here are five steps to implement. If you follow these, you should really begin to see a difference in the quality of the questions your team asks about how your content is performing:

- *Set appropriate KPIs (Key Performance Indicators)*: KPIs are quantifiable measurements, which the organization agrees are the right things to measure, and that reflect levels of success (or failure). Choosing those KPIs might also be an iterative process. For example, you may start by thinking that page views are an important metric. But in three months, you may realize that page views have no bearing on content engagement. So change the KPIs that matter.

- *Train your team to understand the different parts of analytics*: Make sure everyone on the team understands the KPIs and how to measure them using the different reporting structures in your organization.

- *Create reporting structures that tell a story*: Structure your reports so they tell a story that everyone on the team understands. Find a way to pull the highlights from your different types of analytics so they narrate your digital content's life in cyberspace.

- *Test your reports*: Distribute your reports on a weekly basis and iterate on them, then refine the reports based on feedback. As your team begins to grasp the full implications of the analytics they will start asking different questions. They will begin to refine the types of information they need.

- *Set aside time to analyze your analytics*: Discuss them once a week for at least 30 minutes and once a quarter for about two to three hours. Consider an offsite meeting or retreat to talk about analytics. And make sure your executives understand the analytics—you may need to pick certain KPIs to concentrate on for them to *see* how the content is behaving.

Some Advice on Key Performance Indicators

Neil Bhapkar, a digital marketing professional, offers a list of KPIs that your content measurement should include:

- *Reach*: Unique visits, geography, mobile readership

- *Engagement*: Bounce rates, time spent, heat maps and click patterns, page views

- *Sentiment*: Comments, social sharing (Bhapkar, 2013)

ENGAGEMENT METRICS

Engagement metrics measure and gauge how well your audience is interacting with specific content. This will help you determine how people are interacting with you on social media channels. Look at how many followers retweet Tweets, how many people like and interact with posts, and how many "repins" you might get. The important engagement metrics are the ones that tell a story about how your target audiences are using your content to further their own goals or convert to customers.

SITE SEARCH ANALYTICS

Looking at your own site's search analytics is a valuable tool for understanding "users' expressions of what information they want from your site in their own words" (Rosenfeld, 2011). A search log analysis is looking at which search terms your audience uses when they're querying your own website's search engines. By performing a search log analysis you can:

- Improve the search results your own search engine returns

- Make the site easier to navigate

- Make your content more effective

Why? Because by analyzing your search engine's returns of relevancy (how the search term aligns with what the audience intended) as well as precision (how many items were returned that matched what the audience really wanted), you can determine how to improve your content, as well as the overall customer experience.

GOVERN

Governance across the web is so vital because we want our customers to have a consistent experience throughout our digital properties. We'll learn more about governance in Rule #5.

SUMMARY

Think of yourself as a publisher—you create, monitor, and update information constantly. To make this process effective and meaningful, you implement content strategy tactics, which include performing content audits, creating the content, publishing it, distributing it, analyzing its performance, and governing the entire process. There are many tools to use so that everyone on the team is on the same page and understands how the content is created. Above all, make sure you have the right people in the best roles for their talents.

Ready to talk about content governance? Keeping the customer experience consistent across channels is key to building trust and engagement. Let's see how in Rule #5.

REFERENCES

Bhapkar, N. (2013). *8 KPIs your content marketing measurement should include*. Retrieved from http://contentmarketinginstitute.com/2013/02/kpis-for-content-marketing-measurement/.

Bowen, S. (2012). *Presenting "The Magic Layer" at Confab 2012*. Retrieved from http://www.pybop.com/2012/05/the-magic-layer-confab-2012-content-strategy/.

Detzi, C. (2012). *From content audit to design insight: How a content audit facilitates decision-making and influences design strategy*. Retrieved from http://uxmag.com/articles/from-content-audit-to-design-insight.

Halvorson, K., & Rach, M. (2012). *Content strategy for the web* (2nd ed.). Berkeley, CA: New Riders.

Jacobs, M. Personal communication.

Leibtag, A. (2010). *Content mapping: A different way to audit*. Retrieved from http://onlineitallmatters.blogspot.com/2010/06/content-mapping-different-way-to-audit.html.

Leibtag, A. (2011). *Getting started with analytics: How to get buy-in from your team*. Retrieved from http://contentmarketinginstitute.com/2011/03/getting-started-with-analytics/.

Leibtag, A., & Watkins, A. (2011). *Johns Hopkins and the healthcare content conundrum: Aligning business strategy with user goals*. Retrieved from http://www.slideshare.net/aaronwatkins/johns-hopkins-medicine-the-healthcare-content-conundrum-aligning-business-strategy-with-user-goals.

Linn, M. (2010). *How to put together an editorial calendar for content marketing*. Retrieved from http://contentmarketinginstitute.com/2010/08/content-marketing-editorial-calendar/.

Morville, P. (2012). *The definition of information architecture*. Retrieved from http://semanticstudios.com/publications/semantics/000010.php.

Railton, D. Comment made to the author.

Rosenfeld, L. (2011). *Search analytics for your site conversations with your customers*. Brooklyn, NY: Rosenfeld Media.

Withrow, J. (2006). *Competitive analysis: Understanding the market context*. Retrieved from http://boxesandarrows.com/competitive-analysis-understanding-the-market-context/.

MAKE GOVERNANCE CENTRAL

RULE 5

WHY DO WE NEED SYSTEMS?

Think about some of the systems you have in place in your own life—you probably don't think of most of them as "systems." For example, dental care. You brush your teeth twice a day, floss once a day, and visit the dentist twice a year. Why? Because dentists have done an excellent job of educating people about oral hygiene.

Now think about family dinners. How do you plan dinner? Do you plan each meal you will have that week, make a list, and go to the grocery store and buy all the items? Or do you get home at 7 p.m. exhausted and just eat a frozen dinner and a pint of ice cream?

Now think about how you manage your finances. How about your bills? Do you have a system in place to pay them on time? Do you use automatic bill pay? How do you keep track of your spending?

Whether you realize it, your life is full of systems that keep you organized and allow you to get through your day with, hopefully, minimal chaos.

SYSTEMS CREATE FREEDOM ... AND SECURITY

Almost every organization has a process in place for finance, accounting, procurement, human resources, and so on. On a person's first day of work, she meets with a human resources manager, receives an information packet, goes through an orientation, and learns about her new position.

In matters of public safety, the government and other governing bodies have created systems to ensure the safety and security of people. Planes don't fly unless engineers have examined them thoroughly and given them the go ahead. There are checklists and systems in place to ensure that disaster does not occur. When there is a major accident we often find out that part of a system was not thoroughly examined or reviewed. These are, thankfully, few and far between. Why? Because all industries understand the importance of creating checks and balances as a form of control within systems so mistakes do not happen.

If serious things require systems and controls to ensure they are consistent, should our content be any different?

GOVERNANCE WILL IMPROVE YOUR CONTENT
AND THEREFORE YOUR CONVERSATIONS

We have touched on content governance several times in previous chapters and rules. Now we are going to examine why governance is vital to an overall content strategy.

Is your content:

- Unorganized?
- Lacking a clear voice?
- Consistently confusing to customers?

Then you should be interested in content governance. (*Note:* We are specifically speaking of content governance in this rule and not web governance, which mandates consistency across content *and* technology *and* design.)

WHAT IS CONTENT GOVERNANCE?

Content governance is the day-to-day detailed management of content delivery and style, as well as the long-term execution of content strategy tactics. Think of content governance as an overall structure that:

- Determines priorities
- Provides detailed guidelines and standards on how content should look, behave, and interact with your customers
- Assigns ownership to people within the organization so they can make strategic decisions about content

WHY CONTENT GOVERNANCE?

Some think of governance as a phase of content strategy, similar to Plan or Create. However, I firmly believe that governance belongs at the center of any content strategy (Figure R5.1). This is because governance:

- Creates a consistent customer experience across channels
- Avoids content bloat
- Sets internal organizational controls

CREATE A CONSISTENT CUSTOMER EXPERIENCE ACROSS CHANNELS

If content is a conversation, then we absolutely must know to whom we are talking, which is why we use Personas and other tools (Chapter 6). We must know who *we* are, which is why we use Identity Pillars, Messaging Architectures, and voice and tone guidelines (Chapter 7). These must-have tools have a

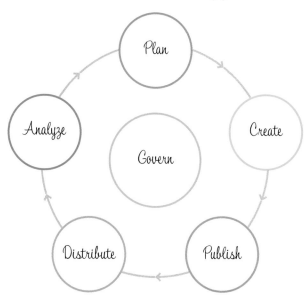

Figure R5.1 The lifecycle of content strategy. Ahava Leibtag. All Rights Reserved.

dual purpose—they help us create outstanding content, but they also form a consistent structure for the team. This allows for strong governance because everyone who touches content uses the same tools. It also provides a certain sense of regulation, without which you'd end up with content bloat.

CONTENT BLOAT

Content bloat is when your content meets in dark corners and expands overnight without knowing how "that happened." This department *had to create a page* that talks about the *same exact product or service* on another page, but from *their* point of view.

But it's not the department's view that we care about, is it? We only care about the customers' points of view. The department head probably went screaming to the VP of Communications and got his content posted, thoroughly confusing your customers. Now your customers have no idea which content provides reliable information about that particular product. How is this a good situation?

SET INTERNAL ORGANIZATIONAL CONTROLS

Governance standards help you set a consistent customer experience across all channels. By following them, you avoid replicating content, muddying your main messages and confusing your audiences.

Governance is also critical in setting internal organizational controls. Most conflict in offices stems from not knowing who is in charge. (Most conflict in life stems from the same reason.) By setting up a clear governance model for content within an organization you can set clear internal organizational controls. This avoids the "I'm the one in charge," arguments that often happen around content and leads you to a home page seven scrolls long.

So, governance is helpful in institutional politics as well in establishing clear guidance on content ownership and process.

Lock Up the Home Page

I once worked as a freelance writer at a hospital where the Web Standards Committee made the decision that no one department would be featured on the home page. Instead, they would revolve through a 12-month calendar process based on campaigns.

I cannot tell you how many arguments I had with different stakeholders over this rule. "But we bring in the most revenue for this hospital," "Patients tell us they can never find us," and my favorite, "If you're not on the home page, you're not important." However, the rule proved to be steadfast and upheld by the entire web department. No one ever was able to scream loud enough or stomp their feet in a way that changed the policy. There was just no getting around it.

Is that an effective governance standard? Well it's only effective if the rule is supporting an overall business initiative. It was successful in the fact that it was a rule that no one ever was able to find a way around.

GOVERNANCE TOOLS

The tools involved in content governance may include, among others, content workflows, editorial guidelines, style guides, taxonomies, web content committees, and archiving standards.

Let's examine a few of these. We talked about many of them in Chapter 8; however, now we are going to examine them in the context of their usefulness as governance tools.

CONTENT WORKFLOWS

Knowing who will touch the content at each point in its production process is critical to keeping content consistent. That means you must map content production from beginning to end. Mapping and publicizing content workflow should avoid people running around in a panic asking why so-and-so made a change at some point in the process. If everyone follows the workflow, certain people will have input at certain points. By knowing who is doing what when, you achieve the golden triad of a productive web content team: Less stress and uncertainty, more generosity of spirit, better teamwork. (More about that in Chapter 10.)

EDITORIAL GUIDELINES

Editorial guidelines are to words what brand guidelines are to design—they set a standard for the words and tones we use when talking to our customers. That is why messaging and voice and tone fall under this category. The guidelines should be detailed, provide clear examples, and offer important information for how to write and create content.

STYLE GUIDES

As we mentioned in Chapter 8, style guides are important, living documents that contain critical information related to all types of content and design standards. Editorial style guides direct written communications and brand guidelines direct design: logos, typefaces, photographic positions, and so on. However, if you want to be effective in using style guides or brand guidelines, you should combine them into one document—this will give your team just one referral guide to use. The sidebar will tell you about other elements you should include in your style guides.

TAXONOMIES

Taxonomies are vocabularies that organizations use to organize their content. It's what librarians call subject headings—a common language that helps us organize and find information. For each book that a librarian catalogs there are several subject headings. If you are looking for a book on cooking in Italy, you can find it under "cooking" and "Italian food." Likewise, in the case of massive documentation systems, content is assigned a few different labels so that people looking for it in only one place will be able to find it.

If you have ever tagged content, then you understand how taxonomies are used—they provide a common and shared vocabulary about content identity. They also relate dynamic content. For example, let's say you run a parenting website and you want related articles about a particular topic to appear so that customers stay on the site. You would tag that article with terms from your taxonomy: sibling rivalry, discipline, blended families, and stepparents. This way if someone is reading an article about sibling rivalry, other articles that relate to that topic will also appear.

ARCHIVING STANDARDS

Stale is a big turnoff to your audience. Remember to keep your content fresh and people will want to come back to see what is new. Therefore, you need to have standards in place for when content is published, so you know to check it monthly, quarterly, or annually. You can program your content management system to do this or you can set up documentation that gives content owners the responsibility to do this. Rolling audits, as we described in Chapter 8, are another way to manage archiving standards.

CHECKLISTS

By far, one of the most important governance tools you can use is checklists. After reading *The Checklist Manifesto* by Atul Gawande, MD, I was inspired to create my own content checklist. In the book, Gawande describes how many industries use checklists: Airlines, construction, and medicine to name a few. The idea of a checklist appealed to a consistency standard that I knew was missing from my own work.

I found that writing the same types of content again and again made it all too easy for me to miss certain small details. Once I established a checklist that worked for me—one that focused on certain areas—and didn't have too many steps, the consistency of my content improved tremendously (Figure R5.2).

The Ten Essential Elements of Successful Style Guides

1. *Centralized and Distributed*: Distribute your style guide to the *writing and publishing* workforce within your organization. If they are not professionally trained writers, then spend time explaining how to use the style guide, why it is important, and how to access it (shared drives, Google docs, printed once a year, etc.).

2. *Grammar Rules*: Most corporate style guides direct writers to *other* style guides for grammar rules. Why? Because there are very basic grammar rules that people ALWAYS get wrong—even trained professional writers, so why not include three to four pages on some basics? These might include the differences between the commonly misused words affect/effect, who/whom, bad/badly, complementary/complimentary, and so on.

3. *Punctuation Section*: Punctuation can be a matter of style. For example, different organizations use the labeling of dates in various fashions, especially internationally. Make sure to explain the style your company has decided to use, and if you need to, prepare a cheat sheet of the most common issues (commas, quotes, dashes). I know this sounds archaic, but have them print it out and post it near their desks, so that they can easily refer to it. If it's easy to do, they'll do it.

4. *Branding Guidelines*: While you may think that branding guidelines (design, use of logo, etc.) belong in a separate document (and you may be right), I would argue both written and design style elements should be bundled. As we move toward an increasingly versatile workforce, where digital practitioners will be required *to know how to write and code*, branding guidelines within a traditional written style guide will gain importance.

5. *Voice and Tone*: So important. So overlooked. Knowing how to write a redirect page vs. a sign-in page is critical when voice and tone may vary depending on the situation. Style guides can help with this, most critically by saying, "This is how we say it" and "This is NOT how we say it."

6. *Channel Distribution Guidance*: How do you personify your brand's voice and tone in 140 characters? Well, it had better be in your style guide. How many social media properties are you managing currently? Five? Six? Eleven? However many there are, make sure your style guide gives distinct instructions for each one. For example, your brand may allow you to say something like "Will we C U there?" Your brand may not. Note it in the style guide.

7. *Mobile Section*: Have a section in your style guide that addresses your mobile properties and their distinct styles—now content is divorced from design and style on mobile may be different.

8. *Titles, Naming Conventions, Degrees*: These are all important elements of a style guide most often ignored. Because I write so much in the healthcare space, I cannot tell you how many times within the SAME bio I have encountered MD and B.A.

9. *Last Published*: Update and distribute the style guide once a year. Make sure the last published date is ON THE COVER and every other page, too. That tells people they are working with the most current version.

10. *Customer Personas*: Make sure your customer personas are included in your centralized style guide (that means you should place them where everyone who touches content can view them). Knowing with whom you are conversing makes for better dialogue, no?

CREATING VALUABLE CONTENT™
A Step-By-Step Checklist

IS THE CONTENT:

DOES THE CONTENT INCLUDE:

Findable
Can the user find the content?

- An h1 tag
- At least two h2 tags
- Metadata, including title, descriptors & keywords
- Links to other related content
- Alt tags for images

Readable
Can the user read the content?

- An inverted pyramid writing style
- Chunking
- Bullets
- Numbered lists
- Following the style guide

Understandable
Can the user understand the content?

- An appropriate content type (text, video, etc.)
- Reflection that you considered the user personas
- Context
- Respect for the audience's reading level
- Articulate an old idea in a new way

Actionable
Will the user want to take action?

- A call to action
- A place to comment
- An invitation to share
- Links to related content
- A direct summary of what to do

Shareable
Will the user share the content?

- Something to provoke an emotional response
- A reason to share
- An ask to share
- An easy way to share
- Personalization (add hashtags to tweets, etc.)

Figure R5.2 Creating valuable content: A step-by-step checklist. Ahava Leibtag. All Rights Reserved.

SETTING UP A CONTENT GOVERNANCE PROGRAM

Governance, at its core, requires behavioral change within your organization. For change to occur at the broader enterprise level, individuals within the organization also need to change.

In order to publish content that sustains the brand identity, all content professionals within the organization must understand the importance of governance and associated tools. In order to run a successful content governance effort, we must move through four phases:

1. Convincing others in the organization that governance matters
2. Setting up governance bodies
3. Choosing and creating the right tools for your organization
4. Training

Let's examine each of these in depth.

CONVINCING OTHERS IN THE ORGANIZATION TO FOLLOW GOVERNANCE STANDARDS

How on earth are you supposed to figure out your business objectives, figure out your CMS, decide on identity pillars and voice and tone, set up a content strategy, and now convince everyone in the organization to stand in one straight line and kick at the same time?

Wait! Before you throw the book across the room, like my daughter with her pencil during math homework time, remember that behavioral change only happens when people truly believe they will benefit. Therefore, you need to demonstrate the benefit of content governance for the people within your organization.

Sell It to Them

Remember when you were determining your audience? You did research to develop a persona (or a number of them) to represent your target audiences.

Well, now it is time to create a persona of the people within your organization—the ones who have influence. Why would they care about messy, boring, incorrect content? Are they attorneys and therefore worried about legal issues? Are they grammar freaks and embarrassed that their brand does not know the difference between who and whom? Do they want content to appear in the right places at the right times in order to sell more of their products?

> Behavioral change only happens when people truly believe they will benefit. Therefore, you need to demonstrate the benefit of content governance for the people within your organization.

Discerning what will matter to different content professionals within your organization is a critical piece of selling governance to them. Here are a few different ways to approach this.

Find a Head Cheerleader

Jonathan Kahn recommends this approach, "Get a sponsor: someone senior in the organization that cares about this problem and wants to fix it. Let's find that person, and get them to teach us how change happens: who should we speak to, when, and how should we present our case?" (Kahn, 2011). Usually cheerleaders will advocate for content governance, but will not necessarily direct the process. They are usually people within the organization that are well-connected and have clout.

Show the Mistakes

Nothing gets people's attention like showing them the mistakes. Show examples of where content was tagged poorly so it didn't show up where it belonged. Give your colleagues pages where words are misspelled or voice and tone are completely off the mark.

It is tough to do this exercise because people get defensive and want to blame someone, or worse, point fingers at their colleagues. You need to deflect that by introducing this as an organization-wide problem, not something where a particular person or team is at fault.

It might help to give examples of other companies (competitors!) whose websites have similar problems, to defuse any tension. In the end, you should present this as an opportunity to have an honest conversation with your digital team about how you are going to manage the problem of content that is unruly, wild, and growing without any controls.

Behavioral Change Comes in Steps

Another way to sell content governance is to follow a set of rules made famous by a popular weight loss system. I have found their approach works because they approach weight loss in the same way you should approach setting up content governance rules: Slowly, with persistence, and with your eye on small milestones, until you reach the final goal.

Here are the rules:

- *If you bite it, write it*: Focuses on strict documentation, both inside and outside of the CMS.

- *You can choose not to count it, but it counts*: Every piece of content matters, so you need to emphasize the importance of the entire content enterprise committing to governance.

- *Schedule it into your life*: Schedule regular check-ins of governance efforts and governance guidelines—this helps keep the system on track.

- *Find strong support systems*: Find the people in the organization who champion and support governance.

- *Claim it as a lifestyle*: Everyone within the organization needs to understand their part in the workflow, how that role helps to support governance efforts, and live it.

Try a Pilot Project

Anytime you want to try anything—especially things that involve behavioral change—you should start small. Rome wasn't built in a day, after all. So focus on something small, where you can prove that using governance standards will positively influence the way your audiences interact with your content.

You might also want to spend some time analyzing how content is managed currently, without strict governance rules. Take a recent content project and track how it progressed—make sure that everyone is in the room. This will show your team how chaotic the process is and let them speak about problems with the current system, or lack thereof. This conversation provides a starting point for making the case for governance standards. These standards will improve internal interactions within the organization and save valuable time avoiding arguments about whose content is more important.

PEOPLE AND GOVERNANCE: WHO IS IN CHARGE?

After choosing the types of governance you will institute, you need to decide which people will contribute and run this effort. It should be a multidisciplinary team with many skill sets and functional areas represented.

Ideally, you should create two teams, one with *strategic authority* and the other with *implementation authority*.

- *Strategic authority* refers to the more bird's-eye-view decisions, such as site objectives, resources and budgeting, audience definition, and annual planning.

- *Implementation authority* refers to decisions related to day-to-day operations, such as requests for home page real estate or new content, content maintenance, and editorial oversight (Casey, 2013).

There may be crossover between the two teams and they must meet together often to share ideas and findings. However, their authority falls into two very different realms based on differing access to executive level information within the organization.

Alternatively, Seth Earley, a taxonomy and governance expert, recommends three types of governing bodies (Earley, 2011):

- *Steering Committees*: They have strategic authority and "typically make business decisions about priorities and allocation of resources. It is the entity that decides on priorities when there are conflicts among business requirements and business drivers. There is representation from various stakeholders throughout the business."

- *Work Teams and Working Groups*: These groups have day-to-day implementation authority and make sure the magic happens when it is supposed to. They report to the steering committee and should present to them often.

- *Task Forces*: Groups that manage a unique project for a limited duration.

WHICH PROFESSIONALS?

Seth Earley recommends the following areas and professionals:

- Marketing
- Product management
- Business intelligence
- Creative/editorial
- IS/library
- IT
- Site management
- Web content management
- UI/UX
- Legal
- Training

Here are a few roles that may be represented:

- Executive sponsor
- Taxonomy manager
- Content creators/editors
- Content managers (someone who has oversight for the system or repository) (Earley, personal communication)
- Librarians
- Regional representatives
- Line of business/functional area representatives
- Search specialists
- System owners

Earley also points out, quite wisely, "Remember to limit yourself to people in roles that will be affected by or need to have a say in content matters. You can always add people later, but it is hard to cut people once they are included" (Earley).

I would also recommend assigning staggered appointments with term limits. This way, people can serve on different working groups, task forces, and committees but for a limited amount of time—say two years. Some appointment rotations should occur every year—that way you always have a mix of people who have done this for one year and people who are just starting in a given role. And perhaps there are some people who are always a part of these conversations and efforts: Captain Content comes to mind, as well as other members of the web team, like the content strategist or head copywriter.

WHICH CONTENT GOVERNANCE TOOLS SHOULD YOU USE?

The right tools for your organization are rooted in your culture and attitude. If you work in a place where people are generally supportive of trying new things, then you'll probably have a pretty smooth time introducing the concept of governance to your colleagues. If people don't wash their dishes in the kitchenette, even though there are three signs in red, underlined, bold font telling them to; well, you're in for a bumpy ride.

Start with a style guide. That's something most people can understand—say it like this, not like that. Focus on one part of the style guide—maybe voice and tone is what you pick for the first task. Demonstrate that following the directions makes life easier.

TRAINING AND MEASUREMENT

In order for governance to take hold in an organization, you need three things: Consistency, training, and measurement. Consistency is the name of the game here: If you don't take the time, and train others to do the same, to make sure that message, voice, tone, style, and taxonomy are consistent; you will not win this race. In fact, it isn't even a race—it's just an ongoing process you and your team must believe in.

People need training, but more importantly, people need to understand why you are asking them to change the way they have always worked. Once they believe in the need for the change, they will be on board.

When it comes to skills training, make sure your team knows how to use style guides and why they are important. The CMS isn't going to show them *how* to tag content and use the right taxonomies. Particularly if you have a distributed content force, invest in quarterly training and make at least one session a year mandatory. Otherwise, you will never be able to maintain any type of real consistency, as people move throughout the organization into new roles and responsibilities, handing their content-updating roles to others.

Measurement will make or break your governance efforts. If you cannot accurately represent that governance is making a difference, you won't have convinced anyone that this is worth the effort. Remember our weight loss rules? If people don't see an impact on the scale every week, they are bound to return to their negative habits around food once again. (Even if they do see a change, they may go back to their bad habits.) So make sure you constantly publicize the governance wins. Lead them back to the business objectives to show bottom-line impacts.

SUMMARY

Introducing governance into your company's corporate mindset might not be easy. After all, governance is "about building support and awareness among other people in the organization. It takes a long time to turn an oil tanker" (Kahn). What you need to do, as a content manager, is to understand the critical importance of governance, and then communicate it to everyone on your team and to the C-suite or whoever approves the budget.

Once you do that, and everyone has bought into at least a trial period, create the necessary style guides and other tools, and try it. You'll soon see that life becomes less, not more, complicated, and that everyone relaxes, knowing where they stand in the process with a full understanding of the rules.

Once governance is part of your daily life, make sure to keep measuring how it is working, as you will probably have to keep making the case for it repeatedly. But all of this effort is worth it. Your team will be happier and more productive and your content will be the better for it.

REFERENCES

Casey, M. (2013). *Get your content strategy out of the drawer with governance*. Retrieved from http://uxmag.com/articles/get-your-content-strategy-out-of-the-drawer-with-governance.

Earley, S. (2011). *Developing a content maintenance and governance strategy*. Retrieved from http://www.asis.org/Bulletin/Dec-10/DecJan11_Earley.html.

Email between Seth Earley and Ahava Leibtag, February 13, 2013—Clarification between content manager and content creator.

Kahn, J. (2011). *Web governance: Becoming an agent of change*. Retrieved from http://alistapart.com/article/web-governance-becoming-an-agent-of-change.

CASE STUDY: HIPHOPDX

I don't think I'll ever forget this moment: I was walking in a parking garage when a California number came up on my phone. Thinking it was my sister at her new job, I answered and an uneasy voice asked if I was Ahava Leibtag.

When I answered in the affirmative, he told me he'd found my name and contact information on a website for ConFab, the content strategy conference. Then he asked me if I knew any hip hop content strategists.

I had a hard time suppressing my laughter. I said, "We're a pretty new field—you're going to have a hard time finding someone who fits into such a narrow niche."

We proceeded to have several conversations over the next couple of weeks. Sharath Cherian, CEO of Cheri Media, ran a site called HipHopDX.com. He became intrigued by the idea of content strategy after reading Kristina Halvorson's book, *Content Strategy for the Web*, and wanted to understand how to implement some of these ideas within his organization.

HipHopDX.com is a popular website devoted to producing and disseminating content about the culture of Hip Hop, including music, personalities, and history. The site has been in operation for 10 years. Staff at the time included three editors, a social media manager, an art director, a developer, and a salesperson, as well as freelance and staff writers.

BEGIN WITH DISCOVERY

As with all content strategy projects, I started with discovery. If your discovery lacks depth, you will fail; only by truly understanding the organizational challenges will you be able to develop a robust strategy.

People

Sharath had several challenges with his staff. First, there was some change coming (one of his long-time reporters was leaving) and the journalists were not aligned in the most productive way to manage the daily tasks of producing a hip hop news site. Most of them had come from working together at another music website and had migrated many of those practices to DX.

Furthermore, the staff didn't buy in to the idea of content strategy, mostly because they didn't understand it. I knew that part of my discovery had to include education. After talking them through some of their challenges and describing some of the tools we could use to help them, they warmed to the idea.

To understand the full picture, I interviewed every member of the editorial and social media staff—about seven people in all. As usual, disparate views on what needed to change to improve the journalistic standards at DX, as well as how to organize the staff into a well-oiled journalistic machine, emerged from these stakeholder interviews.

Process

Process was lacking for several reasons:

- *Organizational structure challenges*—the editorial team's structure made it difficult to communicate clear direction.
- *Time management*—every staff member complained of having too much to do and not enough time to do it. Many also complained of having to manage production issues like posting pictures or audio mixes that they felt took away from their creative writing time.
- *Lack of expertise*—team members found it difficult to execute on the overall editorial vision of the site, for a variety of reasons that had to do with training and journalism experience.

Technology

Luckily, Sharath had invested in a content management system that was easy for the staff to use. However, they lacked search engine optimization (SEO) training and were not entering in all the meta descriptions that were so critical to publishing findable content.

DISCOVERY FINDINGS

After discovery, I presented the following findings to Sharath and his executive team. DX had five pressing challenges tied directly to content, including:

1. *Cohesive direction for the editorial staff*: Communicating that production of content must be tied to revenue as well as what the customer wants
2. *Clear identification of market*: Educating the staff about who the real audience of the site is and how best to attract and retain that market
3. *Identify bottlenecks and issues in the publication process*: The right talent was not in the right roles; writers were uploading photos and wasting precious time everyday

4. *Better utilization of staff*: Structuring the editorial staff to produce the above goal, as well as their long and short-term activities, so that efforts were not replicated or wasted

5. *Web writing*: Educating staff about better web writing practices, including SEO, style guide, and headline use

GET EVERYONE ON THE SAME PAGE

We proceeded with a State of the Union debrief and training at the company's annual CheriCamp retreat.

First, I presented a State of the Union, using multidimensional content audits that detailed the following:

- Traffic patterns
- Top pages by section—showing where the bulk of the audience was spending their time
- Top content pages
- Heat maps that showed where on the pages users were reading and interacting with the content
- Top 100 pages by artist
- Top news content by artist

By analyzing the content and using multidimensional content audits, we were able to draw certain conclusions about the types of content that most interested DX's audiences. We also built a solid business case for spending more time on creating content formats to which the staff had previously assigned a low priority.

KNOW YOUR AUDIENCE

With all the writers and editorial staff present, we created personas during a workshop by cutting out pictures from magazines. Each member of the editorial staff "presented" their different ideas of the personas for DX, and other members commented and critiqued their findings.

Solidifying the personas was critical, as there was some disagreement among the staff about who their target audience was. This exercise was invaluable for the team: It built consensus, creatively engaged them, and helped them come to a certain understanding about whom they were talking to on a daily basis.

The below table shows two of the personas we created—one male and one female—so the writers could truly envision who was consuming their content.

Persona #1	Tyler	Talia
Photo	 Tyler persona.	 Talia persona.
Age	16	18
Lives	NJ suburbs	Houston, TX
Hangs with friends	Friends' houses, skate park, home, and mall	School, home, mall, sports practice, friends' houses, church, and movies
Listens	Lupe Fiasco, J. Cool, Kid Cudi, Kanye West, and Whiz Kalifa	Rihanna, Nikki Minaj, B.o.B, Bruno Mars, Kanye West, and Drake
Watches	Family Guy, Skins, and Plays video games (Call of Duty)	Jersey Shore, America's Next Top Model, 16 and Pregnant, and Vampire Diaries
Eats	Taco Bell, Family dinners, and microwave food	Family dinners, Chili's, and Chick-fil-A
Social Networks	Facebook	Facebook
Sex	He says he hooks up and lies about it	Guys take her to the movies
Education	High school	College
Content most interested in	Audio, Video, and some news	Audio, Video, Mixtapes, and some news if it concerns artists she cares about

BRANDING: WHO IS DX?

Most important, Sharath gave an impassioned speech at the beginning of the day that really set out his expectations for the brand. By doing so, he set the stage necessary for knowing who DX was supposed to be.

Sharath also identified three specific goals for the brand—business objectives:

1. *Produce quality content* for the audience
2. *Grow the site to increase revenue* through increased page views
3. *Influence the audience* through the uniqueness and integrity of the brand

By knowing who they were talking to, as well as what the brand was supposed to represent, we were able to map the following inverted pyramid based on business goals.

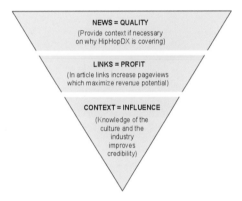

HipHopDX Inverted Pyramid.

By training the content creators to think like journalists—put the most important information at the top—but also as business people—by embedding business goals into the content—we were able to ensure they executed each piece of content according to business objectives.

UNDERSTAND THE BUSINESS MODEL

The staff did not understand how their choices of articles and what to write about affected the business of the site. Sharath established a bonus program based on traffic and other engagement metrics. Tying employee's performance to the business model was a critical part of what made this content strategy engagement a success.

Eleven months after DX instituted the content strategy, they saw their traffic rise by 24%, which contributed to a direct increase in revenue.

Here's an example of a chart the social media manager, Mike Trampe, made so he could have an at-a-glance content strategy at his disposal:

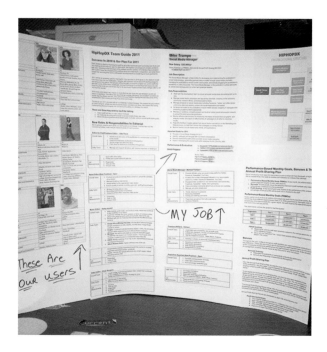

HipHopDX Mike Trampe's content strategy chart.

Now that we've learned about content strategy, we're going to learn about the amazing power of content marketing. We'll also talk about design and dream content teams, as well as how to hire the right consultants when you need help.

CREATING CONTENT: TALKING AND LISTENING

Part 4

Thus far, you have learned how important content is as a business asset, as well as how to structure your content so it can float everywhere. You now understand your target audiences clearly and can frame and distribute content that drives your sales cycle. By clearly defining your content strategy, you are now ready to produce content—great conversations that will affect your bottom line.

CONTENT MARKETING ATTRACTS, NURTURES, AND CONVERTS CUSTOMERS

In Chapter 9, we are going to discover content marketing. Content marketing fuels the conversation by consistently engaging your audiences with your content. Your customers communicate and keep in touch through various content vehicles, such as email newsletters, blogs, and traditional print forms of media.

After you learn about content marketing, you will learn how to structure your internal teams to create great content that works for your business in Chapter 10.

Then, you will learn Rule #6, so you can execute your content programs effectively. After Chapter 11, we will explore our final Rule #7.

READY TO TRANSFORM?

Transforming the way you think, produce, and manage content will change your organization internally, as well as move you with the propulsion of a rocket toward your achievement thresholds.

Now to content marketing. Let's understand what it is, why it's so important in today's marketplace, and how you can introduce and sell the concept within your organization.

CONTENT MARKETING SUSTAINS THE CONVERSATION

Now that you have the tools and theory behind content, we are ready to talk about the power of content marketing. Content marketing centers on the idea of having a conversation, the natural give and take that happens when people communicate. It is the difference between saying "Buy a Toyota," and "Hey, it looks like you are interested in buying a new mid-sized car—this particular model of Corolla might be perfect for you, but I'd like to hear more about your car needs." The first is forceful, the latter is more about give and take, which gives the customer a chance to make up his mind based on the information you provide.

Let's talk about the concept of content marketing in regard to party planning (because who doesn't love a party). I use a small business to illustrate how every organization can use the access the Internet provides to nurture and convert customers.

Daphne and her sister run an event design business called À La Mode. They specialize in distinctive parties with handcrafted pastries and desserts and unique presentations. When you look at pictures of their events, their creativity comes alive in amazing detail. Their parties are truly one-of-a-kind masterpieces (Figures 9.1 and 9.2).

Recently Daphne asked me, "Where can I place a good ad to get more customers?" I looked at her and without missing a beat said, "Nowhere." Is advertising dead? No, but it's only one method of the many that marketers use to attract and retain audiences. In today's age of social media and social sharing, it may not be the most effective way to attract and nurture customers.

PROMOTING A BUSINESS IN TODAY'S MARKETPLACE

I started to explain to Daphne that she needed to start a blog, share recipes, and publish pictures from her parties at least twice a month. She also needed to capture email addresses of former clients and possible leads and send them an email newsletter to continue nurturing those leads. Her response? "Well, first, who has time for that? Second, we would do that, but we've started to notice

Figure 9.1 À La Mode table presentation.

Figure 9.2 À La Mode sweets presentation.

that other event designers are copying our work. So if we publish too many of our pictures, we're worried that people will continue to copy us, and our designs won't seem unique anymore."

Daphne hit on the two major objections people have to content marketing:

1. How do you truly measure the return on investment? (Who has time for all that work?)

2. Why should we give stuff away for free? (People will copy our pictures or our ideas and we will lose our competitive advantage.)

The responses to both objections are that when you freely share information that solves people's problems, you engage with them in a very nonthreatening way—a conversation; the opposite of an obvious sales pitch. Remember, people are, for the most part, suspicious of the hard sell.

Prospective customers are looking for a company or service to trust. You want them to come to regard you as an expert on a subject and then as a *trusted* expert. If you're strategic, eventually they will also regard you as a friend. By sharing stories and solutions, people will look to your brand as the answer to their problem and engage with you.

Once they regard you as a friend, you have created a member of a brand community who will advocate for you and spread positive comments about you all around the web. Content marketing exists to pull people into your customer loop (lead funnel) by providing practical, useful information that leads to continued engagement and interest.

Findable, shareable, trustworthy—they are the hallmarks of great content marketing. Let's explore more.

WHAT IS CONTENT MARKETING?

We defined content marketing earlier, back in Chapter 1. So, let's revisit the concept.

Joe Pulizzi explains, "Content marketing is a marketing technique of creating and distributing relevant and valuable content to attract, acquire, and engage a clearly defined and understood target audience—with the objective of driving profitable customer action" (Pulizzi, 2012a).

Debbie Williams, from Sprout Content, explains it from the perspective of the customer, "Content marketing is about timeliness, connection, response, and results. It allows businesses to connect with and grow their audience by providing compelling, helpful, and purposeful information that their audience is looking for. Content creation and marketing offers a more personal approach to business, and helps build trust, which ultimately creates longer and more meaningful consumer/brand relationships. Brands can also promote their expertise in an industry and become a valuable resource to people that consumers look to for guidance, advice, and trusted information on a topic. Unlike traditional advertising that is largely one-sided and disruptive, content marketing creates conversation and empowers both sides with a voice" (Williams, 2010).

CONTENT MARKETING GOALS

By combining both Joe and Debbie's definitions, we see that content marketing has very specific goals when it comes to developing a rapport with a clearly defined target audience (which is why you must create personas, as we talked about in Chapter 6). Here is a list of those goals:

1. *Attract*: Create content that will draw prospects like bees to a blossoming flower
2. *Acquire*: Give them the content in exchange for an email address or some other form of potential ongoing contact

3. *Engage or connect*: Continue to engage by creating and sending relevant content about your product, service, or knowledge base

4. *Drive profitable action*: Clearly align your content creation and distribution efforts with your business goals

5. *Build trust*: Provide useful information focused on your audience and on solving their problems. Provide solutions instead of telling them about how great you are; that is how you build trust and friendship.

6. *Listen*: Listen to their reactions to your content. That is how you determine if you are communicating the right pieces of information.

7. *Create conversations*: Do this once you have them interested in you. Then communicate carefully based on their needs and interests, and *continue* to listen.

Content marketing is about creating and sustaining relationships with your customers by sharing content with them, and then measuring and responding to their reactions.

Once again, the powerful concept of conversation takes its rightful place as the foundation for creating great content experiences. Creating content is inserting information you want to share, and finding the right format and distribution channel for it; content marketing is about creating and sustaining conversations. By sharing content with your customers, you nurture your relationships with them and, in turn, can measure and respond to their reactions.

In the case of Daphne and her sister, producing content about their parties, sharing recipes, and creating videos that showcase their creative process would enhance how relatable they are to their target audiences. It also increases their appearance on search engines, because the more robust and engaging content you have online, the more your social networks will share your content. The popularity of your content helps your rankings on search engines, which in turn leads more people to your content.

Sales are when *you call them* and marketing is when *they call you*. Content marketing is *when they call you a trusted friend*—a very powerful concept.

CONTENT MARKETING TOOLS

Creating content requires understanding the different formats available to you, which is what we talked about in Chapter 3. Some of the tools content marketers use to attract and sustain customers are:

- Email newsletters
- Websites
- Blogs
- Webinars
- Ebooks
- Whitepapers
- Infographics

- Podcasts
- Slide presentations
- Videos

Any developed content you use to grab a potential customer and move them into your customer loop serves as content marketing.

CONTENT MARKETING SOLVES CERTAIN PROBLEMS

Before we talk about how to institute content marketing within your organization, let's explore some of the problems content marketing solves. We will examine some of the current frustrations marketers are experiencing and how content marketing can help.

ADS DON'T HAVE THE SAME POWER

The Internet has weakened some of the most common advertising channels of the past, making a multi-pronged approach even more necessary. Certainly print media has suffered most publicly, and, digital advertising is not always effective (McCambley, 2013). People skip over ads using their DVRs (Digital Recording Devices), their eyes roll right over them on websites and they close them out as soon as they pop up. So, *Question #1: Without effective advertising, how do you create brand awareness and reinforcement?*

REDUCED ATTENTION

People are busy, busy, busy. When's the last time you talked to someone on the subway or had a conversation with someone that didn't take place via Facebook or Twitter? We are all so busy looking down at our phones, that we miss a tremendous amount of the world as it streams by us. This means people ignore billboard ads, don't listen to radio commercials, don't retain information about your product and service, and couldn't, honestly, care less. *Question #2: In a world where no one is paying attention, how do we capture the attention of our target audience?*

LACK OF BRAND LOYALTY

There was a time that people only bought one brand of car, shopped at one department store, or bought one brand of home appliances. Those days are gone.

People want deals, they want the best product and they want someone to confirm that they are getting that. Why do you think online customer reviews are so powerful and plentiful? People with bad experiences want to rant in public so that the company that betrayed them suffers. People who had good experiences want to rave about the brand that treated them as though they really mattered. *Question #3: How do we create brand loyalty in a world in which allegiance to brands doesn't really seem to exist anymore?*

SOCIAL SHARING

Remember the flattened white picket fence we talked about in Chapter 1? People share a tremendous amount of information over the web now. Often, brands are not even aware of the conversations that take place—both negative and positive. More than ever, people look to their networks to make recommendations about everything from gel manicures to guitar teachers to mortgage brokers.

Once they ask their friends, they do not search the yellow pages or look at ads. In fact, they may not even care about your brand at all—they are simply interested in your service. All they care about is solving THEIR problem. You only become relevant to them when you provide proof that you have the solution. *So, Question #4: How do we inform our audiences through a trusted community?*

CONTENT MARKETING TO THE RESCUE

Let's answer those four questions, but first let's address something important about content marketing. It isn't really new. Communications professionals have been practicing some form of it for years, been doing it for years, using different parts of it, but never calling it content marketing (some people call it custom publishing, corporate journalism, brand journalism, branded media, brand content, and inbound marketing).

By wrapping a name around it, recognizing it as another type of marketing approach (McDermott, 2013), and associating it with certain tactics, we've tapped into a powerful method that is incredibly useful for attracting, engaging, and cultivating today's consumer.

How Kraft Does Content Marketing

The Kraft brand is ubiquitous—think what it means to you. Gourmet? Perhaps not. Good, comforting, easy to make food? Probably. How do they do it? In an interview with Joe Pulizzi in 2012, Julie Fleischer, Director of CRM at Kraft Foods, revealed how Kraft mines data and monitors trends to create engaging content.

Kraft studies its consumers carefully: "We mine our data, and look carefully at search trends to understand which recipes people are making at any given day of the year, and then we serve those recipes up to our consumers in the manner, and at the moment, they're most interested in."

Continued

Understanding their audience is of prime importance to them, "We spend a lot of time understanding who our consumer is, how she cooks, what kinds of food she wants to cook. Even more, we understand on any given day the kinds of recipes our customers want to make."

Here is a statement that encapsulates perfectly how well Kraft understands its audience, "We use pantry items to know what's already in the house because we don't want you to have to go out and get extra ingredients to make something. We know what produce our customers are more likely to have in their refrigerator, as well as those they're unlikely to ever purchase."

After creating the content, the Kraft team monitors how it is used. "We monitor everything that we put out to see how many clicks and what type of engagement we get. Are customers printing a recipe? Saving it to their recipe box? Adding it to the shopping list? 'Liking' it, emailing it, and pinning it on Pinterest? When we see something hit a spark of high interest, we pull it into our weekly email (which in turn ignites it on Facebook and Pinterest—it's a virtuous cycle)."

Knowing their audience means knowing what turns them on, and what doesn't. She compares Kraft to the more gourmet-ish sites like *Bon Appétit* and *Martha Stewart Living*. The Kraft consumer, she posits, would look at the nice photos on those sites and think that the food is beautiful, but would never consider making it for dinner that night. "At Kraft, we publish in order to sell products, so we want to create recipes our customers really want to make and share."

This is an example of content marketing at its best: The company produces relevant, valuable information to its consumers in service to the company's business goal: Selling more of their products. It's a win–win for everyone (Pulizzi, 2012b).

HOW CONTENT MARKETING CAPTURES TODAY'S CONSUMER

Let's look back at that list of challenges that face the modern marketing or content professional and demonstrate how content marketing can help:

Question #1: Without Effective Advertising, How Do You Create Brand Awareness and Reinforcement?

You create consistent brand reinforcement when you share stories about your brand and distribute the message in a way that encourages sharing among your target audiences.

Great content marketing is helpful information; it gives the consumer enough information to do the research they want to do before they buy. By providing information, you will engage with your customers on a consistent basis (like an email newsletter) forever capturing them in your customer loop (lead funnel) and leading to continued engagement over time.

Question #2: In a World Where No One Is Paying Attention, How Do We Capture the Attention of Our Target Audience?

If you create relevant, interesting, informative, educational content, it will be shared. It may not be shared the same day you publish it, it may only be shared by a very niche market, but, it will make its rounds to the people that matter.

By making yourself into a trusted resource that the consumer can always count on, they will instinctively search you and your services out when they need you. By producing content that can remain evergreen (it's always relevant), you increase the findability of your content. Then when a customer is searching for someone who provides your product or service, you come up first.

"Your key to ignited sales," say Ann Handley and C. C. Chapman, "is to create online content and optimize it so that it appears on the first page of search results when your customers search for you or the products or services you sell. Done right, the content you create will position your company, not as just a seller of stuff, but as a reliable source of information" (Handley and Chapman, 2011).

Question #3: How Do We Create Brand Loyalty in a World Where Allegiance to Brands Does Not Really Seem to Exist Anymore?

This is challenging because part of brand loyalty comes from a product and service that is consistent and positive all the time. As a marketing, communications, or content professional, you may not have any control over this. Brand loyalty is not what it used to be. In a world where, in a matter of minutes, in the comfort of your own home, you can compare prices, read reviews by peers, and see what experts think, your audience relies more on their research when they buy a product or service, than on the comfort of a famous brand name.

Therefore, now more than ever, capturing your audience's attention and trust is about the content you provide. If you produce content that solves people's problems—it explains a product or service so it makes it easier to use—you will gain brand loyalty. Because you come across as being helpful, positive, and willing to provide clear solutions, people will want to engage with your brand more often because they know they will get a certain level of customer service.

Question #4: How Do We Inform Our Audiences Through a Trusted Community?

Creating trust takes time. As Kim Phillips, an information marketing expert, points out, "One of the great marketing lies is that great marketing should be able to turn a prospect into a customer quickly. Marketing should not be looked at as transactional. Instead, marketing's goal should be to build relationships over time with prospects so when it comes time to make the sale, the prospect trusts you and is ready to say, 'yes.'" (Phillips, 2013).

In other words, you build a trusting community by being someone worthy of trust over time. Just as we all typically date for a while before we get married, do not expect your customers to sign on the dotted line before they are repeatedly exposed to your brand. Even more important is the consistency with which you communicate with them—in terms of both time and voice and tone.

Now that we understand content marketing fully, let's talk about how to:

- Get buy-in for content marketing in your organization
- Establish a content marketing program
- Measure and publicize your results

GET BUY-IN FOR CONTENT MARKETING IN YOUR ORGANIZATION

As we discussed previously, content strategy is an online publishing strategy. It lays out a clear strategy and set of tactics for how your organization takes information and turns it into content that you can publish and distribute. Convincing your internal design, web, and marketing teams to follow a content strategy will require having people change the way they think about publishing content. So, let's talk about how to convince them to give content marketing a whirl.

Content marketing will probably be accepted much more easily as a new way of thinking. That is because everyone has read about blogs and social media. What they may require is for you to explain *and demonstrate* the financial return on investment of producing content that speaks to your thought leadership—in other words, giving away your best secrets. What is important to demonstrate is that content marketing is not about giving away your best secrets—it is about positioning yourself as someone who is willing to share.

Think about Paige Holden back in our case study on XONEX at the end of Part 1. Much of the information she and her content team share with their target audiences is information they have spent years accumulating—knowledge that is valuable within their industry. Previously, companies did not want to share that information because they wanted to attract customers by convincing them that they were the experts. *Only* by using their services would the audience have access to that hard-won information. The marketplace has changed significantly. It is crowded. There are many experts—and your audience knows it. So how do you distinguish yourself in the crowd?

First, you have to understand the pain points of your customers, and create content that solves problems. If you generously give people useful information, they come to trust you. Rather than trying to make a go of it themselves, more often they will approach you to help them solve their problems. Why? Because you have demonstrated, in a very transparent way, that you truly know what you are talking about and are willing to share that wisdom.

When you're selling content marketing in your own organization, remind them, "More than anything, marketers want to engage with customers. One of the disadvantages of traditional advertising was the one-way aspect

What is important to demonstrate is that content marketing is not about giving away your best secrets—it is about positioning yourself as someone who is willing to share.

of the conversation: Sales was one of your only measurements to see if engagement was happening. With content marketing, you can have a two-way conversation with your customers and use varied tools to measure engagement. Watching your customers interact with your brand makes social media and content marketing dynamic and enjoyable. And, if you see that you're not getting the results you want, you can quickly change your tactics without a major investment of printing, ad space, and production costs" (Leibtag, 2011).

Two other approaches suggested by content marketing consultant Sarah Mitchell are "When you're talking to any level of management about a content marketing strategy, you have to focus on the benefit of word-of-mouth referrals. Managers, especially C-level decision makers, usually aren't interested in theories or philosophies. Everyone loves customer testimonials and success stories and knows exactly how powerful they can be. Pitch content marketing as the vehicle for maximizing word-of-mouth referrals. The other important point to make is content marketing puts the organization in complete control of their message, especially when using social media. Most managers are attracted to the idea of autonomy" (Mitchell, 2010).

Content marketing gives you the ability to track your customers' interests and change course if you need to, without the massive investment of printed brochures or ads, which in any case do not always let you track return on investment accurately. Content marketing can also provide the most powerful type of sales material there is—the word-of-mouth customer testimonial. And it can help you stay in control of your message, because you are constantly monitoring the communications—and conversations—with your customers.

ESTABLISH A CONTENT MARKETING PROGRAM

As we have said previously, any type of program you start in your organization should probably be a small one—a pilot program. Identify a business initiative that needs a little extra love and attention, so you can prove content marketing is making a difference.

Starting small usually means a blog; but do not start one unless you can truly commit to blogging once a week. Infrequent and inconsistent blogging is not going to give you much content to work with, and it is also going to lose the interest of your audience. Pamela Vaughan of HubSpot has this to say, "Companies that blog 15 or more times per month get 5X more traffic than companies that don't blog at all. And if you're a small business, increasing your blogging frequency can move the needle even more. [In addition] small businesses (1–10 employees) tend to see the biggest gains in traffic when they publish more articles" (Vaughan, 2012).

You might also try even smaller—an eBook, for example. I suggested to Daphne and her sister (the event designers) that they consider publishing an eBook—*How to Design an Elegant Garden Party*. They should write a short, six-page book with pictures, ideas for decorations, several ideas for desserts, and one recipe. Then, they could choose to share the eBook in one of two ways:

1. *Gated*: This means that in order to download the eBook, you must give your email address and some contact information. This is also called a Request for Information Form (RFI). Once the prospect gives her contact information, she becomes a lead, as we discussed in Chapter 2. Daphne can continue to send that person email newsletters or updates about the event design business in order to continue nurturing the lead within the customer loop.

2. *Ungated*: This means that the eBook is freely downloadable and no exchange of any information takes place. Experts bandy about whether to gate or ungate these types of content marketing materials. It depends on the type of business you run, where you are in your content marketing program, and what your goals are for this particular piece of content.

THE 1-7-30-4-2-1 APPROACH

How often should you publish your content? Russell Sparkman, a content marketer, uses a numeric approach in the context of a content marketing program:

*   1: On a daily basis—Tweet, retweet, and share content relevant to others.

*   **7**: On a weekly basis—blog at least once a week. You can also consider sending out an email newsletter once a week.

*   30: On a monthly basis—you should be sending out different pieces of content like: Videos, podcasts, presentations (share on Slideshare), guest posts on another blog, a webinar.

*   4: On a quarterly basis—try some heavy lifting content marketing, like an eBook or whitepaper.

To Gate or Ungate?

Tim Moran, editor-in-chief of CMO.com, summarizes the debate about offering ungated, or free form, content as follows:

*   Pros—enables content evangelism; offers better SEO; creates more inbound links; generates more site traffic.

*   Cons—provides lower quality leads; serves up inconsistent lead volume; fewer conversion events mean poorer lead intelligence; offers less control over lead nurturing (Moran, 2012).

- 2: Twice a year—you should produce bigger events, like a conference or smaller in-person event.

- 1: Once a year—think about doing something that's "a celebration, an event, an announcement" (Handley and Chapman, 2011).

MATCH YOUR CONTENT MARKETING EFFORTS TO YOUR IDENTITY PILLARS AND MESSAGING ARCHITECTURE

Now that you have done the work in Chapter 7, you should plan your content marketing efforts around your identity pillars and messaging architecture. You are applying your understanding of the business case of *why* you are producing content to *actually producing content*.

Remember our American faucet maker, Fawcet, from Chapter 7? They are struggling with increasing competition from European competitors who are designing sleeker, more modern looking faucets that are in fashion now in American kitchens.

Their business objectives were:

- *Show* people that Fawcet's faucets are just as beautiful as European designs

- *Remind* people that Fawcet is a strong American brand and makes excellent products

- *Demonstrate* that Fawcet will last a long time

- *Increase* awareness of Fawcet in Europe to compete there

Current Brand Attributes (What people think of us now?)	What We Want Brand Attributes to Become (What we want people to think of us)	Identity Pillars (How we will communicate our brand promise—both internally and externally)
Nice, but boring	A style to fit any taste (after all, there are people who don't like the modern look)	With so many choices, we'll find the right Fawcet for you
Not as attractive as European competitors	Beautiful to look at	Look at how beautiful our Fawcets are
Will break	Well-made and lasts forever	Competes in terms of longevity with any other type of faucet

The identity pillars are:

- *Personalized*: We'll find the right brand Fawcet for you

- *Beautiful*: Our Fawcets are beautiful

- *High-quality*: Our Fawcets are well-made and stand up to heavy use

The content marketers at Fawcet created the following editorial calendar that aligns content creation with identity pillars and a schedule (Figure 9.3).

	Frequency	Identity Pillar #1	Identity Pillar #3	Identity Pillar #3
		Personalized	Beautiful	High Quality
Daily	1	Tweet 1x	Tweet 1x	Tweet 1x
			Facebook picture	
			Google+ picture	
			Pinterest	
Weekly	7	Share customer testimonial	Run contest for favorite style	Share customer testimonial
Monthly	30	1 blog / month	1 blog/month	2 blogs/month
		Video blog about customer picking right Fawcet		Video blogs that demonstrate how well-made Fawcets are and how they stand up to heavy use
Quarterly	4	ebook about choosing the right Fawcet		Video blog of plumbers talking about Fawcets
Twice a year	2	Webinar about choosing the right Fawcet	In store demonstrations publicized on social media networks	In store demonstrations publicized on social media network
Once a year	1	New product intro	New product intro	New product Intro

Figure 9.3 Editorial calendar for Fawcet.

By aligning content creation to business goals, the content marketers at Fawcet can better track the results of their efforts.

Let's look at the calendar a bit more in depth:

- Each identity pillar has its own column
- Each identity pillar has a clearly defined time period when content is created and distributed to reinforce that pillar
- By choosing the content formats that the marketers feel will best reinforce those messages, they are able to plan in advance what content they need to produce: Video, photographs, eBooks, and so on.

MEASURE AND PUBLICIZE YOUR RESULTS

As with any pilot project, it is important to show your success, even if it is minimal. Let's say Daphne's eBook was downloaded by 18 people. This would be a very modest success, depending on how many different social media channels were used to distribute the eBook. However, those 18 downloads, assuming they are 18 different people, do not result in 18 separate leads that Daphne will pursue. Instead, they are moved into an email newsletter database.

Each of those 18 leads receives an email newsletter twice a month from À La Mode about their parties—filled with crafty tips to make your next dinner party a success, a fun centerpiece idea for a holiday party, or a recipe that looks

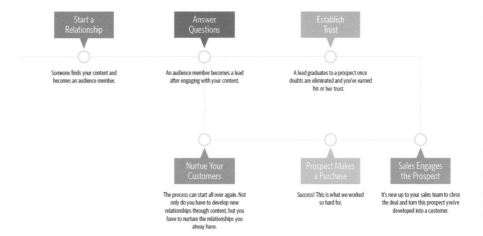

Figure 9.4 The customer loop, which reminds us that we always want to be nurturing our relationship with customers, even after they have bought a product or service.

elegant and difficult to make, but is actually easy. After about six months, one of those 18 leads becomes a customer: After six emails filled with interesting content, the prospect decides À La Mode should be the one to design her husband's 40th birthday party. From one six-page eBook, À La Mode books one party, where six people are so impressed, they book individual consultations.

Let's look at the customer loop (Figure 9.4) again and how this strategy works for À La Mode:

Customer Loop Action	À La Mode Action
Start a Relationship	Prospect downloads the gated eBook (the person trades their email address for the content)
Answer Questions	The eBook provides relevant and unique content about how to make an elegant garden party
Establish Trust	Because of the eBook and the emails that À La Mode uses to connect and nurture the lead, the person comes to see them as a trusted source for how to produce an unusual party
Sales Engages the Prospect	Daphne or her sister notices that someone has opened the emails six times since downloading the eBook. They reach out to ask about possible party requirements
Prospect Makes a Purchase	The prospect says she is indeed interested in producing a party for her husband's 40th birthday and engages À La Mode
Nurture Your Customers	À La Mode continues to send out emails about their parties, recipes, and ideas for centerpieces. People share the content with others, which prompts more people to sign up for the email newsletters, and perhaps download a new eBook on how to produce an elegant and unusual Thanksgiving dinner party

In a larger organization, a success like booking one party and seven consultations needs to reach the C-suite. But, first, you need to do a few things:

1. *Set expectations*: Content marketing programs typically take at least six to nine months to show any success—even modest ones. So set C-suite expectations that there needs to be a commitment of time and patience.

2. *Carefully consider business objectives and resources*: What types of professionals do you need in order to create all of this content? Writers, videographers and photographers? Customers who can give testimonials? Make sure you have the budget and resources in place to execute your plans.

3. *Keep track of engagement*: The number of people who sign up for the eBook, or later open the email newsletter, point to your content marketing program working. While it may take time to lead to direct sales, it won't hurt to publicize the engagement statistics. A monthly report to the executives who approved the project is probably enough.

At the end of the day, your business model and the needs of your audience will determine the content formats you create and produce. What is most important is that you know whom you are talking to, you know what you are trying to say, and you continue to say it in a respectful way that engages your audience and builds trust. As Marcus Sheridan says, "Become the best teacher in the world at what you do" (Murray 2013).

SUMMARY

In today's world, it is all about the conversations we have with our audience. The old-fashioned idea of brand loyalty has undergone a major re-design: Our audience trusts us when we show that we can be trusted, which is when we have proven ourselves. In a world of online customer reviews and social media, proving ourselves means providing content that marketing professionals forty years ago would have considered unimaginable.

Transparency and honesty in content marketing are keys to developing a reliable, trustworthy brand that the audience will revisit. Sell this idea internally within your company and demonstrate to the C-suite that there will be a return on investment.

Now that you know why you need to produce all the content, and how to frame it, let's talk about the people responsible for doing so in Chapter 10.

REFERENCES

Handley, A., & Chapman, C. C. (2011). *Content rules, how to create killer blogs, podcasts, videos, ebooks, and webinars*. Hoboken, NJ: Wiley.

Leibtag, A. (2011). *How to explain the value of content marketing*. http://contentmarketinginstitute.com/2010/11/content-marketing-value/.

McCambley, J. (2013). *Stop selling ads and do something useful*. http://blogs.hbr.org/cs/2013/02/stop_selling_ads_and_do_someth.html.

McDermott, C. (2013). *How your content marketing benefits from a listen, ask, share approach*. http://contentmarketinginstitute.com/2013/01/content-marketing-listen-ask-share-approach.

Mitchell, S. (2010). *How to explain the value of content marketing*. http://contentmarketinginstitute.com/2010/11/content-marketing-value/.

Moran, T. (2012). *Should content marketing get the gate?* http://www.cmo.com/articles/2012/2/23/should-content-marketing-get-the-gate.html.

Murray, D. (2013). Content Marketing World: Is there where we want to live? The Ragan Report.

Phillips, K. (2013). *Marketing lies*. http://www.iocreativegroup.com/blog/2013/2/12/marketing-lies.html.

Pulizzi, J. (2012a). *What is content marketing?* http://www.junta42.com/resources/what-is-content-marketing.aspx.

Pulizzi, J. (2012b). *Mining data for the right content marketing at the right time*. http://contentmarketinginstitute.com/2012/11/mining-data-content-marketing/.

Vaughan, P. (2012). *12 revealing charts to help you benchmark your business blogging performance*. http://blog.hubspot.com/blog/tabid/6307/bid/33742/12-Revealing-Charts-to-Help-You-Benchmark-Your-Business-Blogging-Performance-NEW-DATA.aspx.

Williams, D. (2010). *How to explain the value of content marketing*. http://contentmarketinginstitute.com/2010/11/content-marketing-value/.

THE DREAM DIGITAL TEAM

CHAPTER 10

We have spent a lot of time exploring how to configure your content and digital teams so that you can produce and manage content in the most efficient and effective way possible. The focus of this chapter is to describe and define who should be doing all of this work.

As we've discussed before, most organizations suffer from siloed environments in which content is created without input from important contributors or, even worse, where there is duplication of effort. The goal of this chapter is to help you create your digital dream team—to let you know whom you need and why you need them. They may not all be directly under your supervision (some may be outsourced), but you will manage many of them.

YOU NEED GREAT TALENT

Talent is the mainstay of any organization. It doesn't matter how fantastic your technology is or how tightly your processes run: if you don't have great people who understand and do their jobs creatively and with passion, you will not be able to run a successful organization. Nor will you be able to create great content that engages your audiences with your brand.

Remember, content isn't just about the actual words or pictures on the pages. It's about how that content is planned for, created, published, and distributed. In this chapter, we're going to discover who should be on your digital team and how to configure those teams. Then in Rule #6, we'll explore workflows for content creation, publication, and distribution.

THE DIGITAL STRATEGY TALENT YOU NEED

Here's a list—not complete, but a good starting place—of the types of talent you need. I say "talent" because your company may not be able to hire as many individuals as you would like, but however big or small your team is you will need these skills at the table. It is possible that an individual will wear more than one hat. Remember Jonathon Colman from our case study about REI at the end of Part 2? He does wear many hats—he calls himself a hybrid web professional.

The people on your dream content team will probably fall into three groups of advocates:

- Customer advocates
- Publishing and distribution advocates
- Business advocates

While every member of your digital team is supposed to advocate for all three of these areas, on most web teams you will find that some professionals think the customer is the most important, others think that the business is most important, and still others that the content management system (CMS) is the most important.

The truth is that all three are vital: when you don't ensure that all are being protected you will not have much. The tough part of managing teams who come to digital projects from different places is that you need to remember where everyone is coming from. Be sensitive to each person's take on content strategy and content development, especially as you create the workflow.

Note: You may have some professionals who fall into all three divisions below and advocate for different things at different times on different projects. The goal of this chapter is for us to describe the different roles of a great digital content team. Your situation will constantly flex; make sure you have the right talent who can help you flex with it (a Lycra® content approach, so to speak).

- *Customer advocates*
  - Content strategists
  - Visual designers
  - Information architects
  - Content creators (writers, photographers, videographers, and graphic designers)
  - Usability professionals
- *Publishing and distribution advocates*
  - Developers
  - CMS authors
  - SEO experts
  - Audience engagement strategists (social media professionals)
- *Business advocates*
  - Project managers
  - Analytics experts

- Business analysts
- Reviewers

Before we talk about those different roles, let's talk about some of the challenges inherent to a digital team.

FINDING THE MONEY (SPENDING LIKE A PUBLISHER?)

As we said in Chapter 9, all organizations need to start thinking like publishers. Does that also mean that they need to spend money like publishers? Can every organization possibly have a staff that huge, one that encompasses an entire design and editorial staff? If the organization is unwieldy when it comes to content production, how can you ensure that money is being spent wisely? Well, output matters.

MAKING OUTPUT MATTER

The size of your team should be in direct ratio to how important your digital efforts are to the organization. For most large companies, the way you attract customers and market to them online is central to achievement thresholds, which usually involves getting as many people as possible to visit your digital properties and begin/continue conversations. For smaller companies, having a strong online presence allows you to stand out from your competitors. How do you produce all this content and design all these websites and content projects if you don't have a team?

As we discussed in Chapter 2, you need to make the business case for content. You need to make it in the right way, beginning with a deep understanding of your C-suite and what matters to them. Once you do that, you may be able to hire additional full time employees. Or you may be able to gather some budget money to outsource some of your needs. In fact, outsourcing may be the solution that is right for your company. Luckily, many fine organizations around the globe specialize in content planning, creation, production, and distribution.

HAVING A BACK END AND A FRONT END

To have a great digital content team, you need to have two types of web professionals—those who understand the front end of the web and those who understand the back end. The front end of the web is what the audience sees—the graphical interface (visual design), the navigation, and the interactive elements. The back end is the code, what makes the web run. We talked about code in Chapter 4.

Front End Web Professionals	Back End Web Professionals
• **Captain Web** (How does it all look?) • **Content Strategists** (How does the content look? Does it facilitate interaction?) • **Visual Designers** (How does it look? Does the design facilitate interaction?) • **Information Architects** (How do the navigation and interactive elements look?) • **Content Creators** (writers, photographers, videographers, and graphic designers) (Is the content doing what we want it to be doing?) • **Usability Professionals** (Can people navigate throughout the design and find what they need?) • **CMS Authors** (Is it publishing properly?) • **SEO Experts** (Can people find different content?) • **Audience Engagement Strategists** (social media professionals) • **Project Managers** (Is the project resolving the business case challenge—on time and within budget?) • **Business Analysts** (Is the project resolving the business case challenge—on time and within budget?) • **Analytics Experts** (Do the analytics show that we approached this properly and that the content is performing well?)	• **Captain Web** (Is everything operating the way it should?) • **Content Strategists** (How is the content meta-tagged? Is it behaving as it should in different templates and on other digital properties? Can people easily save it for later?) • **Information Architects** (Does the structure support the interactive elements?) • **Developers** (Is the code working properly?) • **CMS Authors** (What can we do on the back end to publish efficiently?) • **SEO Experts** (Is the content meta-tagged with the right keywords?) • **Audience Engagement Strategists** (social media professionals) (Is it easy to share content and interactive features?) • **Project Managers** (Is everything operating properly?)

What you see is that many of these people/talents overlap. Some do not. That's where you may have some major challenges to work through. The important thing is that each role is somehow represented on your team.

Many teams run into problems when the back end and front end do not communicate. They need to understand each other and work together, but they don't understand the limitations that each role faces. Remodeling a room is a good example: You want to redo your kitchen. You have a certain budget—as my husband, the economist, always tells me, "There are limited resources in the world."

Can You Have Both?

There are hybrid web professionals who do understand the back and front ends. These people are rare—so when you find one, make a friend for life. However, as the digital industry continues to change and grow, more professionals will learn to be comfortable with both.

You can bring in a kitchen designer who has 10 years of experience redesigning kitchens. Or you can try to redo the floor plan yourself. However, to redesign a kitchen, you need to understand the back end of the operation—that is, where does the plumbing go, where are the electrical sources, what are the restrictions of the local building code if you want to make changes?

In other words, you may have limitations and you may have to follow them, even if they have absolutely nothing to do with budget. You might throw all the money in the world at the task, and there are still certain things you just cannot change about the kitchen because of the plumbing code where you live.

This is why it is so important for both sides of your web team to understand the functional requirements of what you're trying to do with content and interaction. One side may recommend a solution that just is not feasible—either because you cannot write programming code that way or because that solution does not solve the business-case challenges.

Work hard to ensure that the back end and front end understand each other's roles. One of the inherent problems on digital teams is that people are usually from very different fields and backgrounds. Plus, there already may be baggage from working together in the past. I can't tell you how often I've seen a copywriter roll her eyes at a developer and a designer smirk at a marketing professional.

You need to help them see the world through each other's professional eyes. They need to understand both ends of the web and not just advocate for who they think their main client is on the project—whether it be the customer, CMS, or business case.

Why? Because your number one goal is to satisfy your audiences so that they keep coming back to your digital properties. Explain it this way to your team: If a customer comes to a gorgeous website that is sleek and fancy but it is hard to find what they want and the navigation is clunky—they're gone. Likewise, if the back end of your site is super-efficient but the site is no fun to look at—they're gone. The two ends need each other.

If your team isn't united behind that goal, then make sure you find the right professionals who do understand this. If your entire team is not internal to your organization, you may need to work even harder to make sure those conversations happen. And speaking of team members not being internal to the organization—even if you hire an outside firm, make sure that those people are invited to meetings and are part of the conversation. Everyone needs to hear everyone else.

MULTIDISCIPLINARY DIGITAL STRATEGY TEAMS ARE BEST

As we discussed in Rule #4, to plan, create, and distribute great content within your organization, you need multidisciplinary content teams. Because of the nature of modern business, and by this I mean the siloed nature of departments within organizations, you need people who span across departments, who can move horizontally within and sometimes outside of the organization. To put it in different words: You need web professionals who know something about everything and everything about something.

As Tiffani Jones Brown says, "As it stands, the boundaries between IA, web strategy and content strategy are porous. They will become more porous later. So, disciplines, kiss" (Brown, 2011).

KISSING DISCIPLINES

It's no longer acceptable for a visual designer not to understand content strategy. A usability expert has to be able to talk to developers about how to solve mobile template challenges. Lawyers need to understand the unique challenges of the online space so they can give appropriate advice about how to create and enforce guidelines.

Your content will be sharper and richer when the different members of your team understand each other's roles better, as well as the broad sketches of their jobs. By understanding certain limitations on technology, distribution vehicles, or sourcing content, members begin to understand what roads are best to follow and what roads will lead to nowhere. By each person understanding what they bring to the table and how their talents overlap, better content projects result.

For example, a visual designer may want to make a template follow certain design best practices. The content strategist, after content testing, knows that people ignore some of the content embedded in modules and would prefer to move that content into the main section. By understanding each other's points of view, a better customer experience emerges because the two professionals put their heads together to solve the problem in the best interest of the customer.

We all must learn to work together—and the good news is—most of us can.

PICK THE RIGHT TALENT

Now that we understand some of the inherent challenges of creating a team, let's focus on the talent and professionals you should hire so you can ensure your team works together seamlessly.

CAPTAIN WEB

Every team needs someone to be in charge, and the head of a digital engagement strategy (or whatever job title that person has) needs to have a unique set of talents. First, she needs to be able to manage people. She also needs to be able to listen to, and have the ear of, executives above her, including the VP of Marketing and perhaps even the CEO of the company.

Depending on the industry, the digital strategy of an organization is going to get a lot of scrutiny. The person leading the team needs to be comfortable with people, technology, and explaining process.

For many, this job is the culmination of some other marketing, technology, or communications job. Captain Web needs to understand:

- The overall strategy of the organization
- The business case
- The back end technology that runs the web
- The marketing strategies in place, both off and on digital properties
- Content strategy
- Design, development, and publishing process
- Talent within the organization
- What's missing from the team so she can outsource
- How to manage perceived mistakes

So basically you're looking for Superman or Wonder Woman. Actually, I've worked with many Captain Webs and I've found all the successful ones to be the same—they are calm under pressure, great listeners, and empathetic to the tremendous demands placed on their teams.

However, what makes Captain Web stand out is her approach to getting it right. First, Captain Web is not the type of person who thinks she is always right. This person is a listener. This person always follows Rule #3, and inherently understands that "to do the web right" they need to work in phases.

A great Captain Web knows how to work with the different people on the team: Customer advocates, the publishing and distribution advocates, and the business advocates. Interestingly, these people may cross over between front end and back end. Your best bet is to keep everyone focused on the idea that success will only happen when everyone brings their best game to the table.

One more thing—Captain Web needs to be someone who believes that each team member has equal importance to any other. This can't be emphasized enough. This means that everyone should be at the table at many points in the process. If the meeting is about the back end, don't exclude the front end team—let them experience each other's expertise first hand. Captain Web should not be the go-between; she should be a great facilitator.

USER EXPERIENCE PROFESSIONALS

The hallmark of user experience (UX) professionals is that they keep the customer at the center of every project. The better the experience customers have, the better chance there is for continued engagement with your brand.

UXers are phenomenal at keeping the focus of the project on best standards in current web thinking. However, they are sometimes so focused on the customer that they forget about the business case; that is, why the project was undertaken in the first place. That can't happen if the project is to be successful from a business perspective *and* a customer perspective.

Content Strategists

Content strategists are responsible for the entire publishing lifecycle of content within your organization. By the way, I find that people often lump content strategists and copywriters together, but that is a misconception. That's not to say a content strategist didn't start as a copywriter—and a great one at that. But just because the word content is in their title doesn't mean they are writers.

Content strategists are critical to web teams as content demands grow and the needs change, ranging from the need for technological expertise to the need for editorial expertise. Most organizations think they need a highly experienced editor, and only later realize that they also need someone who understands the technical end of the picture.

As content strategy continues to develop as a discipline, the lines between those "editorial content strategists" and "technical content strategists" will blur. Or else one will migrate into an entirely different discipline. In any case, it's important to understand the difference between the two.

Technical Content Strategists

Technical content strategists are concerned with many of the back-end attributes of publishing content: Metadata, structured content, adaptive content, and so on. They worry about the form and functionality of content so that it is prepared for multi-channel publishing. Technical content strategists may have technical writing backgrounds, library science training, or some other type of information technology background. These content strategists are invaluable for CMS authoring, as well as working with developers and designers to improve the content customer experience.

Editorial Content Strategists

Editorial content strategists are those who are concerned about the messaging of the content. They are the former editors and writers of the world and often come from a journalism, writing, communications, or public relations background. These content strategists are going to be tightly focused on editorial standards, voice and tone, and messaging.

Both types of content strategists are invaluable within an organization. Hopefully, you can find all of these skills in one person. But if you can't, make sure you can tell the difference between the two so you know who the right person is to entrust with different parts of the content publication process.

Information Architects

Information architects are like building architects—they build a website so that it has all of the support it needs, but so that you can still move things around and rework the layout if you want to, without the whole thing falling down.

Just like a building architect has to make the building beautiful and ensure that all of the electrical, plumbing, and other infrastructure works well, most information architects see themselves as shaping the website's structure and taking into account the back-end file structure and the front-end interactive elements. "As a discipline, IA defines spatial relationship and organization systems, and seeks to establish hierarchies, taxonomies, vocabularies, and sachem—resulting in documentation like sitemaps, wireframes, content types, and user flows, and allowing us to design things like navigation and search systems" (Wachter-Boettcher, 2012).
IAs should also work closely with content strategists so they understand the customer experience from the perspective of content.

In my experience, the most important thing about an IA is that he or she really understands the *business case* behind the digital strategy as well as how the audience will accomplish their goals. Without this understanding, you may end up with an "inside out" website, which is the term we use for a website that demonstrates the internal organization of the business ("See how we're organized!") rather than solving the audience's problems ("How can we get you what you want?").

For example, think of a big bureaucracy, like the government. Those within the bureaucracy understand how that agency is organized and the role they play in the government. Most people don't have that internal knowledge—they just want to understand how to do what they need to do when they interact with the agency on the web.

Visual Designers

In the same way, content creators interpret the business needs of the organization in written, video, or photographic form, visual designers interpret the identity of the brand in visual form. To be a great web designer, though, visual designers must understand usability and the interplay of interactive elements, as well as how consumers interact with all those interfaces. If content is the steak, design is the plating. We never want content to break design, as Margot Bloomstein, a content strategist, says, so it is important for designers and the rest of the team to work together, from the beginning, ensuring a single-minded vision for how the site will look and navigate (Leibtag, 2010).

Visual designers can make or break the success of web projects. When you hand client mockups of web pages, they often go right to critiquing the designs: Colors, pictures, typography, placement of elements, etc. They don't respond to the content as often, usually because the designer has filled content blocks with *lorem ipsum…*, and therefore their eye naturally goes to the design.

That's why the visual designers you hire, outsource, or include on your web teams need to understand that design's primary purpose is to shape and define interaction. If a visual designer is wedded to a particular design because of the way it looks, he's the wrong guy for your team. If he loves it because of the way it *works*, you've got a winner.

We will talk more about design in Chapter 11.

The visual designers you hire, outsource, or include on your web teams need to understand that design's primary purpose is to shape and define interaction.

Content Creators

The people that are a part of your content creation team (writers, photographers, videographers, graphic designers, and so on) may be in-house, or they may be freelancers or firms you hire to manage different content projects.

Copywriters

These people will hopefully run with the content strategy and produce useful, engaging, persuasive content. Great web writers understand all the technical ins and outs of writing for an online audience—SEO, usability, reading on screen—but will also capture the essence of your brand and know what you need your content to do.

Copy Editors

This group can help keep your editorial strategy on target, update style guides, maintain standards, and make sure that your content looks its best. Copy editors can also help refine content in terms of translations and localization.

Videographers

As video becomes a significant part of every organization's content strategy, you need to have people who can create great video experiences. They might team up with other content creators and creative professionals to tell brand stories that captivate your target audience.

Whether you outsource video professionals, or you have them in-house, include them in significant content conversations. Understanding the brand and business objectives will only serve to help them create video that is in line with what you're trying to accomplish.

Photographers

Pictures are invaluable on the web. Not only can they spark a conversation, they can also keep one going. And often pictures can be the central reason a browser converts to a customer.

Unless you run a news site, you probably won't have a photographer on the staff. However, you do need several competent, savvy photographers you can use when you have content that requires visual treatment. Your brand guidelines may specify different types of pictures, headshots, and action shots that are acceptable according to brand standards. Make sure your photographer knows about those standards before the shoot so he or she can plan accordingly.

Usability Professionals

Usability professionals research design, and evaluate the customer experience of products and services. Their main goals are to define and demonstrate how intuitive and easy it is for a customer to interact with a technology type. Usability experts are invaluable on digital projects because they can validate both visual design and content through testing. Remember to use their comments and findings when you are talking to the C-suite—this kind of feedback will be meaningful to them.

Usability testing usually involves watching a participant interact with your digital project—whether an app or website. Most usability tests are performed using a script and asking the participant to complete a set number of tasks. Each of the tasks is scored so after testing a predetermined number of users you know if you are on the right track (Krug, 2009). These tests should be scheduled at intervals throughout the project; you should probably test wireframes, the second iteration of wireframes, the design, and the second and third iteration of design. In this way, you can refine content and design throughout the course of a project so you know if you are moving in the right direction.

In the case of content, you should absolutely test your content, as much and as many times as possible. Testing both design and content together makes the most sense—you will get the fullest results because you will know whether the two are working together as they should; in tandem. So don't test with *lorem ipsum*—it will only hurt the arguments around the table when people claim the design is working or not working. You can't know unless you've also tested the content with it.

Testing content with design also helps to avoid one of the main problems we have described about content—it gets shifted to the end. Your content should be considered from the very beginning—it is the fuel that fires all those important conversations you are having with your target audiences. By demanding that usability testing happens with the actual content you are going to use, you ensure that it doesn't get left till the last minute.

PUBLICATION AND DISTRIBUTION ADVOCATES

The publication and distribution advocates are heavily wedded to technology. They understand that once the content ball is passed to them, they need to move it down the court without hiccups. In short, these professionals are responsible for how your content lives and performs in the outside world.

How your content performs is largely based on how easy it is to share and manipulate it. Therefore, you can expect these professionals to be very focused on providing seamless, technically superior experiences for their audiences.

Developers

Developers are a significant part of the web process but they often are left out of the business case meetings as well as the other planning project meetings. Most inexperienced clients will bring developers in for the requirements phase of a project. Or they will skip right over the business case and move right to requirements—this is a mistake. How can a developer truly understand the requirements if he or she doesn't understand the real goals of a project?

The truth is that developers are a critical part of the business case, design process, and content meetings. Developers know the code—the building code that is. They can tell you where you can put plumbing and electrical wiring without getting into trouble with the inspector at the end of your project. Developers are also helpful for suggesting the best types of programs to use for what you're trying to accomplish. Most importantly, they can tell you what you can't do—and bring everyone back to reality.

When you're using a content management system, you need your developers in the room so they can help you understand the full functionality of that content management system. If your databases aren't working correctly, you're in trouble. So make sure your developers are included in your planning meetings so you can hear and discuss their input.

CMS Authors

Your CMS authors produce your content and make sure it shows up on your digital properties correctly. In some organizations, CMS authors are called content producers, web producers, or web production specialists. These folks manage the content management system, assure content quality once it goes up, make sure it looks as it was envisioned, and that all links are working.

CMS authors are also experts on your CMS, what it can do and what it cannot do. Include them in all content conversations, particularly those that surround workflow and planning. We talked about CMS authors in Chapter 4. Remember, some CMS authors are going to have some knowledge of the CMS based on how often and how much content they are responsible for publishing.

SEO Experts

The first requirement of content is "Is it findable?" If people can't find your content, then they aren't going to interact with it. SEO professionals are responsible for this findability and their jobs are getting harder every day. Not only are the search engines of the world changing their algorithms constantly, but social media has put increasing pressure on optimizing content.

On your teams, the content creators and SEO professionals should engage with each other from the beginning (or they might be the same person). One is not more important than the other, although it is clear that your content should be written and created for people to consume. How you tag and identify the content on different channels is vital, and your SEO professional should be engaged in that process as well.

Once the content is out there, the SEO team should watch and analyze its performance, making tweaks along the way. That's when you iterate—bring the content creators back in for help once you identify potential weaknesses in the way the content was originally optimized for search.

Audience Engagement Strategists (Social Media Professionals)

We talked a lot about distributing content using audience engagement strategies in Chapter 5. After you publish content, you need to distribute it to as many people as possible. Great audience engagement strategists are like hosts at cocktail parties—they make everyone feel comfortable and don't focus all the attention on themselves.

Community engagement is really the interaction of several different parts of an organization: marketing, PR, customer service, crisis communications, and emergency response. Make sure that your audience engagement strategists work with other people in those departments so that you are delivering the best possible experience for your customers as they engage with your brand using distribution technologies, including social media.

BUSINESS ADVOCATES

Many of "business advocate" professionals might not think of themselves as business-focused. However, on digital projects, the reason these professionals are on your team is to keep the focus on the business objectives for the project. They are invaluable for shifting attention from creative differences back to what will ultimately make the project successful—if the feature you're arguing about encourages better brand engagement.

Project Managers

Project managers keep the trains running and on time. In many organizations, Captain Web may serve as the PM on many, if not all of the web projects. Great PMs know that they need to listen to every voice, but as Sheryl Sandberg, Chief Operating Officer of Facebook, says, "Prioritize ruthlessly." In this context, not everyone is equal. The goal of a project is to satisfy the business case for why you started the project in the first place.

I have seen all types of PMs—those that are obsessed with timelines and spreadsheets, those that try to manage everyone's expectations, those that tell everyone they are right. Those are not the great PMs of the world. The great PMs of the world understand the delicate balance between listening, hearing, and getting the work done.

The real reason to have PMs is what Mike Monteiro, a designer and author says, "The project manager also serves as the voice of the client in the room" (Monteiro, 2012). Even if the project manager is on your team, and you are the client, the client in this case is the business case for the project. A great PM keeps the project focused on the original business goals for doing the project.

Analytics Experts

Analytics experts are responsible for watching how the content performs. This may be simple, reporting on how certain pages are performing, or complex, monitoring product sales and customer traffic on a daily basis.

True analytics experts are data geeks. They don't love numbers—they love patterns and mysteries. They want to answer the questions of why, and how, and when. They think data is a god that must be followed into the wilderness. I admire those qualities. However, as with any true discipline, even in digital we must triangulate our research. This means that if we have an assumption, and we have one data point that backs it up, we should look for at least two others to be sure.

Our analytics tells us one part of the story. We need usability testing, customer feedback, and business processes analyses before we can make any true determinations.

Business Analysts

Business analysts are critical to have on your team because they will keep you focused on the business objectives of the organization. They will also tell you how the content is doing from a performance perspective and how well you are doing in terms of the organization's overall goals and metrics. In most organizations, the business analyst for your web team would be the VP of Communications or the Director of Marketing, who reports C-suite messages back to the marketing and digital teams.

In small organizations, this might work well. But in large organizations, you really need this person to be part of the web team so that he or she knows exactly what is going on and can communicate that to all of the business teams within the company.

For example, if you run an e-commerce website, you need someone to be responsible for understanding the constant data that is pouring in. I'm not talking about the analytics of site usage, but about how different products are performing. Can the digital marketing team do anything to improve the situation? Or are you doing so great that they are ready to launch another set of products? How do you prepare for that?

Think of your business analyst as a translator. It is his or her job to move horizontally in the organization and understand what's taking place in other departments. This will help the flow of information moving in the form of feedback and new requirements for the digital strategy team. In this way, the team can continue to build robust digital experiences.

Reviewers

Ah, reviewers. The true bottlenecks on almost every web project I've ever been on. How many times have I heard, "Oh, the developers are holding us up?" Almost never. How many times have I heard, "Oh, legal is holding us up." A lot.

Yet, that said, reviewers are required on any project. They need to review content to make sure it aligns with brand standards, is in keeping with messaging, and is legally compliant (this is particularly important for heavily-regulated industries). In some organizations, it is clear who the reviewers are—they are the subject matter experts who can tell you if what you are saying is factually correct and appropriate. In other organizations, you may need to find reviewers who serve as editors or brand protectors.

The most effective way to manage reviewers is to educate them about digital content. Lawyers, in particular, can be very creative if you explain to them what you are trying to say. They even may help you find a different way to say it that is legal.

Spend time with your reviewers—whoever they are. Teaching reviewers about digital content and what you are trying to accomplish will often speed the process along and make them feel like an invaluable member of the team. If the project is successful, shine some of the golden light upon them. They will be more than happy to help you out the next time you need them.

SUMMARY

Now more than ever you need to align the digital marketing talent you have. Members of digital strategy and content teams need to move horizontally across organizations as well as vertically. One project may not have the same group of people as the project before. Let the needs of the project dictate the roles that should be in the room every step of the way.

There are many different professionals you should have on your team (and in some small organizations, people will probably wear a few different hats). Your digital strategy professionals need to understand the back end and front end demands of the web. They usually fall into three groups—those who advocate for the customer, those who care about the business, and those who care most about publishing and distribution. No matter which group they are a part of, you need all of them on your team because they bring a much needed mix of talents to every project.

Projects are not about ego—they are about serving the client (and your organization) and doing great work. Collaboration is vital to a better product—no matter if the person is a front end, back end, customer, business, or publishing advocate. We're all here for one reason—to reach our achievement threshold. Trusting each other's knowledge and working together will get us there.

Now we're going to learn Rule #6, which addresses all of your questions about how to structure dream content teams so they do their best work.

REFERENCES

Brown, T. J. (2011). *Toward a content-driven design process*. Retrieved from http://thingsthatarebrown.com/blog/2010/05/toward-a-content-driven-design-process/.

Krug, S. (2009). *Rocket surgery made easy: The do it yourself guide to finding and fixing usability problems*. Berkeley, CA: New Riders.

Leibtag, A. (2010). *Content strategy: It's truly a multidisciplinary practice*. Retrieved from http://www.cmswire.com/cms/web-engagement/content-strategy-its-a-truly-multidisciplinary-practice-008733.php.

Monteiro, M. (2012). *Design is a job*. New York: A Book Apart, p. 112.

Wachter-Boettcher, S. (2012). *Content everywhere: Strategy and structure for future-ready content*. Brooklyn, NY: Rosenfeld Media, p. 20.

WORKFLOW THAT WORKS

The goal of the seven rules in *The Digital Crown* has been to give you a framework you can use to create, publish, and manage the content within your organization. The first two rules were about focusing your content on your audience and understanding your stakeholders. The next two rules were about keeping your content processes constantly iterative, as well as creating teams of multidisciplinary digital and business professionals. The fifth rule encouraged you to make governance central. Now we're going to explore combining all of these ideas into Rule #6. Workflow is the beginning, middle, and end of content success; it's where people, process, and technology should all come together in synergy.

WHAT IS WORKFLOW?

Workflow. Two four-letter words put together. Workflow is the process your teams follow to get the job done.

Let me explain workflow a bit. I have two daughters, ages eight and ten, and they love to watch *DC Cupcakes*, a show about two sisters who started a cupcake bakery together. Watching the show with them made me realize how workflow is everywhere and affects every business. When you bake something, there is an obvious workflow. For example, you can't ice a cupcake before you bake it.

Similarly, have you ever tried to put together a Lego playset without the directions (this is where my four-year-old son comes in), the step-by-step, in-color directions that you have to follow carefully to recreate the totally cool toy on the cover of the box? It is impossible—trust me; only a mathematical genius with incredible spatial talents can do it—or a four-year-old.

Content strategists Ann Rockley and Charles Cooper describe workflow as "the way work or tasks flow through a cycle on their way to getting a job done. Workflow helps organizations perform tasks in an efficient and repeatable manner."[1]

Again, you must bake a cupcake before you ice it. Otherwise, no one will eat it, and if no one will eat it, then no one will buy it. Result: The bakery will lose money.

[1] http://www.amazon.com/Managing-Enterprise-Content-Unified-Strategy/dp/032181536X/ref=sr_1_1?ie= UTF8&qid=1377783441&sr=8-1&keywords=ann+rockley

WORKFLOW PROBLEMS: PEOPLE CREATING ICED CUPCAKES WITHOUT THE CAKE

Do you have any content lifecycles that are unbaked, iced cupcakes? Examples in content would be:

- Scrambling like mad to find an author, reviewer, and publisher the day that an important blog post is supposed to post
- Using three different names for your company on three different parts of the website
- Publishing content without metatags
- Using the wrong keywords, so no one can find the content

Those are your unbaked, iced cupcakes.

Meanwhile, that content was created in the same manner in which a frustrated parent tries to put together a Lego toy without the instructions—completely lacking in any logic, backward, and basically impossible.

Why do we treat content this way? Why do we treat our content teams this way? Most important, why do we treat our customers this way?

Ask yourself if you are running your content production teams like you're trying to reconstruct a Lego toy without the instructions. Are you making them eat a raw cupcake with icing?

WORKFLOW CHALLENGES

Let's appreciate the value of workflow, which forces us, frantic though we may be, to go step by step and get it right. But it's not easy, is it? Sometimes we have big teams to manage, and, face it, we are always rushed and some little devil inside our brain is trying to convince us that "just this once" we can skip the workflow steps and "just put it up."

So let's agree that this is not easy—using a workflow has its challenges. We can divide these challenges into four categories; in most organizations, these challenges overlap. See if you can find your organization in one of the following:

- Information flow
- Misplaced talent
- Lack of guidance and clear models
- Lack of training

INFORMATION FLOW AMONG TEAM MEMBERS

Creating and publishing content is challenging because the production, management, and dissemination of content rely on the flow of information

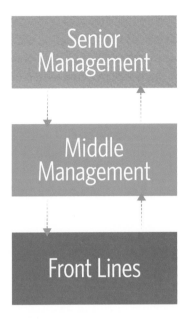

Figure R6.1 Information flow. Ahava Leibtag. All Rights Reserved.

within an organization. And, as we all know, information within an organization does not always flow as it should—freely.

Information flow in an organization should look like Figure R6.1.

Information should flow freely from senior management down to the front lines. Then it should flow back freely from the front lines up to senior management. This is not how things usually work.

Why? Mostly because in many organizations there are many more layers than this diagram shows. Also, information tends to flow sideways and stay within a particular department or larger segment within the organization. This leads to content silos, in which important information intended for a wider audience stays stuck in one place.

Now the bigger question—*why* does information flow the wrong way, resulting in poor workflow? The answer is—people. The information does not move by itself. Someone, at some point, fails to communicate, fails to report, or just plain doesn't get the value of correct information flow, and—boom!—workflow is impeded.

MISPLACED TALENT

I have seen so many content projects go awry because the wrong people were in charge of the wrong things. I'm not talking about your typical, "He shouldn't be the boss," political nitpicking. I mean serious misplacement of talent—not just the wrong people in the wrong jobs, but the wrong jobs in the wrong order.

I will give you an example: I once ran a team of content writers who were writing content for a huge question-and-answer portal. The editorial direction was pretty unclear to begin with, but it continued to shift throughout the project. The project manager running the team was a very talented writer. But, she was put in the awkward position of having to be the project manager on a content project she really didn't love. She didn't have enough time to do this project, plus all of her other work, and so she fell behind on editing our submissions. By the time she got around to editing them, the project was more than halfway done, so we couldn't fix the mistakes in time. It was a disaster all around. Wrong person in the job.

On a different project, I worked as a consultant who hired an excellent writer. She was also phenomenal with code, creating landing pages, and publishing content. (If you find a person like this, marry them to your organization.) Because she was so good with code, and the organization lacked anyone in-house to publish content, they ended up squandering this excellent writer's talent in the production queue. Why, when you can easily find an entry-level CMS author, would you waste the talents of a writer who has worked for some of the largest media companies in the world? This time—right person, wrong assignment. I actually could go on and on with examples like the two above, but the reason I chose these was because they both illustrate workflow challenges: The wrong person is in the wrong role.

In both cases, the two women were talented at their core roles and were better off focusing on those. In the first case, the client should have hired a project manager, which they did end up doing, to their credit. The writer should not have been doing the editing work—that should have been done by a professional editor who truly understood the editorial direction of the project. In the second case, my client should have found a web producer to build the landing pages who would also insert content that the writer created.

These are both clear workflow problems that lead directly back to talent identification issues. A great writer does not make a great editor. A great SEO professional does not make a great project manager. And, a great designer does not make a great writer of microcopy. Icebergs will find your content if you let the wrong people steer the ship.

This is why Rule #4 is so important. Everybody on digital content teams has to wear a few different hats. Pick people who are good at more than one thing. This rule is critical for all of web production, not just content.

In the case of workflow, however, one person cannot perform more than one task at a time. So, make sure the most talented person *at that task* is responsible for it. For example, a nit-picky content editor should do quality assurance on published content so that she can pick up any mistakes or problems with layout. We'll talk about evaluating talent later on in this rule.

LACK OF GUIDANCE AND CLEAR MODELS

This is one of the challenges I see most often when consulting about workflow. Workflow is like a recipe, with a clear set of tasks that must be performed step-by-step. Embedded in the process are checkpoints and approvals, in the same way that in a restaurant, more experienced chefs watch the line to make sure dishes are prepared correctly. When not everyone in the kitchen is aware of the recipe, as well as the correct way to set the plate, mistakes occur.

It would seem then, that if people have guidance and clear models, they should be able to produce, create, and publish content. However, that leads me to my next workflow challenge—training.

LACK OF TRAINING

In many organizations, content is messy because people lack training. Not just in creating the content, but in all areas: Sourcing it, understanding who to go to for clarity, knowing how to use the CMS correctly to publish the content, and knowing they must take it down or archive it according to a certain timeline.

If you have a distributed content workforce, which we'll explain shortly, then training everyone may seem almost impossible. But, nowadays training can be accomplished with short videos, half-day training seminars, and sometimes a simple phone call. You wouldn't expect someone to make a sales call without some training, would you? So why do you expect them to manage and handle your content without training?

Let's learn more about the different types of content teams you may have and how you can structure them to produce the best content for your organization.

DIFFERENT TYPES OF CONTENT TEAMS

There are many types of content workforces and the makeup of your workforce will influence your workflow. You may have any one of the following types of content teams:

- Siloed
- Distributed
- Centralized
- Rogue

SILOED CONTENT TEAMS

When companies don't communicate in an organized fashion about their content, they create siloed content workforces. In fact, the organization may be structured in such a way that there is no reason for different departments to communicate about content. The nature of the web itself can create this problem, because by nature it is disruptive to the way organizations have always compartmentalized information. Content should cause departments to rethink the way they manage knowledge and data from within the organization, as well as how they communicate about it to outsiders. But many organizations have been slow to catch up; they still suffer from siloed communications.

You can see the effects of siloed communication when you find FAQs (Frequently Asked Questions) on one part of a global organization's website, and a PDF file containing the exact same information, but in long, boring paragraphs, on another part of the site. This begs the following questions:

- When did Department A create the FAQs?
- Did they know Department B was creating the PDF Guide? If so, why didn't they collaborate?
- Who is updating the FAQs when things change?
- Who is updating the PDF Guide to reflect those changes?

Chances are neither Department A nor B knew about the other's content. It could be that Department A read Department B's boring guide and decided to break it up into FAQ web pages. That team didn't let Department B know. In any case, consumers are very confused; they are having two different conversations with the same company—and they do not know which conversation to trust. It is *because* they are having two different conversations that the audience will lose trust.

Silos Hurt Organizations

While content silos frustrate content professionals, they do more to hurt the customer—therefore, hurting the business—sometimes to the tune of millions of dollars. As Ann Rockley and Charles Cooper describe, "While organizations suffer from the negative impact of content silos, customers are the real victims. When information exists in multiple areas, it often differs in content, style, tone, and message. Customers don't know which one is correct, most up to date, or comprehensive. When customers encounter these inconsistencies, they become understandably confused. Sometimes confusion leads to aggravation. Inconsistency damages the customer experience."

In other words, if the conversations on your digital properties are confusing and inconsistent, guess what your audiences are doing? They are jumping to your competitors to have conversations with them. That equals lost revenue for you.

DISTRIBUTED CONTENT TEAMS

"Distributed" in this case simply means that your content teams do not sit together in one place. Rather, they are scattered throughout your organization, like so many leaves in the wind. Distributed content teams typically are the hallmark of large, multinational corporations or institutions like government, higher education, and healthcare. Sometimes the different teams exist for political or budgetary reasons— but whatever the reason, if these teams are not well trained and motivated, the content suffers, the consumer suffers, and so the business suffers.

In the model of a distributed content workforce, different departments are given access to certain publishing powers within the content management system (CMS). Depending on workflow, they can hit "Publish" and have the page go live when they are finished. In some cases, there is an extra checkpoint, where presumably a trained editor is looking at the content to ensure it fulfills all of the organizations' standards for web content.

Distributed content teams are usually a necessary evil and they present a variety of challenges. However, they can be incredibly useful in situations where you just don't have enough manpower on your central content team to keep all of your content fresh. Distributed content teams are typically responsible for the assembly line content we talked about in Chapter 4. They may just change phone numbers or names of faculty or update events on calendars. Some distributed content workforces may have much more authority.

Think of a huge multinational organization with offices around the world, offering thousands of chunks of content describing products, services, or support documentation. Those teams create content around what they do and they want to have control over their content. Consider the following scenarios:

- Content must be produced in multiple languages and for multiple cultures
- Content is requested and sourced within that department; for example, they are engineers who produce technical documentation that your team can't produce
- The head of that department doesn't report to your boss, or really to any bosses, as far as you can tell

How do you apply governance standards to that team? How do you know when they are publishing content? Are you responsible for their data and analytics, or can you give them access and expect them to track those conversations? As we see, distributed content teams can be helpful and they can also present challenges.

CENTRALIZED CONTENT TEAMS

Centralized content teams are typically marketing or editorial departments that have complete control over any content published to any of an organization's digital media properties. While complete control sounds like a really fun fantasy, in actuality, centralized content teams can suffer from any of the following:

- Not enough resources or staff to cover all of the content
- Massive backlogs of content because of bottlenecks in workflow

- Confusion over priority on creating and publishing content
- Lack of clarity about who owns certain types of content
- Lack of subject matter experts who will help clarify content

Centralized content teams are also usually comprised of a motley crew of individuals: Former journalists, marketing managers, data analysts, and designers and developers. This can typically lead to in-fighting about who is more important (you all are!) or whose projects deserve priority. Also, depending on the size of the organization, centralized content teams may be exhausted all the time because they just have too much content to manage.

ROGUE CONTENT TEAMS

Of all of the different types of content teams, rogue content teams are my favorite because I love rebels. Did you know that Thomas Jefferson said, "A little rebellion now and then is a good thing"? However, in the case of rogue content teams, they can cause a tremendous amount of trouble for you if you are responsible for the brand and content floating out there on the currents of the web.

Rogue content teams typically surface in organizations like hospitals and higher education. Doctors want their own Facebook pages, faculty members want to publish research on their own websites—and who can blame them? The web is a self-publishing medium and the doctor wants to get the word out about his services. A professor doesn't want to hear that she can't directly publish her research to her site—it's "publish or perish" (pun intended here) in her world. Why should she be at the mercy of your governance standards? She doesn't necessarily care about the brand of the university—she cares about her own personal brand.

In my experience, you can actually learn a lot from rogue content teams, and turn those lessons into a positive experience. Consider the fact that they had the gumption to go out there and create their own digital properties. This means that they:

- Are extremely motivated to converse with their target audiences
- Understand the innate importance of communicating using digital technologies

That makes them potential advocates in helping you persuade your senior leadership for better publishing standards within the organization. It also means that you may have to give them extra attention by giving their content priority in the beginning of your seduction process. However, if you manage it right, they will reward you by letting others in the organization know they should trust you.

Rogue content teams are also valuable because they are often creative, unhampered by political content concerns, and just trying to put a stake in the sand. While they may call your brand something it is not, use a logo their teenager created using illegally pirated software, violate every rule of social media etiquette, and do other obnoxious things that make you tear your hair out, chances are they may have created engagement with their customers because they are REAL. If they are having success, try to understand and appreciate the creative part of what they are doing as a model for your content teams.

That said, by definition they will probably not want to conform to your (or any) standards, and certainly will not want to adhere to a workflow. Managing their needs means having to convince them of the value of working with you—this is a tough sell for them.

WHICH CONTENT TEAM IS RIGHT FOR YOUR ORGANIZATION?

The truth is, any of the above models except rogue may work for your organization. You may have to use a blended mix from all three. You can have a distributed content workforce that has access to some minor parts of the CMS and a centralized content workforce that does most of the heavy lifting on content. You may have rogue content teams that you need to get under control. Here's a table to sum up our comparisons:

Type of Content Team	Pros	Cons
Siloed	• A lot of content gets created because there is no over-arching process to go through	• Departments do not communicate with each other • The audience is confused • The departments are confused
Distributed	• Can be useful in situations where you don't have enough manpower on your central content team to keep all of your content fresh • For multinational organizations, can deal effectively with language, culture, and other differences	• Difficult to govern • Difficult to achieve consistency • Need careful, thorough training
Centralized	• Have complete control over content	• Not enough resources or staff • Massive backlogs of content • Confusion over priority • Lack of clarity about ownership • Lack of subject matter experts
Rogue	• Are extremely motivated to converse with their target audiences • Understand the value of web content • Unhampered by political concerns	• Almost impossible to govern • No interest in adhering to workflow • No stake in overall quality or consistency

Iterate, Iterate

A point about iteration. No one is expecting you to create the perfect team. But you may feel you have done so. Great! But remember—be flexible. Iterate. If something is going wrong, sit down with the team and find the problem area—more than likely it will be that someone isn't really capable of the assignment, isn't interested in it, or isn't doing it well. Find the problem, reorganize, and move on. Iterate the workflow, the team, and the process.

In a perfect world, you would create your dream content team based on your business objectives, as well as what your C-suite expects you to deliver digitally. However, most organizations already have legacy content, demands for new content, and talent and teams in place. So, your job is to find alignment between the amount of content you are expected to manage, and what the right amount of content truly is for your organization. And, like everything else on the web, configuring the right type of content team is an iterative process. What works today may need to be altered tomorrow.

However, even more important than the type of team you have, is the workflow you have in place for putting the right talent in the right roles. So let's analyze workflow and figure out how to identify the right talent for baked AND iced cupcakes.

WORKFLOW BASICS

When we look at our content strategy lifecycle next to our editorial structure for planning, creating, publishing, distributing, and analyzing content, we see a reflective process (Figures R6.2 and R6.3).

At each point in a content strategy phase, we have people who are responsible for moving the content to the next phase. So too, in the workflow, we have people who move the content from one stage to the next. This would be highly coordinated baton tossing of content, which works—as opposed to uncoordinated baton tossing. Let's look at these roles.

THE PEOPLE

Any team creating content needs to have a clear picture of where the content is coming from and how it is published to the site. In every content production chain, there are typically eight different roles:

- Requesters
- Providers
- Creators
- Reviewers

Figure R6.2 The lifecycle of content strategy. Ahava Leibtag. All Rights Reserved.

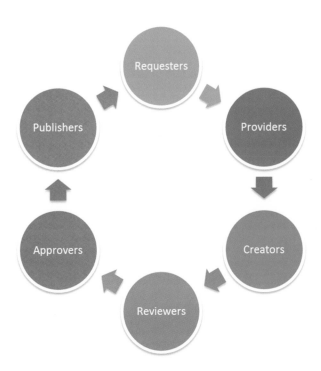

Figure R6.3 Content publishing workflow structure. Ahava Leibtag. All Rights Reserved.

- Approvers
- Publishers
- Distributors
- Analysts

Requesters

In most organizations, content requests come in from the C-suite, from executives throughout the organization, and from data analysts requesting changes. In a proactive content team, the team makes content requests because, by analyzing data, they realize they need to change the conversation.

Providers

Providers are the people in the organization who give you the basic raw facts or data to create the content. They may be subject matter experts, sales people, product specialists, or marketing managers who understand their product or service lines.

Creators

Once the request comes in and the content is sourced, it needs to be created. This is when content is handed to your creative content producers: Writers, photographers, videographers, and so on.

Reviewers

Content needs to be reviewed to make sure it is in line with brand and editorial standards. Legal may need to review for compliance on regulatory matters. The original requesters and providers should probably review as well to make sure the content is not only factually correct, but satisfies the original business intention.

Final Approvers

These people can finalize the content and say that it is ready for publishing.

Publishers

These are the CMS authors, web producers, and content publishers who ensure the content goes live and looks good.

Distributors

The social media and audience engagement specialists are responsible for publicizing and using the new content to drive engagement.

Analysts

These are the people who answer the question, "How is that content performing?" That is the most important question in the minds of analysts. Content supports the sales process and whatever it is that you're selling; analysts are going to focus on how the data shows an ROI from having a robust content team.

Review of Roles

Roles	Definitions
Requesters	Create Assignments
Providers	Source Content
Creators	Source and create
Reviewers	Edit
Approvers	Give Final Approval
Publishers	Prepare content for distribution
Distributors	Distribute content
Analysts	Analyze content performance and behavior

The above is a very simplified version of a content workflow lifecycle. Within those roles are thousands of tiny details that need to be performed. To truly understand your content lifecycle so you can create an efficient workflow, you need to understand all the tasks that the people in each of these roles perform.

EVALUATING THE WORKFLOW

Before you begin to structure your content teams for greatest efficiency, you need to sketch your current workflow. Here are some questions you need to answer for a basic sketch:

1. Who currently fills the above roles?
2. What is the current process in place for that role?
3. What happens when that person is unavailable?
4. Who gets to make decisions about changes in process?
5. How does information flow from one role to the next?
6. How does information get shared? (Files, shared drives, project management software)

A basic sketch might look something like this:

Roles	Tasks	Who?
Requesters	• Request content	
Providers	• Source Content—could be multiple subject matter experts	
Creators	• Write and Source • Edit Video (if necessary) • Edit Photos (if necessary)	
Reviewers	• Edit • Legally approve • Approve for messaging and branding	
Approvers	• Edit final copy	

Roles	Tasks	Who?
Publishers	• Prepare content for distribution	
Distributors	• Distribute through different digital channels	
Analysts	• Analyze the content over time to see if it is performing well	

Now that we understand what the current workflow looks like, we need to apply one very basic principle—*who* the baton is passed to is just as important as *how* the baton is passed. It's the people AND the process.

So take some time to analyze the table you've created and see if the personality and skills of the people in the "Who" column match what you need. If they do—great. If not, make some changes.

PUTTING THE RIGHT PEOPLE IN PLACE

The most important part of workflow is making sure you have the right professionals doing the job. As Erin Kissane says, "divide up the work in a way that takes advantage of your colleagues' various skills. Got a data nerd handy? Put her on that content audit and gap analysis. And your content specialist who used to edit a magazine? Let him lead the feature design recommendations and voice and tone work" (Kissane, 2011).

In other words, you don't want a baker icing a cupcake. You want someone who is really good at icing to decorate the cupcake and someone who is really great at baking to bake the cupcake. Now, that person might be great at both, or he may not. It takes good management and effective leadership to understand how to organize and structure workflow.

In order to put the right people in the right roles, you need to do the following:

- Evaluate talent fairly
- Structure for experience and personality
- Don't be afraid to experiment

It takes time to set up an effective workflow and in small companies, some people, if not all of them, may wear multiple hats. At the end of the day, you have to be honest when you're evaluating your talent and watch carefully how different people and personalities work together. Mix and match people—if it is a horrible idea, you will learn early on in the process that it may not work. Do not forget what we learned in Rule #4—everybody on the team has to be prepared to understand and know something about other professionals they work with.

If you find you are consistently having a problem getting your team to work together, then you need to troubleshoot and find the source of the tension.

Otherwise, you'll keep serving unbaked, iced cupcakes to your customers. And we're going for yum—not yuck.

Now that we've talked about content teams and how to structure them to create and manage content most effectively, we're going to talk about design and the fabulous interplay that needs to happen between the two to give your customers the best possible conversational experience.

REFERENCE

Kissane, E. (2011). *The elements of content strategy*. New York: A Book Apart.

TALKING ABOUT DESIGN

Remember the movie *Splash*? She's a mermaid; he's a lonely guy in New York looking for love. They meet and begin a passionate love affair. One day he brings her a beautiful music box wrapped in the famous Tiffany's box. Now, remember, she's a mermaid, so she isn't familiar with Tiffany's. When he presents her with the box, she looks at it lovingly for a long time, kisses it, looks at him and says, "It's beautiful. I love it."

IT'S WHAT'S INSIDE THE BOX

We have a tendency to act like that mermaid sometimes. We think that a beautiful design will bring success. However, we need to know that it's what's inside the box that brings the digital wins. Understanding the content that goes inside all of the boxes on your digital properties is the first step toward providing your customers with a satisfying conversation.

HOWEVER, LET'S GET REAL

In the real world, however, people *do* react to design. In *Splash*, the iconic blue box that signifies luxury was so beautiful that a mermaid believed *it* was the present.

We sometimes forget how many things around us are designed: cities, roads, traffic patterns, wait times in the doctor's waiting room, grocery store aisles, department stores within malls, and so on. Everything is designed—sometimes well and sometimes not so well—in investment of a business process. "Design is an investment in infrastructure and keeps the wheels of business running smoothly. Good design equals a more effective product or service. Design equals profit!" (Monteiro, 2012).

Design equals profit. Well, so does content.

Which one should you focus on during the digital strategy process: design or content? (Because you've already read the entire book, you already know the answer.)

THE RELATIONSHIP OF CONTENT TO DESIGN

Let's take a walk down memory lane. Remember, in Chapter 1, when we talked about how information becomes content? I'm going to make the same type of parallel about design and content as I did about information and content: design is to content as content is to information.

Just as design is supposed to hold, display, and structure content, content is doing the same thing for information. Information is what people want and need—content is just an entertaining, educational, informative way to give it to them.

While reading these chapters and rules you've learned how to take the information you want to convey to your audiences and select the right content format and distribution so that it resonates. Now we're going to talk about how the visual design process fits into that framework.

MARRY CONTENT AND DESIGN

There's no point in arguing about which is more important: content or design. I try to compare the two to an engagement ring: A beautiful diamond needs a stunning setting to set off all those facets so they sparkle with every turn of the light. No matter how beautiful the diamond, if the setting is ugly, it will lose its vivid appeal.

Content, too, will lose its sparkle if not set properly in the right design. But even more than that, content also has to support customers in accomplishing their tasks. If content and design are not well matched you mar the customer experience. By now we know what happens when you do that: you lose sales, or the chance to make an impression, or the opportunity to convert a lead into a customer.

When we think about content as a conversation, we understand how important it is to have the design of the conversation supported vividly. As Ginny Redish says, "For successful conversations, you must develop design and content together. Waiting until the end and just pouring content into a design that was created without real content is a recipe for disaster" (Redish, 2012). As we said earlier, the design process almost always gets more love than the content process. Let's take a look at why that happens. Then we'll look at some tools you can use to smooth your design/content process.

DESIGN BEFORE CONTENT REASON #1: PEOPLE REACT VISUALLY

As did the mermaid, people react visually. They see something and they think the totality of what they are seeing is the experience. I can't tell you how many meetings I have sat in with web teams where they look at the design and start breaking it apart, design element by design element. The most often heard phrase in a design meeting: "Can you just make it blue?" Or visual designer Jeff Rum's second favorite, "Can you make the logo bigger?"

People react visually and they often measure the value or usefulness of something based on how it looks. But—and perhaps this will become even more true as years go by and consumers get savvier about the web—today's audiences do not surf the web looking for beautifully designed websites. They're too smart for that. I've seen them hang out on the ugliest website you've ever seen for the promise of GETTING the thing they came to the website to get.

Customers come to websites for content: Text, pictures, slideshows, videos, status updates, purchasing power, personal information updating, and the list goes on. Design *supports* those tasks.

DESIGN BEFORE CONTENT REASON #2: BRINGING IN CONTENT TOO LATE

We need to think about the types of content that exist BEFORE we create the design. Dan Brown, Information Architect (not that Dan Brown), explains how a content strategist functions as a type of designer in his post, "Letter to a Content Strategist." He does a GREAT job suggesting the intricacies of how information architects and content strategists can work together to build better websites. Dan explains, "Ultimately, my job is to design structures. These are structures that establish navigation pathways, search frameworks, and business rules for governing how to display information. In order to design those things, I need insight into what you want the content to be, how you want it to behave, and what structures will let the content thrive" (Brown, 2010).

Content breaking design is a critical issue for digital content professionals. One of the goals of content strategy is to make meaning out of content BEFORE the design process begins (if possible) so that you don't end up with the problem described so well by Charlie Peverett:

> And when does a 'content person' get involved? Usually at what is, effectively, the last minute. When the *lorem ipsem* (that placeholder copy that's just stuck there by a designer) needs to be magically transformed into sparkling, all-singing, all-dancing 'copy.' At this point you'd be better off with an alchemist than a writer.
>
> (Peverett, 2010)

Content is the starting point, the building blocks of a website. For many, it's a paradigm shift in the way we think about building websites and creating content that will float on the currents of the web.

If we don't shift our focus to content, we are going to miss our audience. They come because they are looking for something. When you don't think about how to set the content in those structures so that it will thrive, it doesn't. It dies. And then content breaks design—it takes an elegant design and trashes it—usually because design comps were approved before the REAL content was inserted into the appropriate structures. This leads us to our next major problem …

DESIGN BEFORE CONTENT REASON #3: LOREM IPSUM

Lorem Ipsum is this Latin stuff that people put in as "filler content" until they have the actual content ready. It doesn't work well. If you're showing people digital mockup, doesn't it make sense to show them a digital mockup with all the right content and microcopy (the content that tells people what to do, like "sign in here").

I once encountered a designer who inserted the following into a website page mockup to give the client the sense of what words might occur on that page (Figure 11.1).

Visuals convey critical information to the customer without getting lost in the marketing gobbledygook that so many organizations insist on putting on EVERY page. So, how do you avoid that huge old mess? In other words: How can content professionals inform designers to know what to expect so they can move ahead with competent, appropriate design work?

Before we answer that question, we should probably understand how design works—so let's look at the design process a little more in depth.

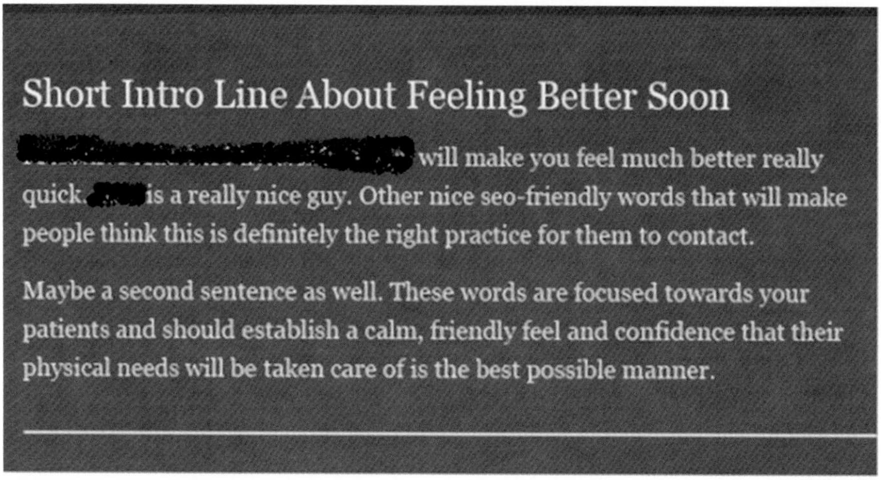

> ## Short Intro Line About Feeling Better Soon
>
> ████████████████████████ will make you feel much better really quick. ████ is a really nice guy. Other nice seo-friendly words that will make people think this is definitely the right practice for them to contact.
>
> Maybe a second sentence as well. These words are focused towards your patients and should establish a calm, friendly feel and confidence that their physical needs will be taken care of is the best possible manner.

Figure 11.1 Bad "advice" from a designer. Can you imagine? I, as the copywriter on the project, was less than thrilled.

THE DESIGN PROCESS

The design process is different for every content format in which you choose to embed your information. But let's take the redesign of a section of a website. That is probably the most consistent design process in digital strategy, and a good starting point for talking about how designers and content professionals can work together to create an overall more engaging user experience.

Designers typically use the following tools to demonstrate design to clients. They also use these tools to communicate with each other about design:

- Site Maps
- Flowcharts
- Wireframes
- Visual Designs

Let's explore these a bit so we can understand the tools designers use to communicate about design. Then we can discuss how content professionals can work with designers using similar or retrofitted tools.

Note: We are going to use visual examples from the same website so you can see how the website comes together from site map, to wireframe, to visual design.

SITE MAPS

Dan Brown defines a site map as "a visual representation of the relationships between different pages on a web site. Also known as a structural model, taxonomy, hierarchy, navigation model, or site structure" (Brown, 2007). Site maps work to show how all the information on a site fits together. Site maps visually represent classification of information so that you see the underlying organizational structure that joins all the different pieces of information together. Think of the organizational chart of a company—that is what a site

Don't Forget the Conversation

When we talk about "information flow" what we are really talking about is "conversations." I know that most people don't equate the two, but we need to if we are going to create engaging content, *and* work well within our teams. On the web every day, and in our offices every day, we are engaging in important conversations that support the flow of information.

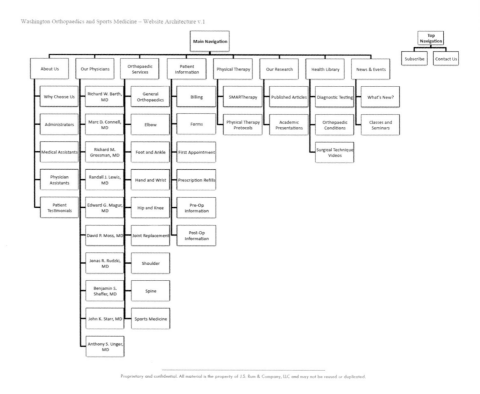

Figure 11.2 Example of a site map.

map looks like. Some people might also call this the information architecture; a visual representation of the spine of a site (Figure 11.2).

The most important thing about site maps is that they show you the interconnectivity of the content on your website. For a content professional, understanding how everything is categorized and linked is vital to communicating with your designer about the information flow people will follow.

Content professionals should absolutely be engaged when creating site maps and should also be engaged in naming pages. As we learned with Jonathon Colman's group at REI at the end of Part 2, you need to combine enterprise SEO with information architecture to get the most bang for your buck. You may want to name a page "Hypertension." Then you find that when you do the keyword research, high blood pressure scores higher. As a content professional, if you're involved in building and refining the site map, you will create a more findable, usable product.

FLOWCHARTS

Flowcharts are important for understanding what a customer will do in the course of interacting with a site. Also called user flows, designers use flowcharts to show how people will walk through a task step-by-step. For content professionals, flowcharts are incredibly helpful because they demonstrate the conversation a person is probably having in his head with himself while he is interacting with the site. We used flowcharts in Chapter 6, but there we called them decision journey maps. Those maps inform content—flowcharts help to inform design. Truthfully, you can use them to inform both—as long as designers and content professionals work together to create them, so both are bringing their concerns to the table and create a shared tool you use to shape interaction.

You can think of flowcharts for use in any situation in which a customer has to give a piece of information to get to another screen or task. For example, shopping carts, forms, and payments can all be visually represented using flowcharts. For content professionals, flowcharts can be incredibly helpful for pointing out where microcopy (copy that is used to give direction) can be modified to make a better task-completion experience.

WIREFRAMES

Designers use wireframes to visually represent where different content types will "live" on a page or template without applying a visual design treatment. Wireframes are a critical part of the design process because they show you the relationship between different content elements on a page or template itself.

Wireframes help you visualize the way a page or template will look without seeing any colors, logos, or graphics. In stripping away visual elements, you are able to comprehend the information flow inherent on one single page or template, thereby understanding the totality of the customer experience on that one page. Content professionals should be fully engaged in this process, as they can help determine hierarchy. We'll talk about hierarchy later when we talk about page specs (Figure 11.3).

Wireframes should be tested and retested to ensure you are using the best possible design for the information flow you want to represent. Often what an internal team (or consulting firm) thinks the target audience wants to see first or second is not right.

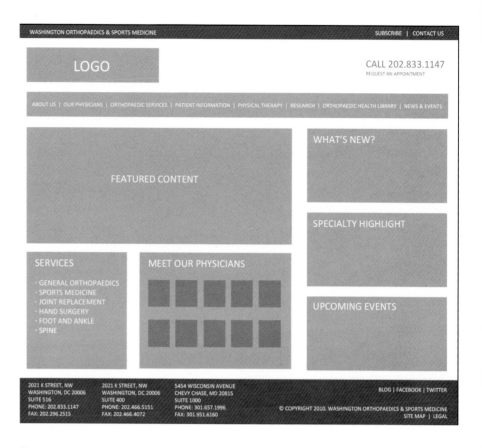

Figure 11.3 Example of a wireframe.

By testing wireframes, you can determine if you are having the appropriate conversation with your audience. Testing wireframes is also cheaper than testing visual designs because if you have to make changes, you are simply moving boxes around a page. Once you apply the visual design overlay, you probably have to spend a lot of budget dollars to keep tinkering with the visual treatment.

VISUAL DESIGNS

Visual designs are what the website will look like once it's redesigned. Use the real images that will be used when the website is launched, real copy, real microcopy, and anything else that helps fully represent the branding and messaging so that everything works together. If you do not have real photography ready yet, use pictures as similar as possible. Presenting visual designs to a client with as much "done" as possible, will help you get a real response that won't be changed once the real content is slipped into its placeholders. Plus it will make it much easier to test, as we will discuss (Figure 11.4).

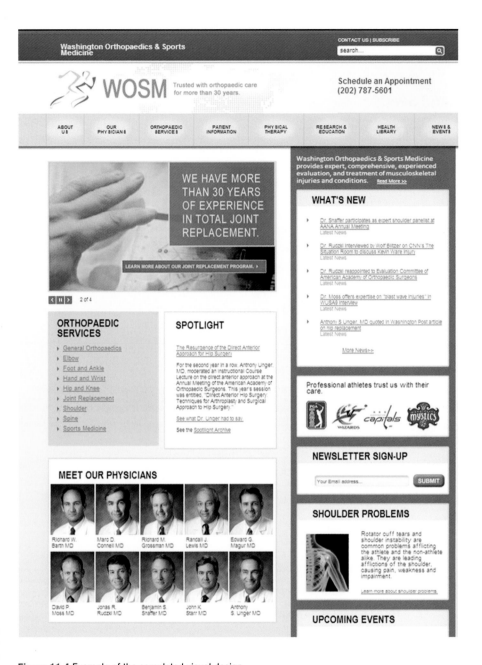

Figure 11.4 Example of the completed visual design.

CONTENT TOOLS TO THE RESCUE

There are several tools we can use to help the design process flow more freely while still using real content, including:

- Page Specs
- Content Testing

- Usability Testing
- Microcopy Testing

PAGE SPECS

Communicating with designers about content has everything to do with explaining which types of content a person might want to consume, and in which order they want to consume them. This is known as a hierarchy—in other words, what really matters when?

One of the best ways to do this is with a page spec or a page template. A page spec gives the designer the "specifications" for what should be on the page. Your specs should include keywords and character counts. In this way, you may give the designer the room to create interesting, well-designed templates that take into account what your target audiences need to know.

Many information architects and designers might refer to a page spec as a wireframe. They are definitely similar; below, I discuss the differences.

What Does a Page Spec Look Like?

A page spec is a lot like a wireframe, except that it demonstrates information flow throughout a document. It can be a list, diagram, etc. It needs to be a document that summarizes:

- All the different sections of the site
- Types of content that each section holds
- Description of the different types of content each page will have on it

For example:

About Us Section

1. This section will encompass the following six pages: X, X, X, etc.
2. Each page must have the following elements:
   - Three paragraphs no more than 250 words each
   - Two ad holder spaces
   - Two award graphics
   - A picture placeholder
3. Headlines should hug content
4. Social media icons should be clearly visible
5. A print this icon is necessary

By giving such clear content directions in the page spec, the visual designer has enough understanding of information flow on the page that he can design a spectacular setting for your diamond of content. Without knowing how many words each part of the content will have, how many pictures need to be on the page and so on, designers design templates that look good, but don't necessarily accommodate the needs of the content. It's like designing a house without knowing how many people are going to live there. Would you ever do that?

CONTENT TESTING

Content testing is a step many organizations skip, but it will absolutely improve the final product. All of this testing is dependent on engaging a content professional early on in the process. I'm a huge believer in content testing for three reasons:

1. You learn a lot about what your content needs to do to support the sales, interaction, and engagement process

2. You convince your executive leadership that what they think their audience wants is not the same as what their audience actually wants

3. You truly see information flow from section to section and are able to refine the content to provide excellent movement for your audiences

Testing content can be done in several ways, but I think it makes the most sense to test it three times:

- *Outside of the wireframe*, so you're actually *just* testing the content. Remember, as we learned in Chapter 4, content must be divorced from display, so you want to make sure you are testing your content without relying on the visual design.

- *Inside of the wireframe*, so you can see if making any changes to where content is on the page, the hierarchy, makes a difference to the way your audience consumes the content.

- *Inside the visual design*, so you can observe if any of the colors, logos, or design attributes of the actual visual design interfere or compete with the content or microcopy.

The most effective way to test content is to use a variation of usability testing, which we will now discuss in brief.

We talked about content testing in depth in Chapter 8. Briefly, content testing should help in finding answers to these questions:

- Can customers find the content they need?
- Can they read the content?
- Can they understand the content?
- Will they act on the content?
- Will they share the content?

We also need to know:

- How relevant do they find your content?
- Will they act on the information from the content?
- Did they find this content useful?

USABILITY TESTING

Usability testing sounds exactly like what it is; testing to make sure the site is usable. (We talked about usability testing in Chapter 8.) Typically, you write a script of tasks you want an individual to complete. Then you can record them using software, a camera, or writing down how they perform each task. Your results will reveal to you whether content is clear, is in the right place in the design, and gives the person enough information to move deeper into the site or complete the task at that page or template level.

Many usability experts will tell you to test in small groups so that you can continue to iterate as the design process moves along. Typically, testing 10–12 users will get you the same results as when you test with 25 users. Now, testing a lot of people will always give you varied and individual results, but you probably don't have the time or budget for that. So, test in small groups, and use the findings from each of those usability tests to adjust the content, design, or their interplay.

MICROCOPY TESTING

Testing the small copy that instructs people what to do on a website is often ignored. Yet, that copy is sometimes the most critical copy on the site—think of a shopping cart or a sign up process. Make sure when you test microcopy you test:

- Meaning of each phrase
- Placement on the page
- Placement within a design feature, like a button

If the microcopy leaves a doubt, then your audience will not be able to complete their tasks. That's bad.

SUMMARY

This entire chapter can be summed up as the following: Before you think about what the site will look like, think about what you want the audience *to be able to do.*

Start from there, communicate often with the designers, and give them the information, structure, and background they need to make your content sing.

Because if you don't, you'll end up with content that breaks design, an audience who can't find what they're looking for, and a CEO who wants to know why the numbers at the bottom of the spreadsheet aren't green and round.

Now for our final *Rule—Invest in Professionals and Trust Them*.

REFERENCES

Brown, D. M. (2007). *Communicating design: Developing web site documentation for design and planning*. Berkeley, CA: Peachpit Press/New Riders, p. 94.

Brown, D. (2010). *Letter to a content strategist*. Retrieved from http://blog. greenonions.com/2010/06/05/letter-to-a-content-strategist/.

Monteiro, M. (2012). *Design is a job*. New York: A Book Apart, p. 27.

Peverett, C. (2010). *You can stick your lorem ipsum right up your CMS*. Retrieved from http://www.travelblather.com/2010/06/why-content-strategy-matters.html.

Redish, G. (2012). *Letting go of the words* (2nd ed.). Waltham, MA: Morgan Kaufmann, p. 46.

INVEST IN PROFESSIONALS AND TRUST THEM

There is so much to do in digital strategy. Planning, creating, publishing, distributing, analyzing, and governing your content are several full-time jobs, particularly if you are part of a large organization. Rarely is it possible for one company to have all of those roles in-house. That means you may need to outsource many of these functions.

I have been both in-house in agencies and a consultant in my career. There is a massive flaw in the system that I hope Rule #7 will help to correct. It has to do with listening. When it comes to listening, the C-suite can make two serious errors. Sometimes they fail to listen to people in-house who have good, solid ideas and are making perfect sense. The second error, which is sadly, so common, is that the executives will decide to go outside of the organization and hire expert consultants. No problem with that—but, then, they fail to listen to *them!* Why does this happen?

When I was getting married, my parents planned my wedding and went with me to the florist consultation. My fiancé was otherwise occupied because he could not have cared less. (His favorite line? "I care deeply but I have no opinion.") The florist was part of a famous floral design company based in Manhattan. A man in his forties, he opened up his sample book. Each picture looked the same—a waterfall of a variety of white flowers spilled over on the tables.

I didn't want to hurt his feelings, but being the direct person I am, I said, "I hate white. Can't you do anything in color?"

He got so excited; it was as if I told him he'd never have a hard time finding peonies in December again. He was very willing to incorporate color. I had specific ideas about the flowers and I began to object to his. My father interrupted me and said, "When you hire an expert, you give them a basic idea of what you want, and then you let them do the creative work. If you don't micromanage him, he'll do his best work for you."

You know what? People talked about the flowers at my wedding for a long time. They were beautiful, original, and a statement. Because I trusted the florist and let him do his best work, the result was beyond my expectations. Yet so often in digital marketing and strategy we get in the way of the florist. We tell him how to arrange this bloom or that centerpiece. This is a mistake and it must stop.

Brian Kardon, a seasoned chief marketer, offers a great tip, "My kids once told me, 'When you go to a pizza place, don't order a bagel.' The pizza place is passionate about pizza and is highly experienced in making it. Sure, it could make you a bagel. But why would you want one? Get the most out of your partners by trusting their instincts and learning from them" (Kardon, 2013).

How do you get the most out of your partners? Well first, you need to choose the right ones. Then you need to understand if what they are saying makes sense.

WHY HIRE CONSULTANTS AND EXPERTS?

There are three reasons to hire consultants and experts. They:

1. See things you don't
2. Have experience you don't
3. May be able to create internal consensus when you can't

LET'S LOOK AT THIS ANOTHER WAY

To prepare for the 1998 Winter Olympic Games in Nagano, Japan, Japan Railways won a contract to build a tunnel between Tokyo and Nagano. The tunnel was designed to hold a train that would run back and forth between the two cities.

Unfortunately, every time the company dug, water kept filling the tunnel. The company brought in engineers who created a system of aqueducts and waterways to divert the water from the tunnel.

In the meantime, one day one of the maintenance workers was thirsty. Because he had no bottled water close by, he simply dunked his bucket into the water within the halfway dug tunnel and drank it. He told his bosses it was the finest water he had ever tasted and they agreed. Now Oshimizu bottled water is sold from every vending machine in the railway's system and is available for home delivery. What could have been a major loss for the company turned into a major profit maker (Niven, 2002).

There are countless stories like this one from all over the world. When you are thirsty, you may just bend down and drink water that others would not. There are a million ways of looking at things, but it all depends on your perspective. That's what consultants do—they look at a problem from a different point of view.

I often joke that content strategists are the people who, upon entering a room with a metaphorical elephant, only want to talk about the elephant in the room. They want to touch it, describe it, sketch it, talk about it, and make everyone else in the room aware of it. That is because most content strategists are problem solvers and they are not afraid of challenges. In fact, they like solving puzzles because it motivates and inspires them.

Most people really don't want to talk about the elephant in the room. They'd rather brush things under the rug and pretend they don't exist. It doesn't make sense for them to bring everything into the light because it's doing just fine right there in the dark. Many people lack the confidence to describe the metaphorical elephant in the room because it scares them. However, that is exactly what consultants are paid to do.

If it's your responsibility to hire consultants to help you run your digital strategy teams better, then you need to understand that they may give you bad news. Conversations with them may not be enjoyable. They are going to ask many hard questions and there will be pain. They will analyze:

- People
- Process
- Technology
- Workflow
- Decision making
- Data

Consultants challenge your assumptions. They point out the flaws—sometimes in systems you created. They can aggravate you. They may make you look bad in front of your boss. (Good consultants know not to do this.)

Embrace this as a necessary step toward digital strategy excellence. If they are not challenging you, then you hired the wrong consultants. You don't want them to stroke your ego. They are not looking to make you feel good about yourself or your choices. *Their job is to recognize what can be fixed in service of your organization's goals.* If they are not asking tough questions and pointing out challenges, then they are useless digital strategy consultants and you should fire them.

When someone goes out of their way to give you constructive criticism, they are giving you a gift. While consultants are not giving you a gift (they are paid to tell you what the problems are), their view from the outside is incredibly valuable. So listen to them—even when you disagree. I'm not saying you have to implement their solutions or strategies—but listen to them. Hear what they are saying. Digest it. Don't get defensive and try to explain to them why the problems exist. Take some time to think it through with precision. Discuss it with other executive management. Then, make a move based on the information you have in front of you right at that moment.

THEY KNOW STUFF YOU DON'T

In the words of Erick Spiekermann, "Clients need to understand that they've hired us to do something they are not good at. And that they need to pay us for our knowledge, skills, experience and yes: attitude" (Monteiro, 2012).

Very few people are good at every single thing they do. There are some, but they are rare. If you are one of them, then maybe this section doesn't apply to you. But, if you are somebody that knows that you need help in certain areas, you need this rule. So read on.

Consultants and experts are usually people who consult with a wide variety of clients, even though they may always consult with companies within the same industry as your own organization. This doesn't matter—what matters is that they've seen many different sides of the same coin.

I was once asked at a pitch, "Do you find that our vertical is different than the other verticals you've worked in, like healthcare?" I sensed at the time that the questioner was asking if there was something special about content production in his industry that made it a more challenging project than others in different industries.

I answered as truthfully as I could, "Actually what I find is that when it comes to planning for content and content production, it's a spectrum of dysfunction wherever I go." This is true—no matter the industry—no matter the players. No one has the Holy Grail for how to do this right—I promise you. The question is, how far are you along the path to getting it as right as possible for your organization? (I won the pitch.)

You can compare this to a doctor who has performed 30 procedures, and a doctor who has performed 3,000 procedures. Which one do you want taking the knife to your body? Consultants with experience are like surgeons with 3,000 procedures under their belts. They know what to do when things go awry. They have seen almost everything there is to see. Does that mean your project will be easy or lack any challenges? No, but a consultant with experience will come at that challenge with perception and wisdom.

If you choose the right consultants, trust what they tell you. You will not regret it. We will talk about how to choose the right consultant later in this rule.

CREATING INTERNAL CONSENSUS

Consultants can often create internal consensus because they are outsiders. Sometimes your team can be arguing about one particular part of a project, or what the best practices in the industry are, how the changing nature of digital communications requires you not to make a decision right now and so on. But when an external consultant comes in, he can say, "Based on my experience and read of the situation, this is what you should do." Teams will often respond to that authority better than they do to your own.

CHOOSING THE RIGHT CONSULTANT

You could probably write an entire book on choosing the right consultant for all the different professionals and roles we discussed in Chapter 10. (I will not be writing that book next.) Instead, I'm going to describe the basic characteristics I think good digital strategy consultants have:

- Excellent listening skills
- Compassion and empathy
- Attention to detail
- Willingness to try a different approach
- Superb negotiation skills
- Modesty

EXCELLENT LISTENING SKILLS

Obviously, you need a consultant who can listen and hear what others are saying. You should look for these things:

- Do they interrupt when someone on the team is speaking?
- Do they act impatient when I bring up something they say they already know?
- Do they give each person on the team the same amount of listening respect and attention or only those that are more senior?

The way someone listens will tell you a lot about him. Remember, during the discovery phase of a consulting project, it is the job of the consultant to absorb as much as possible. How can she do that without listening effectively?

COMPASSION AND EMPATHY

Digital strategy projects occur at the intersection of people, process, and technology. This means that people are going to be prickly when talking about their roles, responsibilities, and projects. Good digital strategy consultants know that they are hitting people's sensitivities. As such, they show compassion and empathy when they listen *and when they talk.*

ATTENTION TO DETAIL

There are so many things to understand about how an organization attacks its content lifecycle that a good consultant must pay attention to every detail. No matter is too small to consider—I have seen entire projects flounder because consultants didn't pay attention to details. If you have to keep reminding the consultant about important details that you've already discussed, it's a bad sign.

WILLINGNESS TO TRY A DIFFERENT APPROACH

Many people would say the willingness to try something different is a form of creativity. I agree that you need a creative consultant, but I doubt there are people in the content field who don't think of themselves as creative.

Sometimes consultants find a winning formula and look to use that repeatedly. That doesn't always work—obviously. Organizations are like people—no two are alike. You need to hire a consultant who is willing to turn the ship if the tide begins to shift.

SUPERB NEGOTIATION SKILLS

Great content consultants will need to have hard conversations with executives, team members, and others who touch content in the organization. I once had one of the most difficult conversations of my professional life, negotiating a new org chart between the Editor-in-Chief of a digital publication and his Chief Executive Officer. Both had valid visions, but radically different ones about how to move forward. Negotiating between the two successfully was critical to ensuring the success of the entire content strategy engagement. Make sure your consultants know how to negotiate.

MODESTY

Arrogance is the enemy of productivity. No one trusts an arrogant consultant. They may think they are all that. That attitude of "Because I said so," or "Do you know who my other clients are?" just hurts the team—it never helps them. So find a consultant who understands that each time she takes on a new project, *she* is going to learn something new also. I am no longer surprised by how much I learn—every single time.

SUMMARY

Putting together a flexible, responsive digital strategy that encompasses iteration at its core requires a strong team, a constant analysis of your performance, and a complete focus on your target audiences. You may have deficits within your organization when it comes to talent and resources. When you hire an outside consultant to help your team, pick the right one and then trust them to do their job with excellence and passion. You will not regret it.

REFERENCES

Kardon, B. (2013). *Content marketing best practices: 5 tips for the modern CMO*. Retrieved from http://contentmarketinginstitute.com/2013/02/content-marketing-best-practices-modern-cmo/.

Monteiro, M. (2012). *Design is a job*. New York: A Book Apart (Foreword).

Niven, D. (2002). *The 100 simple secrets of successful people: What scientists have learned and how you can use it*. San Francisco: HarperSanFrancisco.

CASE STUDY: STEFANIE DIAMOND PHOTOGRAPHY

We're going to end *The Digital Crown* by showcasing a woman who truly deserves to wear it. In this case study, you will meet Stefanie Diamond, who transformed her professional life by creating and distributing powerful content that grew her business from a part-time gig to a full-blown photography business in just 2 years.

Can you imagine deciding you want a major life change and then actually acting on it? Stefanie spent 13 years in marketing and public relations, her last role as the director of marketing and communications for the American Cancer Society. While she loved her career, there was always a voice in the back of her head yearning for something different. After years of dreaming about it, she decided to pursue photography.

Stefanie reminisces that as far back as she can remember she had a camera in her hand. "I loved taking pictures of friends, of places, even trying to capture my 'favorite rock' at camp. So many of my memories are based on photos I have." As the mother of three girls, she has tried to document so much of their lives in photographs. Her mother would often tell her to put the camera down and actually watch her kids with her eyes, not through the camera lens, but to Stefanie that's how she sees life—in the photographs she takes, in the memories she captures.

Stefanie started by taking newborn portraits. She called two friends who were at the end of their pregnancies and asked if she could take pictures of their newborns to start her portfolio. Twenty-four months and 240 clients later, Stefanie works full-time as a photographer at Stefanie Diamond Photography, photographing newborns, children, families, and events. She books weeks and often months in advance and is the most sought-after photographer in her area.

Stefanie has never advertised—not one time. Her entire business grew by word of mouth through recommendations passed from friends and families who were satisfied customers, as well as by posting her highly entertaining photographs on Facebook and her blog. Stefanie says, "Quality is your best advertisement. When you deliver a consistent product and your heart is behind it, that's all the advertising you need." Stefanie says that people come from all over and will drive for hours with their children to have family portraits taken by her.

Stefanie saw the popularity of her Facebook posts soar when she began writing a blog. She blogs after most sessions, as a way to showcase her images and tell her clients' stories. "I was born a writer," she said. "Everybody has a story and now I can tell it in both images and words." Stefanie's clients share their blog posts and photographs within their own social networks, creating exponential reach for Stefanie's business, something we talked about in Chapter 5: Engagement Strategies.

Because of her marketing training, Stefanie knows she can't manage what she cannot measure. She spends time every week analyzing her metrics, seeing which posts people shared and what blogs are most popular. She likes the stats package on her Blogger blog and checks Facebook metrics as well. Stefanie posts on Facebook daily so she stays top of mind for clients and potential clients. She blogs throughout the week, although she only promotes each image and blog post once because she wants to be respectful and not over-clutter her clients' news feeds.

Stefanie Diamond Photography
April 16

So this morning I meet 3 year old Izzy. She refused to look at me, cried instead of laughed at my shenanigans, and buried her head in mom's shoulder. This image is proof that you don't need a perfect pose or a winning smile for an image worthy of a canvas.
♥

With posts like this one, it's easy to see why Stefanie's content is so popular.

"Sharing your content is a balance between tooting your own horn and focusing on your clients. I don't say I'm the best—I need to focus on my customers. Instead of saying, 'I did an amazing job making her eyes look blue, instead I say, look at how blue her eyes are'."

"To me the customer experience has to be center to everything I do," Stefanie says (Rule #1: *Start with Your Audience*). "People really care about the experience they have and the attention you give them," she said. "When you make them feel like their experience is the only one that matters that day, they truly appreciate it."

Stefanie's relatable style makes her posts fun, even when you don't get pictures of goose poop.

Right now Stefanie wears almost all of the hats in her business. She does have a process in place for managing and distributing her content: she writes her blogs and her sister edits them, as well as helps her choose the right accompanying images.

Stefanie knows that there are thousands of other photographers out there doing newborn shoots, cake smashes, and lovely family photos in autumn leaves. As she says, "Everything has been done. The challenge is putting your own spin on things and making them yours. My work has a unique look that customers recognize and come back to again and again."

Just look at this cake smash. It's hard to know who or what you want to eat first.

No matter what the size of your business, as we've seen in all of our case studies, content is challenging for everyone. Mastering it requires finding the sweet spot at the intersection of people, process, and technology.

CONCLUSION

In October 2010, I wrote a blog about the television show *Mad Men* and content strategy:

> Anyone who has ever worked in an ad agency setting should watch *Mad Men*, a television series about advertising set in the 1960s. Jon Hamm, the lead, plays Don Draper, the creative director of a fictional ad agency, and watching him spin creative magic is—well—magical. However, this season, Don and his partners are faced with the possible dissolution of their firm, following the loss of a huge account. When his protégé, Peggy, asks him, 'Isn't there anything we can do?' Don responds, 'No, we're creative … the least important, most important thing there is.' What struck me most about this comment is how it applies to web content (and having worked at an ad agency, about creative, as well). After all, isn't web content the least important, most important thing there is on a web project? Kicked to the curb, until the designers and developers actually need real words and pictures to fill up the modules, content is mostly ignored. As content professionals, we evangelize the need to change this project cycle so content gets the focus first. But web specialists are entrenched in their process. How can we convince them content strategy is necessary to improving the outcome of the final product? (Leibtag, 2010).

Here we are, in the middle of 2013, and companies are finally starting to get it. They are beginning to realize that what Lisa Welchman describes is, in fact, true: "The Web is managed as if it were a less important version of a traditional business artifact, that is, a technically rich brochure or a virtual storefront, rather than being managed as if it were one of the most powerful business tools an organization has to leverage" (Welchman & Pierpoint, 2009).

Organizations around the globe recognize the power of content—it isn't the least important factor in digital strategy anymore. In fact, according to the Altimeter Group Report, the average brand organization is responsible for the content demands of 178 social media properties, plus websites, blogs, and live events (Levine, 2013). Denial is no longer a strategy: The demand for content is real. After reading *The Digital Crown*, you can describe both of the major challenges inherent to content within your organization. The first: How do you capture and transform the information you need from your internal resources?

The second: How do you create a publishing system to release that content into the vast currents of the web? Once you describe the problems, you can solve them. Prepared with everything we have learned together, you are no longer reactive. You can be proactive about your content. You are prepared to engage your audiences and prove that your content fuels the entire sales and achievement cycle in your organization.

You probably started this book thinking, "What are we doing?" You might also have been thinking, "What are we doing wrong?" Now you know that cohesive, consistent, and controlled content is the goal. You can and will make that happen.

The other night I was flipping through the channels and I noticed the movie *Titanic* was playing. An old favorite (go ahead, judge me) I settled down and was immediately riveted by the well-known story of Rose and Jack and their ill-fated love.

I stayed up late to watch it, wondering why the entire time. I knew how it ended. In fact, we all knew how it ended, and yet millions of us poured into movie theaters during the winter of 1997 to watch it. Here was a film anchored by the building blocks of any great tale: a fantastical love story, a true-life disaster, and human tragedy. We watched it then and we watch it now because it isn't the actual ending we care about. It's the unfolding of the story that captures us.

Everything we have talked about in *The Digital Crown* has been about getting you to a point where you can stop focusing all of your energy on the execution and tactics of your digital strategy. Now that you are prepared to master those, you can focus on what you really want to do with your content: Craft and weave great, compelling stories centered on your audience's needs and wants. In producing and disseminating those stories, you provoke a conversation.

All the great artistic works of the world are a conversation—they create a dialogue between us, the artist, and our truest selves. When we see a beautiful painting, when we read an inspiring novel, when we are touched by an ancient verse, we are responding to content. Content is a conversation but it is so much more than that. It is the exquisite ability to reach out to another and inspire them to reach back.

All of the greatest artists in the world sketched, and rehearsed, and tore up and wrote again, and scratched out, and persevered until they got it right. Your content is an iterative process, meant for you to repeat so many times until it becomes the *art* of conversation. Follow all seven of these rules and you will have a guiding system in place to create content that will support your sales process, spread your message, and inspire your customers to become brand ambassadors. Every conversation has a give and take, a cycle, so to speak, that moves it forward, breaks, and begins again.

Digital communications will continue to change and evolve. The power of these rules will always remain the same—people, process, technology. Master those and you will master the cycle and art of the content conversation.

We will end this book exactly as we started but in a completely new place. We now understand that content operates in a repeatable cycle, that we control and orchestrate. So, we end with the same words we used to start: Shall we begin?

REFERENCES

Leibtag, A. (2010). *Why Don Draper would embrace content strategy*. Retrieved from http://onlineitallmatters.blogspot.co.il/2010/10/why-don-draper-would-embrace-content.html.

Levine, B. (2013). *Altimeter Group report: How can companies feed their content marketing needs?* Retrieved from http://www.cmswire.com/cms/customer-experience/altimeter-group-report-how-can-companies-feed-their-content-marketing-needs-020693.php?utm_source=GPlus&utm_medium=MP&utm_campaign=SocialMedia.

Welchman, L., & Pierpoint, C. (2009). *Web operations management: A primer*. Retrieved from http://www.welchmanpierpoint.com/sites/files/WOMPrimer_2009.pdf.

ACKNOWLEDGMENTS

I still remember a 2-day Web Writing Workshop I took in 2005. Watching Ginny Redish teach people how to think about organizing and writing information for online readers made me think, "I want to do that one day." Ginny, you've been such a generous advocate, friend, and inspiration. Thank you.

Kristina Halvorson: I am so lucky to know you and be a part of the amazing content strategy community you helped create. Thank you for everything you have done to help me and for writing this foreword. We all know what people really think when they see the word *content*.

My amazingly sharp-eyed reviewers: Matt Grocki, Diana Railton, and Jayme Thomason—this book is better and stronger because of your keen, thoughtful comments. I hope you will reread it one day to see how much you helped to improve it.

I also want to thank the following people who reviewed certain chapters and helped me work through some of these ideas: Michael Hogenmiller, Kevin Potts, Sally Bagshaw, Jeff Eaton, and Jeff Rum. Thanks to Jonathan Kahn for letting me use his brilliant quote to set the stage for this topic. Thanks also to all my case study participants: Paige Holden, Jonathon Colman, Sharath Cherian, and Stefanie Diamond.

Susan Leibtag—this book would simply not be here without you. Thank you for all your hard work, encouragement, and guidance.

To my fellow content strategists and content marketers—you inspire me, challenge my ideas, and excite me to do better work. I'm so proud that we have all chosen to make the digital world—and by extension, the real world—a much improved place. In particular, I want to thank Margot Bloomstein, Sara Wachter-Boettcher, Chris Moritz, and Joe Pulizzi for extending their friendship and support.

Thank you to Meg Dunkerley, Heather Scherer, and the team at Morgan Kaufmann for shepherding me through this process.

I am blessed to have learned from the wisdom of the following teachers and leaders: Bryna Levy, Matthew Tinkcom, Sally Laroche, Kathy Smith, Anthony Kalloo, Stuart Seides, Courtney Doyle, Miriam Clayton, Sharon Applestein, and Corbin Riemer. Thank you for showing me how to turn over a problem to see it in a different way. And, Aaron Watkins, you changed my world by extending an opportunity. It still means so much to me. Ditto to Sharath Cherian, who will always be the only client I will Skype with at 11 p.m.

To Kim Walsh-Phillips—who always has the right answers, and manages to save my day.

To my wonderful community of family and friends: Thank you for putting up with me this last year as I booked-out. My parents have always encouraged me to follow the beat of my own drum. A special thank you to my sister, Ariella Aaron Ives, who is all the things a big sister should be. Also, thank you to my older brother who is *also all of the things* a big brother *thinks* he should be. Rhubarb is still a plant.

I could not get through any day without the incredible team I have at Aha Media Group. Christine O'Neil, Nancy Stewart, and Talia Eisen keep me sane every day. I have the best writing team in the business—a special thank you to Shuly Babitz and Gila Rose, who have been with me since the beginning.

Para la niñera fantástica, cálida y maravillosa, Griselda Romero. Con tu apoyo, me voy a trabajar todos los días, sabiendo que mis hijos están felices, seguros, y protegidos. Si hubiera dicho "gracias" un millón de veces, nunca sería suficiente.

To my children: Tzophia, Amaya, and Navon—it is my sincerest hope and prayer that one day you will find something that inspires you enough to pour everything you've got into it. Thank you for sharing your valuable time so I could write this book.

To my husband, Ephraim Leibtag—who edited every page and listened to every doubt: The worst days of this journey became the best, because when I curled up into a fetal position, you curled up right beside me.

And finally—an endless amount of gratitude to Seena Chettiveettil, who rescheduled lunch.

Ahava Leibtag
May 13, 2013
Silver Spring, Maryland

Ahava Leibtag is a well-recognized content expert and writes thought leadership about content strategy and content marketing. She is the president and owner of Aha Media Group, LLC, a content strategy and content marketing consultancy founded in October 2005. You can reach her at www.ahamediagroup.com.

Ahava lives in the Washington, D.C., metropolitan area with her family.

INDEX

Note: Page numbers followed by *f* indicate figures, *t* indicate tables and *b* indicate boxes.

A

Adaptive content
  conversation, 110
  multi-channel publishing, 111
  reusable content, 111
  structured content, 111–112
Aggregated content, 84*t*
Analytics data, 213–214
Audience
  conversation, 23
  customers need, 24–25
  digital strategy roadmap, 23
  "Know Your Audience", 24
  people/customers, 23–24
  tools
    CNNMoney article, Nike, 30
    customer (*see* Customers)

B

Branding
  amalgamation, 9–10
  attributes *vs.* identity pillars, 181–182
  brand communities, 11
  consistency, 13–14
  and content marketing (*see* Content marketing)
  and content strategy (*see* Content strategy)
  copywriter and photographer, 9
  definition, 10, 12, 181
  employees, 12–13
  good brand management, 11
  image and tagline, 9
  management, 11–12
  messaging and, 187–188
  people, 10
  promise, 9

  short history, 9*b*
  "United Breaks Guitars", 11
Brand loyalty, 243–244, 246
Business advocates
  analytics experts, 268–269
  business analysts, 269
  description, 256–257
  digital projects, 268
  project managers, 268
  reviewers, 269–270
Business objectives
  achievement threshold, 36–37
  C-suite (*see* C-suite)
  decision makers, 40
  definition, 36
  description, 34
  General Electric (GE), 35, 35*b*
  media, types, 39–40
  professional, 35
  sales and business cycles, 37–39
  workshops, 35

C

Channels
  audience, 130–131
  content distribution, 124
  definition, 125–126
  description, 123–124
  digital, 126–127
  "Facebook status", 124, 124*t*
  mapping, 212
  and platform, separate content, 124, 127*f*
Co-created content, 84*t*
Community building
  audience engagement, 136
  C-suite, 138–139
  customer loop, 135

Community building *(Continued)*
  email open rates, 136
  measurement, 138
  mind-shift, culture, 136–137
  reiterate, 139
Community engagement
  audience segmentation, 128, 129*b*
  brand community, 128
  and channels identification, 129–131
  conversation, 132–134
  entertainment and relevance, 132
  invitation, 134
  marketing—trust, 128
  steps, 131
Consultants
  attention, 307–308
  compassion and empathy, 307
  constructive criticism, 305
  conversations, 305
  description, 304
  different approach, 308
  excellent listening skills, 307
  flaws, 305
  internal consensus creation, 306–307
  knowledge, skills, experience
      and attitude, 306
  maintenance workers, 304
  metaphorical elephant, 305
  modesty, 308
  negotiation skills, 308
  profit maker, 304
  strategists, 304–305
  tunnel, 304
Content
  business objectives (*see* Business
      objectives)
  consumption, 105, 119–120
  C-suite (*see* C-suite)
  customers, 74
  definition, 108–109
  distribution, 72
  divisions, 73
  floats, 106
  format, 72–73
  framework, 71
  information, 33, 71, 72*f*
  misleading hotel web page, 34*f*
  modeling, 115–116
  newspaper, 74*b*

  people research vacations, 34
  platform and channel and format, 74, 74*t*
  professional and publisher, 103, 107
  projects, 48
  sales process, 33
  types, 84–85
  typical objections and possible
      responses, 47, 47*t*
  website, 74
Content audits
  information architecture (IA),
      200, 200*f*, 201
  mapping audit, 201–202
  mind-numbingly boring and time
      consuming, 201
  multidimensional, 202–203
  qualitative audit, 201
  quantitative audit, 201, 202
  rolling audit, 202
  thin slice audit, 202
  time and budget, 202
  use, 204–205
  UX professional, 200
Content authoring
  advantages, 117
  and creativity, 117, 118
  description, 117
Content creators
  copy editors, 264
  copywriters, 264
  people, 264
  photographers, 265
  videographers, 265
Content framing
  brand values, 179
  centralized style guide, 192
  conversations, 180
  description, 180
  guidelines, 191–192
  identity pillars
      American faucet maker, 183–184
      vs. brand attributes, 180–182
      brand definition, 181
      creation, 182
      description, 180
      hospital cure, 182–183
  messaging architecture, 184–188
  metaphor, 179
  organization, 192

reviewing, 192
structural integrity, 179
voice and tone, 188–191
Content management systems (CMS)
content authoring, 118*b*
definition, 109, 116
governance, 117
multi-channel publishing, 115*f*
templates, 108*b*
usable interfaces, 111*b*
Content marketing
A La Mode, 239, 240*f*
awareness takes root, 18–19
blue-collar industries, 44–45
brand community, 241
brand loyalty, 246
C-level decision makers, 248
communications professionals, 244
competition, 43–44
consumers, 19
content strategy, 247
conversations, 19
create brand awareness and
reinforcement, 245
create online content and optimize, 246
customer personas, 43
customers, 45, 247
definition, 241
description, 18, 239
goals, 241–242
Kraft brand, 244*b*
measure and publicize on results,
251–253
online customer reviews and social
media, 253
online 'surfing', 18
organization, 247–248
Paige Holden back, 247
people objections, 240
printed brochures/ads, 248
priorities, 43
problems
brand loyalty, 243–244
the Internet, 243
people, 243
social sharing, 244
program
1-7-30-4-2-1 approach, 249–250
blog, 248

eBook (*see* eBook)
identity pillars and messaging
architecture, 250–251
prospective customers, 241
return on investment (ROI), 43, 44*b*
sales impact, 44
SiriusDecisions, 44
tools, 242–243
transparency and honesty, 253
trusted community, 246–247
Content strategists
description, 262
discipline, 262
editorial, 263
technical, 262–263
toolkit
analyze phase (*see* Phase analysis)
content strategy procedures, 215
create phase (*see* Creating content)
deliverables, 197–198
distribute phase (*see* Distributing
content)
execution, 196–197
governance, 214
people, process and technology, 198
plan phase (*see* Plan phase)
publisher, 195–196
publish phase (*see* Publishing content)
stages, 198
trust the process, 197
types and phase, 199
web teams, 262
Content strategy
Brian's experience, 18
business objectives and users' tasks, 17
customer, 17–18
"information", 15
production cycle, digital strategy, 14
purposes, 15
repeatable lifecycle, 15–16
systems create freedom, 14–18
weather widget on home page, 15
Content teams, workflow
centralized, 279–280
distributed, 278–279
organization, 281–282
rogue, 280–281
siloed, 277–278
types, 277

Content testing
  finding answers, 299
  reasons, 299
  times, 299
Conversation
  basic unit, construction, 70
  content (see Content)
  content framework, 71
  content mix, 81–84, 83b
  content professional, 70
  controlled content experience, 80b
  Google's research, 79–80
  information, 70b
  the Internet, 69–70
  loop stage and activity, 81, 81t
  organization, 80
  sales and buying process cycle
    (see Sales cycle)
  smoothie maker, 69
  substance and structure, 70, 70b
  web, 69
Creating content
  editorial guidelines and style guide, 209
  goal matrix, 208–209
  tools, 208
C-suite
  business objectives, 41–42
  cares, 43
  content marketing (see Content
    marketing)
  content project, 43
  customer engagement and content
    strategy, 38f, 46–47
  executives, 43
  selling content and C-level executives
    chief executive officer (CEO), 45
    chief financial officer (CFO), 45–46
    chief information officer (CIO), 46
    chief marketing officer (CMO), 45
  sign off on content projects, 47
  stakeholders, 42
Curated content, 84t
Customers
  access, content, 29
  ethnographic studies, 29
  interactive data, 28
  personas, 25–27
  research, 27–28

D
Decision journey maps
  content layering, 170
  customer loop, 169
  decision-making process, 170, 170t
  interactive feature, 171, 171f
  job seeker persona, 171, 171f
  refrigerator sorter, 170, 170f
Design
  communication, 300–301
  content breaking design, 291
  content testing, 299–300
  conversation, 290
  customer experience, 290
  digital strategy process, 289
  important, 290
  inside the box, 289
  Lorem Ipsum, 292
  microcopy testing, 300
  page specs, 298–299
  people react visually, 290–291
  process
    communication, 293
    designers, 293
    digital strategy, 293
    flowcharts, 295
    site maps, 293–294
    tools designers, 293
    visual designs, 296
    wireframes, 295–296
  real content, 297
  relationship, 290
  structures, 291
  Tiffany's packaging, 289
  usability testing, 300
  website, 291
Digital communications, 317
Digital strategy roadmap
  content editing and development,
    59–60
  description, 58
  direction, 58–59
  follow-through, 59
  organization and content creation, 58
  plan, 57, 57f
Digital team
  advocates, 256
  back end and front end, 257–259

business advocates (*see* Business advocates)
Captain Web, 261–262
challenges, 260
CMS, 256
customer advocates, 256
different professionals, 270
disciplines, 260
making output matter, 257
managing teams, 256
modern business, 260
money, 257
organizations, 260
project, 270
publication and distribution advocates (*see* Publication and distribution advocates)
siloed environments, 255
talent, 255
UX professionals (*see* User experience (UX) professionals)
Distributing content
channel mapping, 212
policies and guidelines, 212
tools, 212

E

eBook
gated, 249
ungated, 249
Engagement metrics, 214
Engagement strategies
business objectives, 135
channels (*see* Channels)
community
building (*see* Community building)
and channels identification, 129–131
engagement (*see* Community engagement)
content types, 123
conversations, 123
Facebook, 123, 125*f*
social engagement, 135
social media (*see* Social media)
Executives
C-level, selling content, 45
C-suite, 33*b*
goal, 43
leaders, 41
sign off on content projects, 47
Experts. *See* Consultants

F

Facebook
advertising, 133*b*
communities of interest, 131*b*
likes/shares, 132
multi-screen experiences, 127
platform, 124
status, 124, 124*t*
Flowcharts, 295
Framework, content strategy, 198

G

Gated content, 249
Goal matrix, 208–209
Governance, content
behavioral change, 225–226
consistent customer creation, 218–219
content bloat, 219
description, 218
head cheerleader, 225
home page, 220
internal organizational controls, 219–220
mistakes, 225
and people
content tools, 228
professionals, 227–228
strategic and implementation authority, 226
types of governing bodies, 226
phase, content strategy, 218
pilot project, 226
successful style guides, 222*b*
systems
content and conversations, 218
freedom and security, 217
target audiences, 224–225
tools
archiving standards, 221
checklists, 222–224, 223*f*
content workflows, 220
editorial guidelines, 221
style guides, 221
taxonomies, 221
training and measurement, 228–229

H

HipHopDX
audience
disagreement, 233
personas, 233
Talia persona, 233, 234*f*
Tyler persona, 233, 234*f*
branding, 235
business model, 235–236
content strategy conference, 231
description, 231
discovery
findings, 232–233
people, 231–232
process, 232
technology, 232
producing and disseminating
content, 231
state, union debrief, 233

I

Information architecture (IA) team
digital marketing skill, 152
external traffic perspectives, 151
infrastructure, website, 152
organic search data, 152
Iterative process
art of practice, 88*b*
business objectives shift, 90
change and improvement, 92
content as product, 93–94
content management, 87
content teams and organization, 92
criteria, organization, 88
description, 87
digital and content, 97
digital technologies, 89–90
product and market, 97
roadmap
captain content, 96
design, 95
process evaluation, 97–98
review past projects, 98–99
staff and process changes, 90–91
step to success, 91–92
types of conversations, 87
web design culture, 93
workflow, 97

J

Journey maps
decision (*see* Decision journey maps)
description, 168
interactive scenarios
audience engagement team, 174
delivering content, 172
description, 172
Lisa's customer scenario, 173, 173*f*
Marcus' scenario, 173, 174*f*
mobile device purchase, 174
seeker
pieces of information, 169
profile, path, 169
types, 169, 169*t*

K

Key performance indicators (KPIs), 213, 214*b*

L

Licensed content, 84*t*

M

Mad Men and content strategy, 315
Messaging architecture
and branding, 187–188
communication goals and priorities, 184
creation, 184–185
high-level statements, 184
pillar establishment, 185–188
Multichannel publishing
adaptive content, 111
applied styles, MS Word, 108*f*
article, 112, 113
"assembly line content", 116, 117
audiences, 102, 104
being platform-agnostic, 104
big blobby field, 114–115
broadcast channels, 102
channels, 120
CMS (*see* Content management
systems (CMS))
"containers", 120
content authoring (*see* Content
authoring)
content consumption, 105, 119–120
content floats, 106
content modeling, 115–116

content professional and publisher, 103, 107
customers surf, 102
definition, content, 108–109
device, 101, 103
different devices, 109
digital technologies, 101
format and display, 108b
HipHopDX.com, 113, 113f
horizontal *vs.* vertical formatting, 109, 109f
messaging, 102
metadata, 115
mobile article page, 113, 114f
"mobile" *vs.* "traditional", 104
parts, content, 102
people, process and technology, 102–103
printing, 101
problem, 107–108
responsive design, 109
reusable content, 111
statistics, 104
strip content, 106–107
structured content, 111–112
tasks *vs.* information, 106b
televisions in China, 107
template, 110b
voice-activated technology, 120
website, organization, 105
Multidisciplinary content
  audience engagement teams, 144
  better ideas, 146
  brains, 142
  breaking down silos, 142–143, 144–146
  building blocks, 141
  customers, 142
  description, 143
  different perspectives, 146
  ever-accelerating flow, communication, 142
  great teams, 143
  information and process, 141
  managing audience engagement teams
    committee, 148
    create guidelines, 148
    cross collaboration, 147–148
    people with different skill, 147
  marketing professionals, 143

organizational barriers, 145–146
organizations, 142
personality types, 147b
popular content marketing blogger, 146
right people, 146
rules, 141
software development, 145b
technologies, 144
varied talents, 148
web experts, 143
Multi-screen world
  and multi-threaded conversations, 127, 128b
  US consumers, 126

O

Original content, 84t

P

Personas
  audience, 158
  brand, 158
  content development, 175–176
  creation
    characteristic-based constrictions, 164
    data reinforcement, 163–168
    "image", 164
    knowing, audience, 167b
    life insurance, 165–166
    Lisa, 164
    organization's business objectives, 166
    product/service, 166
    questionaries, 162–163
    style guide/brand guidelines, 163
    wealthy professionals, 166
    workshop, 161–163
  description, 25, 159
  journey maps (*see* Journey maps)
  marketers, 159
  marketing, 26
  "marketing-up" syndrome, 26b
  in organizations, 175
  passion and deep curiosity, 26
  people represent, 159–160
  tools, 157
  usage, 160–161
  UX professionals, 159

Phase analysis
  analytics data, 213–214
  description, 212
  engagement metrics, 214
  site search analytics, 214
  tools, 212–213
Plan phase
  centralized style guide, 205
  competitive analysis, 207
  content audits (see Content audits)
  content testing, 205–207, 206b
  description, 199
  tools, 200
Professionals
  consultants and experts
      (see Consultants)
  C-suite, 303
  digital marketing, 303–304
  digital strategy, 303
  floral design company, 303
Publication and distribution advocates
  audience engagement strategists,
      267–268
  CMS authors, 267
  content performs, 266
  description, 256
  developers, 266
  professionals, 266
  SEO experts, 267
Publishing content
  archiving guidelines, 211
  CMS documentation, 211
  editorial calendars, 209–210
  tools, 209
  workflows/publishing guidelines,
      210–211

Q

Qualitative research, 201
Quantitative research, 201

R

REI
  cross-functional talent, 153
  customer engagement and loyalty, 152
  decision makers, 152
  digital marketing skill, 152
  enterprise-wide IA team, 151
  Google searchers, 153

  infrastructure maintenance
      and support, 153
  ingredients, content teams, 151
  SEO description, 151
  taxonomists, 152
  website, outdoor-oriented people, 151

S

Sales cycle
  and buying process, 76–78
  content, 75, 76
  "content mix", 75
  convert prospects to customers, 76
  "customer loop", 75, 76f
  customers, 76
  description, 74–75
  "funnels", 75, 75f
  relationships, 79
  trust law, 78
  vegetable garden, 76
Seeker persona
  customer loop, 170
  decision journey, 171f
Site search analytics, 214
Social media
  communication technologies, 126
  community and channels identification,
      129–131
  digital marketers and content
      professionals, 127
  multi-screen experiences, 126
  multi-threaded conversations, 127
Stakeholder
  audience and C-suite, 49
  content, shared asset, 50–51
  definition, 50, 50b
  gathering, facts, 55–57
  as information sources, 54
  internal stakeholders, 51–52
  management, 49
  personas, internal, 52
  prioritization, 53–54
  publishing lifecycle, 55
  roadmap, 57–60
  uncovering group dynamics, 57
Stefanie diamond photography
  advertisement, 311
  cake smash, 313f
  log posts and photographs, 312

managing and distributing, content, 313
marketing and communications, 311
memories, 311
newborn portraits, 311
posts and content, 312*f*
professional life, 311
relatable style, 313*f*
sharing, content, 313
training, marketing, 312
Structured content, 111–112, 111*b*

T

The Digital Crown
cohesive, consistent and controlled
content, 316
description, 315–316
digital strategy, 316
Tone
company's voice, 188
definition, 189–190
gogo in-flight internet, 190–191
graphic smiley faces, 188
reflection, feelings, 188

U

Understanding content
anatidaephobia, 7*b*
branding (*see* Branding)
build great relationships, 8
company issues, 6
conversation people control, 6, 8
development and management, 8
digital marketing strategy, 7
digital properties, 3
effective digital content program, 19
great conversationalists, 8
information transformation, 6–7, 6*f*
organization, 3
problems, 3–4
salespeople, 3
TV shows, 7–8
web challenge
actual physical world, 4
business, 6
crowdsourcing, 5–6
exchanges and conversations, web, 4*b*
the Internet, 4, 5
marketplaces, 4
starting conversation, 4*b*

Ungated content, 249
User experience (UX) professionals
content creators (*see* Content creators)
content strategists (*see* Content
strategists)
customer, 262
information architects, 263
usability professionals, 265–266
visual designers, 264
User-generated content, 84*t*
UX professionals. *See* User experience (UX)
professionals

V

Visual design, 296
Voice
brand's personality, 188
definition, 188–189
gogo in-flight internet, 190–191
hardness/softness, 188

W

Wireframe, 295–296
Workflow
analysts, 284
challenges
categories, 274
guidance and clear models, 277
information flow, 274–275
misplaced talent, 275–276
training, 277
value, 274
content strategists, 273
content strategy lifecycle and phase,
282, 283*f*
content teams (*see* Content teams,
workflow)
creators, 284
description, 273
Digital Crown, 273
distributors, 284
editorial structure, 282, 283*f*
evaluation, 285–286
final approvers, 284
Lego playset, 273
problems, 274
providers, 284
publishers, 284
requesters, 284

Workflow *(Continued)*
   reviewers, 284
   right people, 286–287
   roles, 282
   rules, 273

X

XONEX
   B2B corporate relocation company, 61
   content marketing, 64
   content organization and business
      objectives, 62–63
   description, 61
   marketing and organization
      level, 63
   multi-channel publishing, 65
   research, 62
   sales-y, 61
   success, 64
   targeted audiences, 61